C000172072

Gordon Burn was the author of f
(winner of the Whitbread First No
North of England Home Service an
also the author of the non-fiction titles *Somebody's Husband, Somebody's Son, Pocket Money, Happy Like Murderers, On the Way to Work* (with Damien Hirst) and *Best and Edwards*. His last book, *Sex & Violence, Death & Silence*, was a collection of his essays on art.

David Peace – named in 2003 as one of *Granta*'s Best of Young British Novelists – was born and brought up in Yorkshire. He is the author of eleven novels including the *Red Riding Quartet*, adapted for television by Channel 4 in 2009; *GB84*, which was awarded the James Tait Black Memorial Prize; *The Damned Utd*; *Red or Dead*, which was shortlisted for the Goldsmiths Prize in 2013; *Patient X* and, most recently, *Tokyo Redux*. He lives in Tokyo.

Further praise for *Best and Edwards*:

'Burn excels as a chronicler of real lives, a skill evident in this study of two very different Manchester United players: Duncan Edwards, cut down at Munich when set to dominate the game, and George Best, who lived out a long public death. The contrast allows Burn to trace a familiar pop cultural arc – one apt to forget substantial achievement in favour of soiled celebrity. Burn is never less than interesting.' *Observer Sports Monthly*

'This eloquent, sorrowful and angry book adds much to our understanding of what the game has lost.' *Independent*

'A thoughtful, intelligent and moving tale of two young men whose talents were overcome by far greater powers . . . Superbly written.' *Literary Review*

'Eschews footballspeak and attempts to define an era where innocence gave way to cynicism in this hugely successful account.' *Herald*

'A lyrical and often moving read.' *FourFourTwo*

GORDON BURN

Best and Edwards
Football, Fame and Oblivion

February 1958

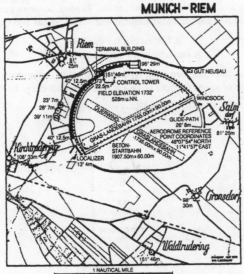

MUNICH – RIEM

faber

First published in 2006
by Faber & Faber Limited
Bloomsbury House, 74–77 Great Russell Street
London WC1B 3DA

This paperback edition published in 2020

Typeset by Faber & Faber Limited
Printed and bound by CPI Group (UK) Ltd, Croydon CR0 4YY

A CIP record for this book
is available from the British Library

Every effort has been made to clear illustration copyright. In the
event of an inadvertent omission please contact the publisher.

ISBN 978—0—571—35364—4

FSC
www.fsc.org
MIX
Paper from
responsible sources
FSC® C013604

2 4 6 8 10 9 7 5 3 1

In the English Twilight,
with the Living Dead

by David Peace

> . . . *for what*
> *You are alone has, to achieve*
> *The rank of fact, to be expressed*
> *In terms of others, or it's just*
> *A compensating make-believe.*
>
> 'Best Society', Philip Larkin, 1951

He's always already there, at the table with his pint, a sip and then another, steady never hurried, too busy listening, watching the room, the bar and the door, men going out, men coming in. That's where you first met Gordon, down a Bloomsbury backstreet, in the Duke, in a wooden booth by the window, afternoon turning to evening. Where you still see him now, at the table with his pint, in the twilight, the English twilight, neither night nor day, dark nor light. Where you sit down and you say, say something stupid like, You know, in certain parts of Japan, there is a folk belief that twilight, being a subtle world of the in-between, is the time when things change; they are not what they seem, when monsters and ghosts can appear.

Best and Edwards is a very deceptive book, about many different things, about monsters and ghosts, the things we see and the things we don't; a book about twilight, the English twilight, when some things change; they are not what they seem; were these monsters and ghosts, this English twilight, the reason you wrote the book?

You never quite know why you wrote a book, he says, he shrugs. You're always kind of rationalising after the fact.

You smile, you say, It's like Tony Wilson and his theory of

praxis, at the opening of the Haçienda: We've spent the last year building the place, now we've the next year to decide why we did it.

Praxis makes perfect, he says. Manchester again. Granada-land.

You nod, you ask, Was that part of the motivation to write this book, do you think, Manchester? The city does keep coming back in your work.

Maybe, he says, he shrugs, I don't know. I've always been fascinated by the Munich air crash. I'd been wanting to write about it for a long time and Faber really wanted me to base a novel on it.

Why didn't you?

You think I should have done, he says, staring at me, a flicker of self-doubt in his eyes, the hint of a challenge in his voice, You wish I had?

You shake your head, you say, No, no, I'm just always very curious why some of your books are novels and others are not?

Norman Mailer called *In Cold Blood* a failure of the imagination, but Capote's reply to Mailer was 'What do you want me to do, write about imaginary things?' And that's still my feeling. Until I wrote a novel I'd had no interest in novels whatsoever, no interest in the imagination. I would always fall asleep within two pages of a novel, or ten minutes at the pictures . . . I still do. But there's this quote by John Berger that I had in mind all the time I was writing *Born Yesterday*, that imagination is not, as most people think, the ability to invent, it's the ability to disclose what already exists. And that perfectly sums up my feeling about the line between imagination and so-called reality. I'm interested in how public events and public figures feed into all of our day-to-day lives in ways we're not really aware of.

Like Best and Edwards?

Mailer once told me he'd got to the stage that he wouldn't recognise potential material for books if it smacked him in the mouth. I laughed at that, but George Best used to live near me

8

in Chelsea. I'd see him around at least once a month, but to me he was just this shambolic old codger in a shapeless tracksuit who walked the same streets as me and sat in the same pubs – the Phene, the Wellesley Arms, the Beehive – always with his puzzle book. In the last years, I'd see him sliding down walls and occasionally sleeping on a park bench. If the fire station down the road ever found him the worse for wear, they would give him a bed for the night. He was so much a part of my everyday life that I stopped seeing him as a football star. I never thought of him as this mythical figure. He remained a neighbour, somebody I saw on a regular basis, in the pub and on the street, over a period of twenty years. But the man within the man was scarcely perceptible. I couldn't make sense of him. And publicly, he had achieved the invisibility of that special species of person peculiar to postmodern life, who is so familiar we don't see them anymore. He had disappeared in full view onto Saturday-afternoon television and into the national soap opera scripted by the scandal-sheets, his boozing and birding exploits, his arrests and transgressions so familiar as to be almost reassuring.

You ask, So when did you start to see him differently?

Well, a few years earlier, I'd written a piece for the *Guardian* about sport and literature. I'd realised that sport is central to a lot of my favourite American novels – Philip Roth's *American Pastoral*, Don DeLillo's *Underworld*, Richard Ford's *The Sportswriter* – and in the course of writing the article, around the same time he received a liver from a cadaver donor, I realised that George Best was akin to a character from one of these novels. Like some of them, he no longer resembled a legendary figure—

And there it was: material.

And it all tied in with my long-standing interest in the corrosive effects of fame. I liked the idea of taking someone who was so heavily written about and trying to find something new. I ended up focusing on the gap between the private individual and the public face.

You say, Duncan Edwards was a very private man, extremely shy, spending his free time hiding in the pictures, going from cinema to cinema; was that contrast part of his attraction, too?

It was the slower, grainier times, he says, and particularly the changing nature of fame. Jon [Riley, who had originally commissioned the book for Faber & Faber, along with *Happy Like Murderers* and *The North of England Home Service*] and I were both fascinated with how fame had changed during our own lifetimes.

You nod, you say, And football, too. You still follow Newcastle?

Carol [Gorner, his wife] supports Chelsea, been a Chelsea supporter for thirty years, since long before they became trendy, so we watch more of them. She can't stand the pundits, but I like the jabber, the chat. Then when it's time to go back to the match, I switch off again. So, I wouldn't consider myself passionate about the game, though I loved the way in which the culture of football contributed to the place I grew up in.

You grew up very close to the Newcastle ground, right?

A goal kick from St James's Park, yes, and maybe that's why I didn't care much for football, because it was so close to the house. My parents went drinking on Saturdays to the local working men's club, the Nova Castria, where they'd mix with Jackie Milburn and other Newcastle players. Gazza was the last of them. The Nova Castria became a light-fittings showroom.

You nod again, you say, A different time, a different world.

Yes, it's partly about the days when the players and the people who watched them came from the same place. The players weren't earning £130,000 per week, so there wasn't much distance between them and the fans.

As you often do, you dedicated the book to Carol, but also in memory of your father. When I was reading the passages about Duncan Edwards and Bobby Charlton, I was constantly thinking of my own father. He was at the last league game the Busby Babes played, at Highbury, still has the programme, so I grew up with his stories about that team and about Munich. He also took me to Bramall Lane to see Best, when he was playing for Fulham with Bobby Moore and Rodney Marsh. My dad loves your book, thinks it's the best thing you've written since *Alma*.

My father wasn't really a football fan, he says. He hadn't been to a match at St James's in possibly fifty years. And yet . . . the team is crucial to the fabric and self-image of the city: and the city – its local detail, the particularity of place – was central to who he was. He belonged. Last thing at night, when I'd ask him if he wanted anything else, he'd always say rotely, already nearly asleep, 'Aye, Newcastle to win the Cup.'

You nod, remembering his mother had passed away around the time he was writing *The North of England Home Service*, that his father had died while he was writing the next book, this book, *Best and Edwards*.

Every time I went back to visit Dad in Newcastle, he'd have collected more cuttings about George, he says, stuff I'd missed.

You nod again, you say, My father used to do the same for me, send me an envelope of cuttings every week. But not anymore.

Do you send your own son cuttings, he asks.

You shake your head, you say, Links.

Links, he repeats, he smiles.

You say, All the quotations you use in the book, they act like links, as prompts to an alternative, occult novel, your own sporting *Wasteland*.

You don't like them, do you, he says, staring at me again, that hint of a challenge back in his voice again. All the quotations.

You shake your head, you say, No, no, they're great, apart from the ones by Martin Amis and Foster Wallace. I prefer your words to theirs.

Twat, he laughs.

You smile, you say, You only quote from Larkin once, but he seems to haunt the book, his particular English melancholy which, as you write, Bobby Charlton came to embody. They even look alike, Larkin and Charlton.

Could be the sequel, he laughs. You should write it.

You shake your head, you say, You already did. *Born Yesterday*.

Links, he says and smiles again, then takes another sip from his pint, steady never hurried, still listening, watching the room, the bar and the door, men coming in, men going out, talking about football, fame and oblivion; the life after death of Duncan Edwards and the living death of George Best.

Almost everything I have written has been about celebrity, he says, and how for most people celebrity is a kind of death.

You nod and think, but do not, dare not say, Premature death.

Bye-bye, everybody, he says, and then, and now, is gone again, in the twilight, the English twilight, on the table, beside the glass, the empty glass, just the books he left behind. Bye-bye.

SOURCES AND ACKNOWLEDGEMENTS

The text was composed from my own memories of conversations with Gordon, recollections by Jon Riley and Angus Cargill, and from quotes found in the following articles and interviews:

'Putting his Best foot forward', *Scotsman*, 17 September 2006.
Burn, Gordon, '1966? You must be joking', *Guardian*, 25 November 2003.
——— 'The games writers play', *Guardian*, 8 October 2004.
——— 'Living memories', *Guardian*, 11 June 2005.
——— 'Death of a sportsman', *Guardian*, 7 October 2006.
Kelly, Richard T., 'Gordon Burn and David Peace interview', *Esquire*, April 2008. [The full, unedited transcript, thanks to Richard.]
Willetts, Paul, Gordon Burn interview, *Book and Magazine Collector*, October 2006.

for
Carol Gorner,
and in memory of my father

One

The world's champion worrier. It is a face on which worry – more accurately worritability, the under-colour of worry – seems to have been permanently imprinted. It looks like a face incapable of lighting up with joy; a face from which joy, or even the open and unselfconscious expression of pleasure, has been forever extinguished.

Even when England won the World Cup in 1966, bringing to a climax a summer month brimming over with a very un-English sense of carnival and expansiveness, Bobby Charlton brought a mask of tears to show the presentation party at the Royal Box. His first question to his brother Jack, on the pitch sharing the victory with him, had been a ball-aching, worritable one: 'What is there to win now?'

Less than a month later, hailed, alongside Jack, as a returning hero in his home town of Ashington, Bobby arrived late and then spent the processional half-mile from the colliery terrace where he had grown up to the Town Hall looking, according to contemporary observers, anxious and on edge. While Jack perched on the back of the rear seat of the open car, taking the cheers of the crowd, waving to familiar faces from his childhood that he recognized, sending up the fact that he was riding past them as a winner in a Roller, Bobby remained seated and sombre. Even his mother, the ever-exuberant Cissie Charlton, remarked afterwards that their Bobby had looked 'peaky' and 'distinctly uncomfortable'.

Although in north-east legend he is always fused in an unusually close relationship with his mother, a daughter of the goalkeeper 'Tanner' Milburn and cousin of the great Jackie and a long line of footballing Milburns, Bobby actually took after his father temperamentally. Bob senior liked his pigeons and his allotment and his own slow company and, typically,

15

had worked his usual shift at the Linton pit in Ashington instead of watching Bobby play what everybody said was the match of his life in the semi-final of the World Cup against Portugal. He felt well shot of the hoo-ha and the blether.

In 1968, ten years after Munich, when Manchester United finally won the European Cup by beating Benfica of Lisbon at Wembley, Bobby was a no-show at the after-match party. Crowds in their thousands milled around the Russell Hotel in King's Cross that night; the celebrations inside went on until dawn. George Best, who scored the first of United's winning goals in extra time (Charlton got the killer goal, the third after the restart), would later claim to have no memory of anything that happened after the team left Wembley; as was to be the case so often in the coming years, recall was obliterated by the alcohol. 'I don't remember going to the official dinner,' Best later said, 'though I'm told I was there.'

Also invited as guests of the club were the families of the players who died at Munich. But, when it came to it, Bobby, perhaps not surprisingly, couldn't face them. He sent his wife Norma down to apologize for his absence. 'It has all been a bit too much for Bobby,' she explained. 'He is just too tired physically and emotionally to face up to all this. He couldn't take it, with complete strangers coming up and slapping him on the back and telling him what a wonderful night it is . . . He's remembering the lads who can't be here tonight.'

Once in his room, Charlton had felt faint. He was drained. It had been eleven years since Matt Busby – flying in the face of official and unofficial opposition from the English football authorities, who still, at mid-century, regarded continental teams as 'wogs and dagoes' (to quote League Secretary, Alan Hardaker) – had embarked on his renegade European adventure. Eight of Charlton's fastest friends, among them Eddie Colman, Duncan Edwards and 'Billy' Whelan, had met their deaths at Munich. The average age of the players who died in the disaster was twenty-one. Now he had eventually arrived at the destination they had set out for together. Soon, in recognition of the Lazarus act he had performed both professionally and personally, heroically hauling himself back from the appalling injuries he sustained in the crash, the Boss would be honoured with a knighthood.

Every time Charlton tried to ease himself off the bed in the room overlooking the heaving crowd and Russell Square, his legs buckled. *The surge sensation, the leap of people already standing, that bolt of noise and joy when the ball went in.* He felt old prematurely, with feeble limbs and double vision and dizzy spells. Every time he tried to make it to the bedroom door, he fainted. When he swung his legs off the bed, his legs couldn't take the weight of him. And tomorrow would bring only more of the same: the consuming guilt of being a survivor when his friends had perished; the trial of carrying the Cup home in glory to Old Trafford, parading it in convoy past the waving and cheering, screaming-themselves-hoarse Red thousands of the fanatic faithful; glad-handing the silverware, holding the big, bowl-sided trophy up to collect their reflection when, if any of them were doing it, it really should have been Duncan.

'We passed them . . . / All poised irresolutely, watching us go / As if out on the end of an event / Waving goodbye / To something that survived it.' Philip Larkin's lines from 'The Whitsun Weddings', written in 1958, the year of Munich, contain all the melancholy which, in the ensuing half-century, the crestfallen, dutiful figure of Bobby Charlton would come to embody.

So synonymous has he become with sobriety and black-braided ceremonial – the scrubbed-up, bow-headed figure in the unexceptional suit acting as a representative of his club, his sport or his country, not infrequently appearing to be teetering on the edge of one of his dizzy spells – that the other Bobby Charlton, the player that many who saw him play at his peak in the sixties thought comprised the athletic ideal, quick and full of intelligence, his massive goal-scoring power erupting on the run suddenly, out of an inborn, flowing elegance – 'He used

17

to delight people,' his old grammar-school headmaster once said – *that* Bobby seems to have been another person, the inhabitant of a different life.

As a young player, Charlton sported a bobbing, almost Teddy Boy-ish quiff of blond hair. By 1966 he was balding. In the final years of his career he was famous for the long, combed-over single hank of hair which, when he was making a run on goal, the ball miles out in front of him, Charlton tearing after it, flew out behind him like a streamer. In those days, for a modest fee, small planes used to fly the length of Filey and Skegness and other holiday beaches in the north, trailing messages such as 'Ken from Donny thinks Barbara Mills is a smasher – Babs, will you marry me?' Charlton's hair, equally ludicrous and touching, and just as much a period piece, looked like that.

Even when he retired from football, he kept the elaborate artifice of combed-over hair, maybe as a reminder of the time before the polite world of formal courtesies and rigid protocol closed in on him, when he could go with his instinct and explode with a ball, beating all-comers, even when there were others – Denis Law, George Best – yelling at him not be a selfish bastard and pass it to them. He knew that Law and Best could be pretty selfish bastards themselves.

But then, sometime in the 1980s, he cut it off. One day the famous Charlton streamer was gone, in its place a tidy, razor-buzzed, businessman's cut, noticeably flecked with grey.

'Prayerful', 'grave', 'sepulchral'. The words so often used to describe Bobby Charlton in later life have been a reflection of the place where his mature role as sporting 'envoy' and 'ambassador' has so often required him to be. In a strange and rather perverse way, it is as if his early acquaintance with violent death in the lunchtime dark and slush at Munich has doomed him to go on repeating this acquaintance at a seemingly never-ending round of memorial services, funerals, commemorations, dedications, reunions, hospital visits, tree-plantings, wreath-layings and services of thanksgiving. In George Best's final hours,

Charlton made a visit to his bedside in the Cromwell Hospital not because of any deep-seated affection – during their playing days both men were frank about the dislike they felt for each other – but as a representative of the club for which he acts as a goodwill ambassador and of which he is now a director: a visit at that time seemed appropriate and seemly, and Charlton, reluctantly maybe, uncomfortably without question, was doing what was required.

Sometimes the pressures of being a paragon can get to him and he'll go off on one. 'What do they think, that I'm the only person who ever met Duncan Edwards?' he can snap when another interview request to mark this birthday or that anniversary comes in. (It's what he spluttered to me over the phone from his office at Halba Travel, a company that organizes overseas tours for Premiership football clubs and has its base in that part of Cheshire – the Wilmslow, Alderley Edge, Hale triangle – known as Gold Trafford because of its popularity with the current crop of young, McMansion-owning, multimillionaire Manchester United players.) But the record shows that he has been beyond reproach when it comes to anything to do with honouring the memory of the man revered then, and mythologized now, as the most lavishly talented of the Busby Babes.

Charlton and Edwards used to stay with each other's families when they were apprentice professionals at United, and in the nearly half a century since Duncan Edwards's death, the road has taken Charlton back to Edwards's birthplace of Dudley in the West Midlands on numerous occasions, nearly all of them casting him in the role of escort to Edwards's redoubtable, elderly mother, Annie, who died, well into her nineties, in 2003; these occasions were invariably rounded off with small talk over the tea cups in the Lord Mayor's parlour.

Away from the raucous atmosphere of competitive football, Charlton has always resisted being the object of attention. He was horribly embarrassed if recognized, in a cinema queue or restaurant, as one of United's young stars and asked for an autograph. A journalist who tried to speak to him for a Manchester paper in the mid-fifties later described how the whole interview was conducted on the doorstep of the player's digs, with Charlton 'holding on to the doorknob, not being in the least obstructive but blushing and leaving words trailing indistinctly and ambiguously in the air'. Even now, at the age of nearly seventy, he will contrive to give all interviews over the telephone rather than in person. He has always had a particular dread of public speechifying.

Fortunately, for many years he had Matt Busby to take the heat and deflect any unwanted attention. Busby was on hand to unveil the headstone on Edwards's grave in Dudley cemetery. He also played a central role in the dedication of the Duncan Edwards stained-glass windows in St Francis's Church in Dudley, in August 1961.

But Sir Matt died in 1994, the year in which Charlton himself finally received his knighthood. The knighthood was a gesture which was interpreted by many as a mark of continuity and a kind of symbolic act of passing down and handing on. Busby was venerated in Manchester. 'He is not merely popular,' Arthur Hopcraft once wrote. 'People treat Busby in the way that middle-aged priests of compassionate and sporty nature are often treated: the affection becomes rapidly more deferential as they get nearer to the man. Small boys rush noisily towards him, holding their picture books out for his autograph, and fall silent and shy once they get up close and he calls for less jostling and settles the word "son" on them like a blessing. Adults shout his first name and grab for his hand. They wave at him in his car.'

Bobby Charlton was never like that. None of it is Charlton's style. He is in and out of Halba, correspondence collected, diary updated, before nine in the morning to minimize the risk of any potentially awkward social encounter. All his life his shyness has been interpreted as dullness or arrogance. 'Bobby Charlton', I was assured by a Manchester businessman who has amassed several fortunes buying and selling United memorabilia, 'has the personality of a spent match.' His reluctance to give players a tongue-lashing and his natural reticence are why most people assume he failed as the manager of Preston North End after his departure from United in the mid-seventies. According to Mark Lawrenson, Charlton's nerves were so fraught his hand would shake when he read out the team.

For many years, long-distance lorry drivers and Manchester United supporters on their way to or from games in the Midlands have been making detours to visit Duncan Edwards's grave in Dudley cemetery. Once there, they drape team scarves over the six-foot-high black headstone with his image ingrained on it and place red and white carnations in the granite flower stand modelled in the shape of a heavy leather-cased football. For a number of years, Duncan's father, Mr Gladstone Edwards, worked as a groundsman at the cemetery and, while always happy to point visitors in the direction of Duncan's grave, he never announced himself. Many people also seek out the tribute windows at St Francis's, close to where Edwards grew up, and the display of his England shirts and other memorabilia, donated by his mother, which has been installed in the chlorine-drenched foyer of the town's modern leisure centre.

But Dudley Council went for forty years without putting up an official memorial to Edwards where it could be seen as a daily reminder, in the town centre. Then, on 14 October 1999, after an exhibition of football skills from the Borough of Dudley Football Development Scheme Academies, Dudley Little League players and representatives of the borough's Schools Football Association, His Worshipful the Mayor of Dudley Councillor Fred Hunt, accompanied by Sir Bobby Charlton and Mrs Sarah Anne Edwards, mounted the temporary platform which had been erected outside Poundland ('Yes! Everything's £1!') and opposite Woolworth's in Dudley Market Place.

The life-size bronze figure of Edwards was still concealed by a tarpaulin. Its shape suggested an extended left arm and a backwards-lifted right foot. After a brief introduction from the Mayor, Sir Bobby stepped forward to say a few words. 'I find that I think about Duncan a lot. I have seen all the players who in their time have been labelled the best in the world – Puskas, Di Stéfano, Gento, Didi, John Charles and the rest – and not one of them has been as good as Big Duncan. There was no other player in the world like him then and there has been nobody to equal him since. This man was incomparable.' The crowd consisted of true believers, people old enough to have seen Duncan play and who knew Sir Bobby was speaking gospel, and half-curious early lunchers and shoppers, families with babies and small children who drifted away mid-sentence. 'Sometimes I fear there is a danger that people will think that we who knew him and saw him in action boost him because he is dead. Sentiment can throw a man's judgement out of perspective. Yet it is not the case with him. Whatever praise one likes to heap on Duncan is no more than he deserved. He was out on his own at left-half and a First Division player in every other position. There was no one else to start with him.

'I am not a person to dramatize things or dispense fulsome praise. It is not in my make-up. A man is a good player or he is not. A few are great, and they deserve respect. But Duncan Edwards was the greatest. I see him in my mind's eye and I wonder that anyone should have so much talent. He was simply the greatest footballer of them all.'

This was nothing Charlton hadn't said many times before and, indeed, had written in a little manual called *My Soccer Life*, published by a subscription book club forty years earlier.

In his 1973 autobiography, *Soccer at the Top*, Matt Busby paid the following tribute to Edwards: 'He was a colossus. Whatever was needed he had it. He was immensely powerful. He was prodigiously gifted in the arts and crafts of the game. His temperament was perfect . . . His confidence was supreme and infectious. No opponent was too big or too famous for Duncan . . . A wing-half, he could have been a great centre-half or a great forward striker. He would have been one of the great leaders with his sheer inspiration . . . If there was ever a player who could be called a one-man team, that man was Duncan Edwards. His death, as far as football is concerned, was the single biggest tragedy that has happened to England and to Manchester United. He was then and has always remained to me incomparable.'

As he has grown older, Sir Bobby has come to bear a striking physical resemblance to his mentor Sir Matt. Although closer in age to George Best and the lairier, less respectful players who came of age in the sixties – there's nine years between him and Best – Duncan and Bobby and their fellow lodgers at Mrs Watson's boarding house in Manchester in the early 1950s seemed closer to the generation associated with the hard days of the war and rationing – Matt Busby's generation – than to the rowdier, more mobile times that were just around the corner.

Mark Jones, for example, a talented centre half, bred canaries and budgies and was engaged to June, his childhood sweetheart back in Barnsley. He smoked a pipe at eighteen and wore a trilby. Big Duncan wrote articles about football on his own portable typewriter and smoked a pipe. Bobby sang along to his cherished Frank Sinatra LPs, and was planning ahead to the greengrocery business he would run when he came out of the game. In a move that won him particular approval from the Boss, he started saving to get married when he was barely out of his teens.

'Mr Busby's attitude towards my marriage in 1961 was typical,' Charlton recalled in *My Soccer Life*. 'He didn't just smile and say "congratulations" when I told him what I intended. He showed a deep and genuine interest. "It's a fine thing for a player to settle down and start a home," he said. "It will make you more mature as a person and that will help your football." He went on in that vein for some time, stressing the importance of it. His prediction proved right, too. I have been a better player as a married man than I was as a bachelor – perhaps

23

because there's not the temptation to racket around. I have now got responsibility and a deeper respect for the game. I am playing for my family and cannot afford to take chances.'

Compare this to George Best's recollection of being carpeted by the manager and held to account for some drunken escapade or other only four years later: 'I remember seeing that film *Charlie Bubbles* where Albert Finney sat in a conference and shut out all the sound from his ears so that he could see the mouths moving but he wasn't listening. I used to do that with Matt . . . When he sent for me I used to sit and look at the wallpaper behind his head. It was funny wallpaper with animals on and I used to count the animals while he gave me a bollocking. I used to want the bollocking to last a long time so I could finish my counting. One day he got really mad at me and went on at some length and I managed to count them all. There are 272 animals on Matt Busby's wallpaper.'

'He'd have had a heart attack if ever he'd have come on holiday with me,' Best remarked on another occasion. 'I used to go to Majorca and Spain because all the Scandinavian crumpet went there and I am very partial to Scandinavian crumpet, it being generally beautiful, always willing and a bit thick so you don't have to waste time with the conversation.'

Duncan Edwards never went 'gallivanting at night', as Busby put it. 'He was never in an ounce of trouble. The pictures were about his only nightlife. He lived for the game and was concerned only with making himself, and keeping himself, fit for it.'

Edwards was a shade under six feet and weighed about thirteen and a half stone. He had a boxer's build. He was only a year older than Bobby Charlton, but even at the age of sixteen he looked like a man. Off the field, 'Big Dunc' gave the impression of being self-sufficient and something of a man of the world. There were quite specific demarcations between the first-team players who lodged at Mrs Watson's and the rest that new arrivals didn't immediately take in. Sensing Charlton's strangeness and feelings of intimidation, Duncan

Edwards, already a twelve-month veteran of 5 Birch Avenue and only weeks away from being a regular first-teamer himself, took him under his wing. Almost from day one, they were mates, both of them all Manchester United right through.

'Bless, O Lord, this statue which has been erected in his memory and honour. Help us always to remember with delight the skills and talents which you had given him and which were admired by so many people throughout the world.' The Revd Geoff Johnston, the vicar of St Francis's and known locally as 'Father Geoff', began his prayer of dedication as Bobby Charlton, Edwards's great friend, and Annie, his mother, looking small and frail, stepped back from the figure of Duncan which they had just jointly unveiled. 'Grant that whosoever looks upon this statue may find in Duncan's life and abilities a true inspiration and an example of the best of the qualities of youth. We ask this in the name of him who is the author and giver of all good things – Jesus Christ our Lord. Amen.'

Sir Bobby supported Mrs Edwards by the arm and together they gazed at the statue of a moment captured in bronze. What did they see?

His mother had last seen Duncan at the Rechts der Isar hospital in Munich, where he had been taken after the plane bringing the team home from Belgrade had crashed after a refuelling stop at the city's Riem airport on 6 February 1958. Seven United players had been killed instantly. They were: Roger Byrne, David Pegg, Tommy Taylor, Eddie Colman, Mark Jones, Billy Whelan and Geoff Bent. The Manchester United club secretary, Walter Crickmer, coach Bert Whalley and trainer Tom 'Tosher' Curry also lost their lives, as did eight football writers who had been travelling with the team. Altogether twenty-three people, including Duncan, who held on, drifting in and out of consciousness for a further fifteen days, would die.

The England captain Billy Wright was one of the pall-bearers at Edwards's funeral in Dudley on 26 February. Tens of thousands of mourners lined the route from St Francis's to the cemetery at Queen's Cross, although it wasn't the custom then to throw flowers or applaud. The hearse carrying his coffin had passed over the spot where the small platform party and his statue now stood.

Bobby Charlton had emerged from the debris virtually unmarked. After the tail section broke away from the chartered BEA Elizabethan when it ploughed into a house at the end of the runway in Munich during its third attempt at take-off, he had been catapulted into the frozen slush still strapped into his seat.

Charlton was kept in hospital for a week. He was the first of the survivors to leave the Rechts der Isar on 14 February. He looked in on Duncan in an intensive care ward on the fourth floor as he was leaving, and came away in tears.

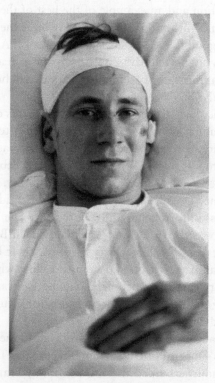

Back home in Ashington, he monitored Duncan's condition through the bulletins in the morning papers. He had broken ribs, a collapsed lung, broken pelvis and a complicated fracture of his right thigh. But it was the unusually high percentage of nitrogen in his blood, the result of a badly damaged kidney, which was giving the most cause for concern. An artificial kidney had been flown from Frankfurt to Munich.

On 15 February, Edwards started to suffer severe internal haemorrhaging. Dr Georg Maurer, Chief Surgeon at Rechts der Isar hospital, explained that the use of the artificial kidney had reduced the ability of his blood to clot. He remained dangerously ill.

On 17 February, Dr Maurer said there was a glimmer of hope that his badly bruised kidney could be starting to work again.

On 18 February, the papers reported a 'restful night'.

On 19 February, the hospital announced that he had taken a turn for the worse and was showing 'signs of distress'.

On 20 February, there was 'a very slight improvement'.

Edwards died at 2.15 a.m. on Friday 21 February.

That morning there was no paper when Charlton sat down to eat his breakfast. 'Duncan's dead, isn't he?' he said to his mother.

For those old enough to remember Duncan Edwards and the bulletins which were issued twice a day by Dr Maurer in Munich, watching Roger Williams, George Best's doctor, giving progress reports outside the Cromwell Hospital in London in the last days of Best's life was to be reminded of the slower, grainier days of 1958 when, in the words of the novelist Don DeLillo, 'things were not replayed and worn out and run down and used up before midnight of the first day' and buy-ups of the principal participants in a tragedy and death-bed pictures, such as the one of Best which had been splashed across the front of the *News of the World*, were an unimaginable thing.

The words the two doctors used to describe their patients were tellingly similar. 'I do not think anyone other than this young man could have survived so long. His resistance made us admire him,' Dr Maurer said of Edwards. 'He was a tremendous fighter. None of us has seen anybody come through as many serious complications as he's had – he must be a very strong person inside,' Professor Williams said, across a gap of forty-eight years.

Sir Matt Busby made it clear many years ago that Best and Edwards were twinned in his mind. 'Every manager goes through life looking for one great player, praying he'll find one. Just one,' Busby said. 'I was more lucky than most. I found two – Big Duncan and George. I suppose in their own ways, they both died, didn't they?'

It was Bobby Charlton's misfortune to be present at both of these deaths, and in Best's case, as Busby predicted, it was a public, very messy, long-drawn-out one. Two more deaths to add to those others that Charlton had seen on that filthy day in Munich.

After coming home from Germany, Bobby Charlton spent two weeks in Ashington just hanging around the house. He never went out. He didn't feel like kicking a ball. He didn't know if he ever wanted to play football again. But then he was taken to see the scratch side of youth-team players, reserves and hasty signings that United put out for their first game after the crash. It was an FA Cup tie against Sheffield Wednesday at Old Trafford, and it took place just thirteen days after Munich. It was a night match. Sixty thousand people packed into the ground; thousands more stood silently outside. Naturally there was weeping. Fans inadvertently shouted the names of dead players when the excitement overtook them. The atmosphere caught in Bobby's throat.

Success, he seemed to decide that night at Old Trafford, with Duncan and Mr Busby still clinging to life in Munich, was a duty. Something to be borne rather than indulged or celebrated.

'Failed success' is something people talk about George Best representing – a gifted and tormented person dreaming of that second act, a second chance. But success had also failed

Charlton when he was still only twenty and some years away from being acclaimed a national hero. This terrible thing had happened to him; he knew it was going to taste of ashes.

'I never heard him sing out loud again after Munich,' one of his Ashington neighbours told a reporter. 'Peggy Lee, Sinatra. He used to be always singing.'

'I knew the road ahead would be different from the moment I woke up in the hospital,' Charlton himself once said. 'Everything had changed.'

The legend of the holy drinker #3

It sometimes seemed that Best lived his life as a series of bumper stickers:

> You're only young once, but you can be immature for ever. I may grow old, but I'll never grow up.

> Not all men are fools; some are single. I'm not playing hard to get, I am hard to get. Few have luck, all have death.

> Heaven doesn't want me and Hell's afraid I'll take over. I'm the person your mother warned you about. Don't laugh; your girlfriend might be in here.

> Girls wanted, all positions, will train. Playgirl on board. Nobody is ugly after 2 a.m.

> You can't take it with you, but I'll let you hold it for a while. Sex is only dirty when you do it right. Liquor up front – poker in the rear. Smile; it's the second best thing you can do with your lips. I'm looking for love but will settle for sex. Bad boys have bad toys. Are we having fun yet?

> Shit happens. I love your wife. Wife and dog missing – reward for dog. Sober 'n' crazy. Don't fence me in. Don't tell

29

me what kind of day to have. Yes, as a matter of fact, I do own the whole damn road. Get even, live long enough to become a problem to your kids.

Don't follow me, I'm lost too. No matter where you go, there you are. Of all the things I've lost, I miss my mind the most.

The water that bears the boat is the same that swallows it up. I love being exactly who I am. Choose death.

Two

Nearly a whole half-century after his death, Duncan Edwards is Dudley's most famous son – or best-known celebrity, as he would be referred to now, here in the age of perpetually streamed reality TV shows such as *Celebrity Love Island* and *I'm a Celebrity . . . Get Me Out of Here!* It is an indicator of how far fame has come adrift from real achievement – of how personality has replaced output as the measure of fame – that Calum Best appeared in the former and Alex Best in the latter purely on the strength of one being George Best's model-cum-tabloiding son and the other his model-slash-breakfast-TV-presenter ex-wife. (Alex's appearance helped win her the title Rear of the Year, although 'Arsehole of the Year' is what she claims Best chose to call her in the brief period between her reinvention as a mini-celebrity and his death.)

In their respective shows, the son and the ex appeared as part of a now-familiar package of personalities that included clapped-out disc jockeys, fresh-from-rehab glamour models, one-hit wonders, daytime-TV chefs, faded comics and barely remembered soap actors, many of them represented by Calum's agent, Dave Read of Neon Management Ltd, who cheerily admits, 'I make my money from the C-List. I go to the back door with my dustpan and brush and sweep up the soap stars.' Celebrities with the shelf life of milk.

For a few months in 2005, Read's most in-demand client was Abi Titmuss, who just eighteen months earlier had been working as a nurse when her television-presenter boyfriend was implicated in a sexual abuse scandal and she hit the head-lines by association. Within months, she had transformed her-self into a tabloid glamour favourite and a staple of the reality TV shows. (As an example of the overlapped processes and transactional cross-pollinations that keep the celebrity engine firing – Read rakes in commission from his clients, the clubs they are spotted at and the snappers who photograph them clubbing – Titmuss bared her all on *Celebrity Love Island* with Calum Best. Calum was also shown 'canoodling' in a toilet with Rebecca Loos, a woman who had made her name selling stories about her alleged affair with David Beckham and masturbating a pig on television.)

It was probably Read who negotiated the fee for the 'world exclusive' ten-page interview/fashion shoot with Calum and his mother Angela, George Best's first wife, which appeared in *Hello!* magazine a few days after Best's funeral at the Northern Ireland Parliament building at Stormont. They shared the cover with Lady Thatcher's daughter, Carol, who had just been crowned 'Queen of the Jungle' in the 2005 edition of *I'm a Celebrity . . . Get Me Out of Here!*

The bargain markdown of fame probably reached some kind of apotheosis at the beginning of 2006, when Chantelle Houghton, an unknown blonde promotions girl from Essex, successfully persuaded a houseful of 'genuine' celebrities that she was a pop star in the imaginary five-strong girl group Kandy Floss ('With a K!') and was voted the winner of *Celebrity Big Brother*.

This is a kind of fame that can be – almost always is – conveniently and irretrievably wiped. It is a thin, weightless thing and mostly exists as a series of electronically generated pulses and pixels. Often it is literally without foundation or substance and is typically memorialized as a brand of designer fragrance or on a T-shirt or a website rather than in the heavy, industrial-age materials of stained glass and granite and bronze. It is an inevitable fall-out of the galloping and still ongoing process which has seen the electronic society of the image – the daily bath we all take in the media – replace the real community of the crowd.

Cyber-age celebrity relates to the kind of old-fashioned renown rooted in genuine public affection and recognized achievement the way the various system-built, semi-prefabricated, part-plastic urban structures we have come to think of as post-modern relate to the heavy Victorian banks, lawyers' chambers and sooty civic buildings that in the great northern cities so often still surround them, like elderly relatives at a rave night.

Dudley gives the impression of being a town which has adapted to the new reality of a deindustrialized twenty-first century without being overly traumatized. Looking eastwards towards Birmingham from the ruins of Dudley Castle, the highest point, the near landscape is dominated by a sprawling business park whose most readable tenants are a Travelodge, Salinger's Bar, the Village Hotel-and-Spa Leisure Club, a branch of Healthworks and the Showcase Cinemas' ten-screen multiplex. There is a giant landscaped roundabout planted with abstract modern sculptures and the broad main road that cuts straight through to Birmingham.

Dudley Castle is the landmark that dominates this part of the Black Country. It stands on a high limestone ridge and it's a steep – and, these days, expensive – climb up through the zoo whose turnstiles provide the only access and whose cages and elephant and polar-bear enclosures have been landscaped into the slope. (One of Duncan Edwards's close neighbours in Dudley cemetery is George Edward Baker, first elephant keeper at Dudley Zoo, d. 1952, aged sixty.)

When he was a boy, the courtyard of the castle was one of Edwards's favourite places to kick a ball about. He'd kick it up through Priory Park to the crumbling priory ruins, header it along the walls towards the town centre and then take the direct route, rather than the softer circular one, up to the castle keep, where the pitch-sized courtyard lawn and the wide-open panoramic views – or, as was more usually the case, the views roofed in with flame-streaked, bituminous black smoke – were laid out far below. It may have been this bit of regular strenuous exercise which formed the foundation for the legendary tree trunk-like mass of his legs.

Edwards had a tendency to carry weight on his thighs and

his backside. He was notorious for the strength and the girth of his legs. The extreme muscularity of his legs is why he always wore his shorts hitched over at the waistband a couple of times, to bring them clear of his thighs. 'Opponents would bounce off him,' Matt Busby once said. 'Just the sight of Duncan blasting his way up the pitch with the ball was enough to scare the bravest goalkeeper to death.' Bobby Charlton remembers a match where Edwards scored four times in a ten-minute spell, 'and, for one of the goals – and I'm not exaggerating – he hit the ball so hard that the goalkeeper started to dive, flinched, and then deliberately got out of the way of it'. The United supporters nicknamed him 'Tank', although he was known as 'Brush' to the players he shared his digs with because of his obsession with smartness and tidying up. (He once offered the following advice to young players: 'The main thing to remember . . . is to see that shirts, shorts and socks are always clean and well darned. A smart team starts off with high morale. They try to play a brand of football as neat as their appearance.')

Edwards was born in Dudley in 1936. Three years before he was born, in the autumn of 1933, J. B. Priestley had wheezed up the hill to Dudley Castle to record what he could see from there for his journal of England in the Depression years. His description of the Black Country from the Dudley ridge has been described in the years since as being 'reminiscent of Brueghel's depiction of Hell, only without the people'.

'I climbed a steep little hillside, and then smoked a pipe or two sitting by the remains of the Keep,' Priestley wrote. 'There was the Black Country unrolled before you like a smouldering carpet. You looked into an immense hollow of smoke and blurred buildings and factory chimneys. There seemed to be no end to it . . . I felt that I was not looking at this place and that but at the metallic Midlands themselves, at a relief map of a heavy industry . . . No doubt at all that the region had a sombre beauty of its own. I thought so then, and I thought so later, when I had seen far more of its iron face lit with hell fire. But

34

it was a beauty you could appreciate chiefly because you were not condemned to live there.'

Priestley had travelled to Dudley from Birmingham via West Bromwich, a jaunt that he described as 'one of the most depressing little journeys I ever remember making': 'All it offered me, mile after mile, was a parade of mean dinginess . . . I saw nothing, not one single tiny thing, that could possibly raise a man's spirits . . . It was so many miles of ugliness, squalor, and the wrong kind of vulgarity, the decayed anaemic kind . . . I loathed the whole long array of shops, with their nasty bits of meat, their cough mixtures, their Racing Specials, their sticky cheap furniture, their shoddy clothes, their fly-blown pastry, their coupons and sales and lies and dreariness and ugliness . . . I have never seen such a picture of grimy desolation. If you put it, brick by brick, into a novel, people would not accept it, would condemn you as a caricaturist and talk about Dickens'.

This was a reference to the visit Dickens had made to the Black Country while gathering material for his 1841 novel *The Old Curiosity Shop*. Despite the luridness of his description – he was clearly excited by the almost subhuman horribleness of what he found – it is worth quoting because the working conditions and environment he describes are very much the ones Duncan Edwards's father was still working in exactly a century later. 'On mounds of ashes by the wayside, sheltered only by a few rough boards, or rotten pent-house roofs, strange engines spun and writhed like tortured creatures; clanking their ironchains, shrieking in their rapid whirl from time to time as though in torment unendurable, and making the ground tremble with their agonies . . . and still, before, behind, and to the right and left, was the same interminable perspective of brick towers, never ceasing in their black vomit, blasting all things living or inanimate, shutting out the face of day, and closing in on all these horrors with a dense dark cloud.

'But night-time in this dreadful spot! – night, when the smoke was changed to fire; when every chimney spurted up its flame; and places, that had been dark vaults all day, now shone red-hot, with figures moving to and fro within their blazing jaws, and calling to one another with hoarse cries.'

All his life at Manchester United – it was a professional career that, because of Munich, lasted something short of five years – Duncan would have the mickey taken out of him for his broad Black Country accent – 'Dood-lie' for Dudley and 'You cor do that!' and the way everybody was 'chief' to Duncan: 'Chook it owver 'ere, chief.' Everybody, that is, except Jimmy Murphy, the man in charge of day-to-day training at Old Trafford, Busby's trusted eyes and ears who many saw as the 'heartbeat' of the club and credit with keeping United going after Munich. He was old enough to be Edwards's father, a peerless drinker and (despite the Irish surname) Welsh patter-man, but Duncan always got away with calling him 'son': 'Don't worry, son – I'll get a goal or two for you this half.' (To everybody else in football circles, Jimmy Murphy was known, of course, as 'Spud'.) A thick local accent was something else Edwards had in common with the young Bobby Charlton, whose indecipherable Geordie 'pitmatic' also came in for a lot of stick from the lodgers.

Parts of the vast, raw-brick Priory estate in Dudley had a reputation for being some of the West Midlands' edgier places to live, even when Edwards was growing up there in the 1940s, and he was a bred-in-the-bone product of that background. Gladstone Edwards, his father, did what a great many of his neighbours did and worked nearly all his life as a metal polisher in an ironworks, in his case beyond the northern perimeter of the Priory estate, at Sankey's of Bilston. He liked the home-made faggots and peas he had been brought up on and his pasteurized-milk bottle filled with tea to take swigs on while he was working. He muffled his neck with sweat cloths against the fierce heat from the furnaces and wore a knot of white scarf at his neck when he wasn't working. Like millions of men in the world of the old industries, he didn't own his house, he didn't drive a car and never had any savings to speak of. To the end of her life, Annie Edwards kept the last £5 note that Duncan had ever given her displayed in a cabinet in the living room that became a kind of shrine to her son.

The Black Country was (in many ways still is) a place of strong opinions and deeply entrenched traditions, not all of them pretty, and the old life that many of the Edwards's neighbours came from quickly took root in the garages and gardens of the modern council houses which were the first permanent homes a lot of these families had ever had. The heavy-set 'pikey' strain of Staffordshire bull terrier was bred competitively. Game cocks were said to be kept and fed on egg and sherry cake to fire them up before a fight. Heaps of scavenged waste metal and scrap picked from under 'tatters' noses littered the estate. Many cottages in Cradley and Cradley Heath had their own one-man chain shop at the end of the yard, belching flames and smoke.

Even today the Priory refuses the uniformity and blandness that are typical of so many similar estates in the rest of the country. It's a short walk from there through an area of woodland to the point where the Dudley canal emerges from a tunnel that, in the past, the boatmen would leg through by lying on their backs and pushing on the barrelled brick roof. Romany and narrow-boat culture is still very much in evidence in the horse brasses and concrete lions and Staffies, and on the vividly painted outsides of many houses in Duncan Edwards's old street. On the afternoon I visited, a man was sitting in a car with all the windows down playing Engelbert Humperdinck's chart-topper '(Lonely Is) A Man Without Love' very loudly down a mobile phone and energetically singing along, his jowls still glazed and mottled from a powerfully pungent aftershave.

Rationing remained a reality of life in Britain until as late as 1954, when the restrictions on the sale of meat were finally lifted. The gradual climb back to prosperity was a long, dispiriting haul. But it would be misleading to paint a picture of life in that part of the Black Country when Edwards was a schoolboy there as being unrelievedly drab, austere and joyless, pustuled with what, in his 1930s novel of working-class life in Salford, Walter Greenwood called 'reality's sores'.

The names of every street on the estate – Bluebell, Cedar, Hazel, Laurel and Elm, where the Edwards lived – commemorated the acres of countryside that had been deforested and concreted over in order for those rows of corporation houses to be built. But the pleasures of the Worcestershire countryside were always close at hand, and Duncan had a black and white collie dog called Jimmy he liked to disappear exploring with and every year he went hop-picking. Miss Cooke, the arts and folk teacher at Wolverhampton Street School, even remembered Duncan being a talented country dancer, nine stone, enormous for his age, 'but so light on those feet with bells at the ankles; so beautifully balanced, so dainty'. He was a member of his school's morris-, sword- and folk-dancing teams and competed at Leamington and Birmingham Festivals.

The nearby hill of the Wren's Nest was pitted with the caves of lime quarries. But what Duncan mainly liked to do when he wasn't playing football – 'and as a boy the only relaxation I wanted from football was to play more football' – was to go fishing. 'Quietly I collect my sandwiches and Thermos flask', he once wrote, 'and sneak off to a river to sit there in peace and quiet with never a thought for the bustling world.'

When Edwards was eleven, after one of the severest winters on record, England enjoyed the glorious post-war summer of 1947. 'To be young, alive and unwounded was a joyous experience,' the former Head of the Home Civil Service, Lord Bancroft, later remembered. 'There was a great relief at the war being won and coming through alive . . . Every Saturday, in that golden summer of 1947, we would go to Lord's with our packets of sandwiches to watch Compton and Edrich.'

Of all British sportsmen, including Stanley Matthews and Tom Finney, gentlemen both, it is probably Denis Compton, the 'Brylcreem Boy' in the post-war hair-tonic adverts, a first-class professional footballer as well as cricketer, who became

the model for every British schoolboy with an ambition to succeed in sport. 'He was touched by the grace of genius in his
cradle,' Sir Neville Cardus wrote of Compton in a pre-echo of
what his colleagues on the sports pages only half a dozen years
later would be saying about Duncan Edwards, by then the
well-known public face of Dextrosol glucose tablets ('Playing
in top gear until the final whistle can really take it out of

you!'). '[His] mastery is easy and young and was not obtained by scorning delights and living laboriously. The strain of long years of anxiety and affliction passed from all hearts and shoulders at the sight of Compton in full flow, sending the ball here, there and everywhere, each stroke a flick of delight, a propulsion of happy, sane, healthy life. There was no rationing in an innings by Compton.'

In the years immediately after the war, the crowds for all sport in Britain were huge. Dance halls were packed, and so were theatres and cinemas. All the pent-up energy of the war years, the sense of waste and being cheated, went into leisure. 'Everybody was absolutely starved of sport,' Compton himself remembered, 'so what was wonderful from our point of view was that we played all our cricket and our football in front of capacity crowds . . . At Highbury, the Arsenal, pretty well every Saturday we used to get 60,000 people and we used to get the young boys, children of even eight, nine, ten, eleven all going with their parents and, in fact, at times not going with their parents, going on to the terraces which were absolutely packed and you used to see them being pulled down over the heads of the crowd to the front so that they could get a jolly good seat. Nobody was ever hurt, the atmosphere I thought was absolutely electric.'

'If you glance at a photograph of a terrace in any football annual dealing with the first postwar decade,' the historian Peter Hennessy has written, 'you are struck by the absence of banners and the homogeneity of appearances.' Young men dressed like their fathers and grandfathers – tweed jackets, mackintoshes, white mufflers and flat caps. Young boys wore school uniforms. 'Not until the first glimmerings of affluence put money into young pockets in the mid-fifties did the external expressions of a youth culture come to distinguish the generations in a sporting crowd.'

Cissie Charlton remembered taking Jack and Bobby down to Ashington FC and parking them behind the stand in their pram. When they were schoolboys both of them went on the bus to watch Newcastle, which is how their 'uncle' – actually their mother's cousin – Jackie Milburn, the Magpies' star goal-scorer, still travelled in to matches up to the end of the 1940s. During the week Milburn worked underground at the Woodhorn pit in Ashington. He used to start at twelve o'clock on the Friday night to finish at seven the next morning, and then turn out at St James's in the afternoon. He'd get on the number three bus at the stand in Ashington town centre at lunchtime with a gang of other miners who were going to see him play.

Because of the family connection, people in the north-east had always assumed that Bobby Charlton would make a smooth transition from East Northumberland Boys and the England Schoolboys team to First Division football with Newcastle United. Similarly, most people who knew him on the Priory had assumed Duncan Edwards would be pulling on the famous old gold of Wolverhampton Wanderers, who he had been supporting all his life. As a player for Birmingham Boys, he had been going for training at Wolves's ground at Molineux two nights a week.

Wolves were one of the glamour teams of the post-war years. Between 1949 and 1960 they won the FA Cup twice and the League Championship three times. In the 1950s, they staged an early series of floodlit friendlies against exotic foreign competition, and these games, which brought the likes of Moscow Spartak, Racing Club of Buenos Aires and Honved of Budapest to the industrial West Midlands, placed Molineux at the centre of a dazzling new era.

Billy Wright, the Wolves captain, was also captain of England, and they had other first-class players, such as Johnny Hancocks and Jimmy Mullen. But it was Stan Cullis, the manager, who could – and, being the kind of man he was, did – claim most of the credit for his team's success.

Cullis was a former Wolves and England captain himself and was known as a hard man – the 'iron manager' – with a puritan's reputation for never swearing. Wolves had one of the most punishing pre-season stamina courses in the game, involving a full-pelt run up a steep hill in part of the tangled heathland of Cannock Chase, and under Cullis no player who could not overcome it could expect to make the first team.

'As long as a player believes the manager is trying to improve him you're in with a chance,' Cullis used to like to say. 'Unfortunately you've got certain players who are like a lot of women – all advice upsets them.' He had come up at Wolves under the tutelage of the notorious Major Frank Buckley, who coached so loudly through a megaphone from the stands that complaints from the neighbours about the obscenities he came out with during training had the megaphone eventually taken off him. Cullis had a reputation for being stern and austere, even a bully, but Wolves set the pace of English football during his years as manager. It was the club George Best supported and dreamed about playing for as a boy.

Wolves won the FA Cup in 1949. Duncan Edwards was nearly thirteen at the time, Bobby Charlton almost twelve. But it was Cullis's great rival Matt Busby's Manchester United who had won the Cup at the end of the previous season, and it was that classic final against Blackpool which made Edwards and Charlton, as they were both to confirm later, converts to the United cause. Runners-up by a single point in the League to Arsenal, 1948 marked the coming of age of Busby's first great Manchester United team. All the neutrals followed United.

'We played for East Northumberland Boys in the morning, and we were invited to go to one of the lads' houses to listen to the Cup Final on the wireless,' Bobby Charlton said. 'We had no television in those days. After a while we went out onto the street to play football – we couldn't get enough in one day – and every so often we would come in to ask the score. I remember United equalizing. The next we heard they'd won. They said it was the greatest Cup Final of all time. I think it was from that day that I wanted to be a footballer and join Manchester United.'

But there may have been other incentives that Charlton

himself was unaware of at the time. His mother said that once it was known that Manchester United had made contact, other clubs had representatives calling at the house almost daily. 'I'd be clearing the fireplace in the morning and I'd look round and there'd be another one standing behind me. There were times when we've had one in the front room and one in the kitchen. They even drank from the same brew of tea without realizing it.'

In his book *The Charlton Brothers*, Norman Harris writes: 'They brought programmes which showed off their well-appointed grounds and the green grass – though Bobby could see the grass was painted in – and they talked of the players who made their club great, and how happy everyone was there.'

United had a disarmingly effective 'procurer' of young talent in their chief scout, Joe Armstrong. He had made several trips up to the north-east to watch Bobby play after a tip-off from a local headmaster who knew the Charltons. This was the time when United had caught the imagination of the country with their youth policy. Seventeen- and eighteen-year-olds were regularly appearing in their League side, and every other club in the country wanted to get in on the act. Clubs that had lived by the cheque book and transfer system suddenly discovered that the raw material was lying around in England's schools. It had taken them a long time to wake up to the fact.

'I don't want to butter you up, missus,' Joe Armstrong famously said to Cissie Charlton the first time he watched Bobby, 'but your son will play for England before he's twenty-one.' But Joe *was* a butter-upperer and a present-bringer and a clever, salt-of-the-earth schmoozer. He was a fixer and facilitator; it was his stock-in-trade. (He also had a good eye. In his report after seeing Charlton play in that first match, in difficult winter conditions, he emphasized his intelligent use of the ball with both feet and also his inclination not to rush forward. He recommended Charlton to Matt Busby, who, when he went to see him play in a trial, noted that 'he did everything with care, almost as if he was sitting at a piano'.)

Offering cash bribes to the parents of young players was, in theory, illegal. But it was no secret it went on. 'One fellow offered £800,' Mrs Charlton said. 'Another said he'd double whatever was the highest offer we'd had. There was another fellow in the front room who said he'd got £550 in his brief-case, and we could have it there and then.' After being visited by the manager of a famous club, the mother of another young hopeful found a parcel containing £2,000 in £5 notes under the cushion of the chair where the manager had been sitting. 'It's not mine,' he told her when she phoned him up. 'I'd keep it if I were you.' Her son signed.

When the education authorities expressed their concern about the pack of scouts who had taken to following Charlton to every school match he played, Joe Armstrong started to say he was Bobby's uncle, and then he'd introduce his wife and say, 'And this is his Auntie Sally.'

Eamon Dunphy, Matt Busby's biographer and, as a former player there himself, a reassuringly reliable witness in regard to most things connected to Old Trafford, believes that the appointment of Armstrong as chief scout in 1949 was as vital as any Busby made in his managerial career: 'If the family was religious Joe would add a Miraculous Medal he'd brought especially from Rome to the other gifts he bore. The medal would be for real, as were the other kindnesses . . . The Armstrong approach worked in many ways, not the least of them being that the greedy, cynical and insensitive [families] would be weeded out at the wooing stage.'

There's no reason to think that what was happening in Northumberland with the Charltons hadn't already happened a year before in the Black Country. 'All the clubs were after [Duncan] as a schoolboy,' Annie Edwards once said, 'and we would have loved him to play for the Wolves, or the Albion, or the Villa. But he said that Manchester United were the greatest club in the country and nothing would stop him from going to Old Trafford.'

In his posthumously published book *Tackle Soccer This*

Way, Edwards tells the tale, now passed into folklore, of how he was dragged out of bed at two o'clock on the morning of his sixteenth birthday to put his signature to the document making him a Manchester United player which Matt Busby in person had motored south from Manchester to deliver, waking up half of the Priory estate with his knocking: 'Still half-dazed, I made my way into the light of the sitting room to come face to face for the first time with Matt Busby, the manager of Manchester United. He had known better than I about the interest other clubs had taken in me, and he wanted to be the first to talk to my parents . . . Of such episodes as these', Edwards concludes, 'are schoolboy dreams composed.' Even the normally irreproachable Arthur Hopcraft sticks to this account in his sixties classic, *The Football Man*.

There *was* a through-the-night dash from Manchester, prompted by the rumour that Bolton Wanderers, who had been in conversation with the family, were about to secure Edwards's signature: his cousin, Dennis Stephens, was already on their books. And he did sign for United in the middle of the night dressed in his pyjamas. But the date was 2 June 1952, not the first of October. And the envoys were the United assistant manager, Jimmy Murphy, and the coach Bert Whalley, who was to be among those killed at Munich.

It is perhaps a clue to the towering stature and totemic presence of Matt Busby that Edwards chose to remember him being there at this major turning point in his young life, even across a distance of only five years. Significantly, Annie Edwards would perform a similar act of misremembering when she placed Busby not only in the room but standing next to her on the occasion when she said her final goodbye to Duncan. It happened in the chapel at the Rechts der Isar hospital. 'We linked arms,' Mrs Edwards said, 'my husband Gladstone, Matt Busby and his wife, when we went in to see him. I can't begin to explain how I felt when I saw him. I expected his body to be laid out, but he was sitting upright on a chair. I went over and held him and kissed him.'

Matt Busby, of course, was in another part of the hospital then, trachaeotomized and sedated in an oxygen tent, fighting for his life.

The legend of the holy drinker #18

I believe in ambition in sport. I believe that a man should aim to reach the top of his class. It keeps the game alive for him. And the first obstacle that stands between you and success at football is that ball – that slippery, mischievous, unpredictable ball. Make it your slave, and you are halfway to success. Let it master you and your football fate is not your own.

Duncan Edwards, *Tackle Soccer This Way*

What is it with ballplayers? What is it about roundness that they understand better than we do? The world is round. They understand that too.

Martin Amis, *Money*

Perfectly round. Even distribution of mass. But empty inside . . . Nothing in there but evacuated air that smells like a kind of rubber hell.

David Foster Wallace, *Infinite Jest*

[His hand] remembers. It remembers exactly. That tan pebbled roundness, the smooth seams between, the little circlet for taking the air valve. A big pebbled ball that wants to fly.

John Updike, *Rabbit at Rest*

The arc of his life progressed as follows: he got into bed with the ball, and then he got into bed with the bottle.

This was literally the case.

As a schoolboy and young teenager, Best was inseparable from the ball. He used to take a ball to bed with him. 'I know it sounds daft,' he once said, 'but I loved the feel of it. I used to hold it, look at it and think, "One day you'll do everything I tell you."'

With the dubbined and laced leather ball secure under the slippery eiderdown beside him, in his dreams he was at Wembley and there were 100,000 people in the ground and it was a Cup Final. He turned on the most incredible show anybody had ever seen in a football ground. 'First I'd take the ball on my thigh and bounce it in the air as I ran the length of the field. Then I'd trap the ball by sitting on it – there'd be a long clearance downfield and I'd control it with my arse. Then we'd be awarded a penalty and I'd walk up to the keeper, point to the underside of the crossbar and say, "It's going in off there." And it would.'

Even when he was tucked up under the candlewick in the upstairs bedroom at Mrs Fullaway's neat council house in Chorlton, a fledgling professional, he kept a ball close by him in his bed at night. Any psychiatrist would have a field day with this information. (The club made him see a psychiatrist when he did a runner from Mrs Fullaway's as a fifteen-year-old, after being away from his Belfast home for something like forty-eight hours. 'I just looked at him and said nothing,' Best remembered. 'Like I used to when Matt had a go at me. Yes, boss, no, boss. Bollocks . . . Look, I wanted to tell him, if I've fucked it up I've done it myself and what's more, I've enjoyed it!')

The sexual symbolism of ball and bed is given considerable weight by the fact that, pre-war – and, at many English clubs, even long after it – a rudimentary rule of coaching was that players wouldn't be allowed so much as a sniff of a ball from Saturday to Saturday. Starved in this way, they would be that much more 'hungry' for it come match day. Training was about instilling discipline and application, developing stamina and strength, and was all gym work and yomping up and down the terraces. The conventional wisdom stated that anything else – basic ball skills, mastery of the ball, heel-training it so that it knew when to obey, when to come and stay; the awakening of skill and talent – was 'continental' and therefore risible. Stan Cullis at Wolverhampton Wanderers and Busby at

United became the most influential football managers in the fifteen years after the war by turning their backs on this nonsense.

A constant in every book by or about a footballer born between the wars or as part of the baby-boom generation in the late forties, is the sentence very near the beginning which is a version of these near-identical ones from biographical sketches of Duncan Edwards and Bobby Charlton: 'I remember the times I used to tell Duncan as a little boy not to bring a ball with him when we went visiting, but no matter how often I said it, he always managed to hide a ball away somewhere. Once we arrived, out would come the ball and away he would go. There was no stopping him then.' 'Bobby always had a soft rubber ball in his pocket. Wherever he walked in Ashington he took it out and kicked it along in front of him through the gutter.' A few pages later comes the arrival of the first pair of grown-up boots: 'One luxury, one that was never forthcoming, would have been a real football. But there did come a day when a real pair of football boots was acquired – a beautiful pair of pigskin McGregors with big, hard, black toes and brand-new laces. They were almost new. Jack took them home and put them on his bare feet and sat soaking them in a bucket of cold water. They would then fit properly, having dried to the feet. This is what he had been advised by Bobby, who knew about these things' (from *The Charlton Brothers*).

Bobby Charlton and his teammates in their junior-school team in Ashington wore shorts made out of wartime blackout curtaining. Duncan Edwards's neighbours used to see him kicking a tin can along Elm Road and into the car park at the Wren's Nest pub. For other players from the same kinds of poor but respectable working-class backgrounds, the ball substitute was rags bound up with string, or balled socks, or even a rock or half a brick. These were hard times. Willie Irvine, George Best's Northern Ireland teammate, who Best roomed with on international tours, has written about the days he was sent to school with no shoes: 'The school was only 300 yards away but that was far enough in bare feet in the snow. But when you had no money, like us, and the one pair of shoes you had was worn through, or had to be saved for best, you thought nothing about it. And we weren't the only ones.'

Best himself has recalled how, as a boy in the fifties, he used to play all the time and in all weathers in thin sandshoes, always called 'gutties' on the Cregagh estate: 'Proper football boots were far too expensive, though every Christmas I got shirt, shorts and socks.' He had to be content with a tennis ball instead of a football most of the time: 'We kicked a ball around at every opportunity, from dawn to dusk, we did it because we loved it, but also because in those days there was nothing else to do . . . If I was on my own in the street, and couldn't knock a tennis ball back and forth with a pal, I would try and hit the kerbstone so that the ball would come straight back to me. With the garage doors, I would try to hit the knob on the doors

. . . My parents had to come looking for me every night. Even when it was pitch black I'd still be there. They had to drag me off the streets.'

When the time came and he got a real ball, he'd take the ball to bed, his most precious possession and the instrument and evidence of his obsession. A close, almost forensic, even fetishistic attention to the plastic fact of the ball – its size, weight, consistency, colour, texture, resiliency and liveliness.

And when the ball stopped doing it for him, he swapped it for the bottle.

'When I arrived back . . . I was confronted with a shocking scene. George was lying in bed surrounded by dozens of empty wine bottles. His face was even more yellow, his feet were swollen and he stank of booze . . . He started drinking brandy as well as wine; [he] would wake up and take swigs from a bottle of Pinot Grigio . . .

'George was lying on the bed. He was naked and surrounded by around ten empty bottles; an overflowing ashtray was on the bedside table.' In her book *Always Alex*, his former wife gives many examples of bottles sharing the bed with George, filling the space where she had once been. 'He seemed to want to surround himself with images of drink,' she said. 'So many pictures he bought for the house were of pub scenes.'

Three

As Joe Armstrong and his team of regional and amateur scouts scoured the country, checking out school and church and youth-club matches in search of promising young talent, so began a ritual which would be repeated for as long as Matt Busby and United ignored the transfer market and continued to pursue their highly effective youth policy. Every June and July, bewildered-looking, poorly dressed, often puny boys, most of them experiencing being away from home on their own for the first time, would step off the train at London Road station to be met by Jimmy Murphy or Bert Whalley ('I'll be standing at the barrier – I'll have a blazer on and a flower in my buttonhole'), who would escort them by taxi to the homes of one of the half-dozen landladies in the suburbs of southern Manchester who had been vetted and approved by the club.

Boarding-house stories are as much a staple of footballers' books as they are of golden-age-of-showbiz biographies. Willie Irvine, for example – 'just 16 and utterly and totally lost and bewildered' – remembers the digs run by Big Jim and Dolly Haworth that he was put into on arriving in Burnley, fresh out of Northern Ireland in the summer of 1960: 'Dolly was a local fortune-teller and her front room was where she had all her paraphernalia and where she took all her clients. We five apprentices were forbidden to enter that room, but we'd see people going in and out of there, usually looking quite embarrassed . . . This was the house that had no inside toilet so the routine we'd use was a pop bottle in the bedroom if we needed to and then empty it the following morning. This worked fine if you remembered to empty it.'

Rogue landladies used to slip through even the Manchester United net. Mark Jones and Jackie Blanchflower shared a room in a house run by a Mrs Browne in Manchester in 1950.

The digs weren't great. Mr Browne liked a drink; pissed, he would fight with Mrs Browne and shout at the two lodgers. They told Bert Whalley. Bert moved them to the 'private hotel' at 5 Birch Avenue run by the fabled Mrs Watson, self-styled official 'mother' to all the Busby Babes. (Mr Watson, it turned out, wasn't such a paragon: his wife would eventually catch him in bed with one of the maids and shut up shop, moving on solo to take up the position of housekeeper to the Lieutenant-Governor of the Isle of Man.)

Neither Duncan Edwards nor Bobby Charlton came from what could be thought of as rustic backgrounds. Despite its proximity to what would come to be known as 'Shakespeare Country' and the Cotswolds, Dudley, as we've seen, was a place of tall black chimneys vomiting blacker smoke. In Ashington, 'the biggest mining village in the world', there was never a season, day or night when soot wasn't sifting down in smuts from the sky; a baby left outside had to have a cloth placed over it.

But, like George Best a few years later, both Edwards and Charlton on their arrival in Manchester were unprepared for the mile-on-mile oppressive grim greyness of what had been one of the nineteenth century's miracle cities – the city from which industrialization had spread across the entire world. Whole areas of the inner-city were under constant threat of being blotted out by smog and pollution. Even as late as the mid-sixties, a traveller arriving by air could register the following impression: 'Looping round in one more curve, the roar of the engines steadily increasing, the plane set a course across open country. By now, we should have been able to make out the sprawling mass of Manchester, yet one could see nothing but a faint glimmer, as if from a fire almost suffocated in ash. A blanket of fog that had risen out of the marshy plains that reached as far as the Irish Sea had covered the city, a city spread across a thousand square kilometres.'

Its closeness to the docks on the Manchester Ship Canal and the giant industrial centre of Trafford Park meant that United's ground at Old Trafford had taken a direct hit during the war and remained a weed-choked bomb site throughout the 1940s. When football returned there at the begining of the 1949 season, the terraces still gave a view on to the Lowry-like landscape of hundreds of spiked chimneys belching smoke into the surrounding atmosphere from the furnaces and coal fires of Trafford Park.

'When we got to the ground there was this smell,' Gordon Clayton remembered. 'It was the fumes from Trafford Park. I'll never forget that Old Trafford smell. When I think of Manchester United, I always get that funny smell.'

Clayton was from Cannock, a small town in Staffordshire mining country. He had played in goal for Staffordshire Boys, Duncan Edwards left half for Worcestershire. They were both

eligible for Birmingham Boys, which is how they met and became inseparable friends. They had gone on to play together for England Schoolboys at a time when Edwards was captain. They had been sold on the idea of a career at United by the club's Midlands scout Reg Priest and were still a few months from turning sixteen when they embarked on the next stage of their life together in Manchester.

'Duncan said he'd meet me on the train,' Clayton told Eamon Dunphy. '"I'll save you a seat," he promised. He got on at Dudley, I got on at Stafford. I can see it now. The train is pulling into Stafford and he is hanging out the window waving. He'd saved me a seat. The train was empty. But he saved my seat!'

When they got to Mrs Watson's, the house was unusually empty. It was June 1952. United had just won the League, the first time the Championship trophy had been back at Old Trafford in over forty years. The commercial travellers and long-distance lorry drivers who lodged with the footballers were off at work (or at the cricket – Lancashire County Cricket Club's ground was a hundred yards away along Talbot Road). The players who were her 'permanent paying guests', as Mrs Watson, a matronly, white-aproned figure, liked to refer to them – Mark Jones, Jackie Blanchflower, David Pegg, Johnny Berry – were on a summer tour of America with the club and would be slightly put out when they got back to find new faces about the place. 'We were a bit disturbed, somebody had broken into our little circle,' Blanchflower said. 'We were a bit jealous, probably a bit too hard on them.'

A rigid hierarchy of age and achievement was in place. The team that won the Championship in 1952 was essentially the team that had won the classic Cup Final against Blackpool in 1948. They were local legends, but they were ageing: Johnny Carey, the captain, was thirty-three; Jack Rowley, scorer of thirty goals that season, was thirty-two; many of the others – Johnny Aston, Henry Cockburn, Allenby Chilton, Stan Pearson – were looking at thirty. The first wave of Babes –

Blanchflower, Pegg, Jones, and local Manchester 'finds' Jeff Whitefoot, Dennis Viollet and Roger Byrne (who, at twenty-two, was three or four years older than the others) – were not only jostling to take their places, they were also tagging along, pissing on their parade during the celebratory trip across the Atlantic on the *Queen Elizabeth*, wearing their bibs and nappies when the team was invited to dinner in the first-class dining room.

'The Great Manchester United!' that was announced over the tannoy to a crowd of 35,000 at Yankee Stadium and to other enthusiastic crowds in Los Angeles, Chicago, Vancouver, Detroit . . . That wasn't a bunch of spotty-arsed youths. It was Carey, Rowley, Aston, the players who'd come back from the war and worked their bollocks off for £12 a week – plus the Boss's fatherly perks of Eddie Calvert and the Crazy Gang at Blackpool Opera House with an overnight at the Norbreck Hydro Hotel on the front, and Mondays on the golf course at Davyhulme with a dinner of the mixed-grill special afterwards – and put silverware back on the table.

Then, on their return, the founding first-wave Babes found the beginning of a second wave of poxy schoolboys already getting its feet under the table at Ma Watson's. 'Here's your toast, done on just the one side, the way you like it, Duncan . . . Are you sure wouldn't like that tea warming up?'

'Looking back', Bobby Charlton would say, 'I can see the subtlety of United's method. When I first linked up with them as a kid fresh out of Ashington, I went into digs with eight or nine other players. It was great fun, everybody ribbed everybody else and gags rattled off like machine-gun fire. But this was something more than a hostel for high-spirited youths. This was where the real business of becoming a United player began.

'You see, we weren't just a gang of kids thrown together to enjoy ourselves. Fourth and fifth teamers straight from school shared those digs with men from the League side. Jackie Blanchflower, Duncan Edwards, Mark Jones and the rest – we all shared the same table and the same conversation, which was invariably about football. Without knowing it, we were learning our business the painless way.'

When he was manager of the England team, Walter Winterbottom claimed that he could pick out a Manchester United player without seeing him. He'd be sitting in a hotel room talking to a friend and he'd say: 'That's Bobby Charlton walking down the corridor,' and he'd be right. 'They have a walk of their own up there,' Winterbottom explained. 'They've all got it – a kind of Manchester United stomp. You can hear their assurance in it.'

Charlton didn't disagree. 'We at United are not so much a team as a breed,' he said.

The ability and determination to become a professional footballer was important in a novice player; a willingness to listen to and act on advice was also crucial. But 'club spirit', a commitment to the club as 'family': these were the qualities Matt Busby and his assistant Jimmy Murphy prized most and worked tirelessly to instil.

Birch Avenue was part of a small villa estate that was only a short walk from Old Trafford. Number five was actually two houses that had been knocked together, and the atmosphere there, given that it was home to a lively group of adolescent, testosterone-charged young men, was remarkably restrained. There was a tablecloth on the circular mahogany dining table which was laid every day for breakfast and tea, the permanent churchy smell of beeswax polish, and a grandfather clock with a clanking mechanism and an audible tick. Mrs Watson prided herself on knowing the players' wives, their girlfriends, their mothers and fathers. She knew their idiosyncrasies, their temperaments, their faddish likes and dislikes, and threw a celebration dinner every time one of 'her' boys moved up from the ranks into the first team to become what, from around the mid-fifties, the press starting calling the 'Babes' (an expression Busby always hated; 'Red Devils' was better; at least it didn't make him wince).

After the multi-span roof of the main stand at Old Trafford, the big white carved plaster gateway to the White City greyhound and speedway stadium was the most visible landmark of the Trafford Park area. Birch Avenue was sandwiched between White City to the north and Old Trafford Bowling Club to the south, with its equally distinctive classic black and white Tudorbethan pavilion. It says a great deal about the temper of the time that the young United hopefuls were more likely to be found killing time with a bit of crown-green bowling than at the dogs (where an added disincentive was the fact that there was a better-than-even chance they could bump into Mr Busby).

Nevertheless, as United players they were entitled to a free pass to the White City, as well as to its long-established rival track at Belle Vue. There were arrangements in place for them to be passed in to all the cinemas in the city, and Duncan Edwards and Bobby Charlton made full use of these to spend long afternoons watching the cartoons and the Movietone newsreel programmes at the News Theatre in Oxford Road. More sociably, if enough of the younger ones wanted to go to the pictures, Mark Jones, the player they regarded as a kind of father figure – 'He smoked a pipe and had a sort of presence,' Bobby Charlton said. 'To us he was an old man; he was only 22' – marched them off on the five miles into town like a sergeant major. Then he'd make them walk all the way back to get the stiffness out of their legs. (Wilf McGuinness, the player who for a brief spell in the late sixties succeeded Busby as manager, once said that the typical sound of a Saturday night in the rear stalls at the Gaumont and the Odeon in town was the sound of United players yelling and suddenly screeching in agony: 'They'd come down with cramp in their thighs and their hamstrings. We didn't have rubdowns like they do today.') After he became known, Edwards would go straight from one picture house to the next, to disappear in the dark. He couldn't get enough of films.

'Duncan was a little bit introverted when he came to

Manchester first,' his good friend, the big goalkeeper Gordon Clayton, said. 'He wouldn't go to the bank on his own, for example. He wasn't a mixer as such. He was shy with people.'

It is a description that seems to have applied to many of the first intake of Babes in the early fifties: 'quiet and distant', 'very moralistic and shy', 'he had an inferiority complex', 'terribly shy type of a lad', 'socially conservative'. The same phrases crop up time and again in accounts of the lives of Edwards, Charlton, Billy Whelan and others among Mrs Watson's finest. What they really seem to have been, a lot of the time, was homesick and intimidated. They were fifteen- and sixteen-year-olds who, up to the day they left home, had been stars in their city, county and even England international schoolboy and junior sides, doorstepped by scouts and courted by the glamour clubs. Suddenly they were anonymous and convinced nobody gave a mousefart whether they stayed or went. Physically they felt inadequate, undersized and puny.

At the age of fifteen, dressed in his first-ever pair of long trousers, George Best would see the imposing physique of Harry Gregg and the other players he met on his first morning at Old Trafford and be off scuttling back to Belfast. 'He looked like Superman. To two kids like [me and Eric McMordie] he was a giant. Even the junior players. They were a couple of years older than us and had spent those years training and building up their bodies so even they seemed enormous. I remember thinking: What chance have two little waifs like us got of making it in a game full of men like these? The size of everyone frightened the life out of me.'

Bobby Charlton also remembers having any of the vainglory that might have come from being the most sought-after English schoolboy player of his generation knocked out of him virtually on arrival in Manchester: 'Jimmy Murphy met me. When we were in the taxi going to my digs he said, "We've just signed this young lad from Dudley in the Midlands called Duncan Edwards and he has a great left foot and a great right foot, he's strong in the tackle, he's great in the air, he reads the game and he can play

in any position, and he is fast and has tremendous enthusiasm."
And then he must have realized that he had gone too far, so he
said: "And when I knock all the rough edges off him, I'm going
to make him a decent player." And I thought, "Bloody hell."'

Players couldn't sign professional papers with the club until
they turned seventeen. Between fifteen and seventeen they had
two choices: to go 'on the brush' – clearing weeds off the pitch
surrounds, cleaning out the toilets, sweeping out the turnstiles,
brushing the car park, cleaning windows (the step up to cleaning players' boots came later) – or take a job in one of the hundreds of joiners and plumbers and small engineering shops
packed in-between and around the docks in Trafford Park.
Boys who went for this option only came in for training two
nights a week. Whichever way you jumped, it was another
massive blow to the ego.

Duncan Edwards was apprenticed to a cabinet-maker but
hated it and left to become a member of the United ground
staff by the end of 1952. Bobby Charlton was working in engineering at first. Swilling out toilets wasn't his mother's idea of
how to earn a living (although that is what her eldest son Jack
was doing as an apprentice at Leeds United). Every morning,
as Bobby left the house at seven to begin his duties as a dogs-
body and tea boy, Duncan would call downstairs, 'Don't slam
the door!'

Edwards had already made his first-team debut, aged six-
teen-and-a-bit, by the time Charlton arrived in Manchester, in
May 1953. In addition to his commanding physical presence,
this gave him added lustre. First-teamers and wet-behind-the-
ears players like Charlton didn't usually fraternize. They didn't
go to the same dance halls or use the same pubs; whole areas
of Old Trafford, including the main dressing room and treatment room, were off limits to boys like Bobby. In *My Soccer
Life*, he admits that, even after he became a first-team regular
himself, he found the highly finessed in-house status details
and demarcations difficult to negotiate: 'Perhaps more than
anything that happened on the field I found the change in my

status at the Saturday night get-togethers bringing my new position home to me. In those days United's reserve and first-team players used to meet in a pub for a drink before we went on to a dance. It became a ritual and, if I was playing in the reserves in the Midlands, I would dash back with the others to be there. But, once I was promoted, I noticed the difference. Then I would arrive with the first-team crowd. It seemed so strange that it took me nearly as long to get used to that as it did to adjust my football.'

Edwards, though he seemed to take his rising-star status as a given (even the older players like Johnny Aston and Jack Rowley were unusually free with their praise), didn't pull rank. In fact, one of his first gestures towards Charlton was a generous one. Seeing how badly off he was for clothes, Duncan made Bobby a present of one of his own shirts. It was miles too big and swamped him, but Charlton was touched.

In any case, their relationship was complicated by the fact that, in addition to turning out in League matches at Old Trafford and being written up in the papers, Edwards was playing alongside Charlton on equal terms in the Manchester United side competing for the Youth Cup. This was an under-eighteen knockout tournament launched by the Football Association in 1952 and, in Busby's and Jimmy Murphy's opinion, it was crucial for United to perform well and win it in order to show that their policy of finding and hot-housing schoolboy players really was, as they repeatedly insisted, the way to guarantee the club's future.

Youth Cup matches were an instant hit with the public. Murphy's daring, open, attacking style drew large crowds to Old Trafford. The Youth team's attendances outstripped most First Division clubs' and, with Edwards in the team, United were simply unbeatable. They were the winners of the Youth Cup for the first five years of its existence and went forty-three games without defeat.

It was this tournament which established Duncan Edwards as one of the outstanding midfield players in the world and ensured that, in 1954, he became the youngest player ever to win a full cap for England, aged eighteen. 'He really was a human tornado,' the Manchester United historian Brian Hughes has written. 'He loved to attack, but because he played in a successful United team he was well covered, and the power and drive he produced time after time brought him vital goals. Nevertheless, he never forgot that his first job was to put the brakes on the opposition forwards. Duncan . . . was a wing-half who proved the accuracy of the old maxim that to have a top-class player in the half-back line was half the secret of a team's success.'

'When Duncan was in United's youth side,' Bobby Charlton said, 'he was alongside a great many other good players. Yet, even then, he looked like an international. The sight of him was enough . . . He was a phenomenon. I think the sight of him in those youth matches used to put the fear of God in some sides. Even if he did nothing in the game (and that was never the case), he still had the ability to put us halfway along the winning path by just pulling on the number-six shirt.

'I liked the feeling. I knew I was in a great side because I could feel it in the play. I didn't need the results to make me aware of it. The speed of the game was breathtaking, and we were faster than most because we had so many good players. Our play knitted together as if it was the most natural thing in the world.'

Another talented player from the youth team who would graduate to the League side was Liam 'Billy' Whelan, a devout, teetotal Catholic from Dublin who was seventeen when he was spotted and brought to Manchester. Whelan's problem was that, unlike Edwards and Charlton, he remained self-conscious and shy on the pitch as well as off it. 'Billy Whelan was an absolute genius with a ball at his feet,' Jimmy Murphy said. 'If he would just believe in himself more he would be sensational.' It was Murphy's job to fire up Whelan's self-belief before a match, but with somebody so naturally nice and sensible and quiet it was difficult.

Murphy got to know which of 'Big Dunc''s buttons to push

in the team talk, very successfully, as Jackie Milburn once confirmed: 'This big lad came up to me at the start of the game and said, "Reputations mean nothing to me and if you come near me I'll kick you over the stand." And that's just what he tried to do as soon as I got the ball. United beat us 5–2 in that game. What a team they had – and what a player that big lad Duncan was. He was a nice lad too, for all his size and power. After the game he came to me and said, "It was a pleasure playing against you."'

Jimmy Murphy, known as 'Tapper' Murphy in his playing days for the ferocity of his tackle, was loud and belligerent, and these were qualities he looked for in a player. A favourite technique was to sidle up to an individual when he was on his own, throw an arm around his shoulder and confide in him something about the man he was meant to be marking. 'Wilf, son,' he said to Wilf McGuinness on the occasion of his first-team debut against Wolves in October 1955, 'you're playing against Peter Broadbent today, now I want you to mark him tightly. This man wants to pinch money from your dear old mother's purse.' What Murphy was referring to, of course, was the loss of McGuinness's win bonus if Wolves beat them. But the young defender took what Jimmy had told him literally. During the kickabout before the game, Broadbent, knowing it was McGuinness's first big match, walked over to him and held out his hand to wish him the best of luck. 'Fuck off, you thieving bastard,' was the reply he got.

'Peter Broadbent was a lovely, mild-mannered bloke,' McGuinness remembered many years later, 'but because of what Jimmy told me, I had him down as a snide, a thief.' But McGuinness had a good match. 'Your dear old mother will be proud of you,' Murphy beamed as the teams came off.

None of his standard repertoire, though, seemed any good at stirring Billy Whelan's blood. During practice matches he'd push him in the back, knock him off balance, pull his jersey, give him an ankle tap, trip him up, urge him to play it hard, but nothing: Whelan would never react.

'Oh, fair,' he'd say when his mother would ask him how he'd played after a match. Always that.

'Billy Whelan was a wonderful inside forward, tall, graceful and tremendously skilful,' Matt Busby said. 'A slow kind of skill. But he was the opposite of Duncan Edwards. Billy had an inferiority complex. He was a terribly shy type of lad. I don't think he knew just how good he was. I remember one day when a section of the crowd were having a go at him and he just could not do a thing right. The following Tuesday I took him to one side and asked, "What was wrong with you on Saturday?" He looked shy and awkward and said, very quietly, "Those people in the crowd were shouting at me." I looked at him and said, "If you're going to take notice of people like that you might as well go back home to Dublin right now."'

Because he was a quiet, inoffensive type of person who never swore, Jimmy Murphy toned down the blistering industrial language he used with the other players when he was with Whelan. 'If you weren't such a great player, you'd make a smashing priest,' Jimmy would regularly tell Billy.

At Mrs Watson's, Billy shared a room with Bobby Charlton, who often said he thought of Billy as 'a big brother'.

'I couldn't stand his holier-than-thou attitude and that image of the fine upstanding athlete. I thought he was too good to be true. I thought he was a bloody misery. I was dying for him to say "fuck" just once.' George Best's feelings of being at odds with Bobby Charlton are no doubt ones that would have also coloured any relationship he might have had with Billy Whelan, had he been spared. But the converse is also true: it is likely that whenever Best turned up for training smelling of drink or failed to report for training or boasted about how many women he'd slept with in a night or totalled a car, Bobby Charlton's mind sometimes turned to Billy Whelan and Tommy Taylor and David Pegg and the other inoffensive types from a quieter time whose bodies he'd seen scattered across the tarmac at Munich.

They'd had a good night. Nothing pious. The United players liked the Yugoslavs, and the Yugoslavs had laid on an official dinner after the game in Belgrade, which had gone on until midnight. Then Charlton, together with most of the rest of the team – it isn't recorded whether Billy Whelan was among them – moved to the British Embassy staff club to have a few for the road.

Many were still nursing hangovers as the plane prepared to take off from Riem airport for the third time, the snow coming down and the slush flying about. Harry Gregg remembered glancing over at Roger Byrne and thinking he looked scared, not like him. Johnny Berry murmured aloud that he thought they would all be killed. 'Well, if that's going to happen I'm ready for it,' Billy Whelan said as the wing of the Elizabethan sliced into the house at the end of the runway where Mrs Anna Winkler was sewing as her children finally quieted into their afternoon nap.

The palpable lure of large events. The story that is tragic and awful and impossible to ignore.

The legend of the holy drinker #16

A drink called a kir. A heavy red syrup, topped up with dry white wine. What George would once have scoffed at as a girl's drink. Very popular in Chelsea, at the Phene, especially in summer, when the outdoor area filled up with noisy rich young people and pairs of girlfriends on the pull, pretty and blonde like Alex, who was at home with her soaps, and somebody had to go out and ask them to keep it down because of the neighbours; they were already on a warning and could have the plug pulled at a minute's notice.

A kir was red and so were the wine gums. He used to fake illness. He'd buy some wine gums and suck all the red ones until his throat was stained, and then he'd go home and pretend to be dying from tonsillitis. It worked so well they made him have the tonsils out.

Failing that – his ma wasn't stupid – he'd play truant. He'd hide in the toilets at lunchtime and then go and play soccer in the afternoon just by himself, using a tennis ball.

Sometimes he'd go shoplifting for a change. Nothing serious. Just a few pens and rulers from Woolie's. Now – another glop of kir into the glass, the gurgle of wine, wine and *gomme*, he'd read that on a bottle – he'd think he sometimes wanted to get caught because he wanted people to notice him.

Four

In his fawn topcoat and brushed Jack Buchanan trilby, smoking his pipe, Matt Busby may have looked like a prosperous bank manager from Alderley Edge. In fact, by the early fifties, he was probably the best-connected man in Manchester. Through his football contacts and the network of relationships he had established in the Catholic community across the north-west, his influence was extensive.

So, for example, when he was looking for employers who would be tolerant of the erratic time-keeping and the lack of application sometimes shown by young apprentices at the club, who after all had come there to be turned into legends not expert fixers of a ball-and-socket joint, he frequently looked to some of his many fellow patrons of the Catholic Sportsmen Club, a favourite charity of the better-off Catholics in Manchester, to help him out.

George Best was a small-potatoes beneficiary of the Boss's ability to swing things. Within a week of arriving at Old Trafford for the second time, Best found himself working as a clerk, a gofer at the Manchester Ship Canal Company, making tea all day when all he wanted was to be kicking a bit of leather about. His protests got him moved to another branch of the same company. He still wasn't happy. Next stop was a job in a builder's yard, where he lasted half a day. United finally got the message and signed him on at an electrical business near the Cliff training ground. There, he used to clock on at nine in the morning, walk over to the Cliff, do his training with the rest of the boys, then go back and clock off. End of.

This early licence given to a young player of outstanding potential would one day look like the beginning of the ever-bigger accommodations the club would be prepared to make in order to keep their most gifted – and, in terms of attendance figures, most profitable – player on-side and performing.

Conscription had been reintroduced in 1947, and this was another area where Matt Busby – the former Company Sergeant-Major Instructor Busby for the duration of the war – was in a position to oil the wheels and make crucial checks and balances. It was a simple (if unofficial) trade-off: the army wanted the pick of the best available young players for its team, and the club wanted the players it had under contract to be released from army duties as and when it needed them for key matches.

Being a football-player conscript, especially one with connections to Manchester United, was, as Bill Foulkes found out, a guarantee of a lot of feather-bedding: 'It was great at Aldershot. The CO was great. He wanted our battalion to win the Army Cup and I was put in charge of the team, played – and was chief scout . . . A captain advised me never to wear battle dress around the camp, but to go around in a track suit and pumps. I took his advice. I never wore that battle dress. In fact, when I came to leave, it was stuck to the door with mould. I was put in a special billet in a little room next to the canteen where the civilians who worked on the camp ate. It was great . . . No one ever knew where I was billeted. They knew I was on the camp, because I used to show my face from time to time and was always running around. But they didn't really know where to find me.'

But on the day he got his call-up papers in 1956, Bobby Charlton didn't know this was the way the world turned when you had United lined up behind you. He had been told by Busby to apply for the Royal Army Ordnance Corps, because their base was within reasonable commuting distance of Manchester, at Donnington, near Shrewsbury. But at the end of his five weeks of basic training at Portsmouth, Charlton received his orders to go out to Malaya, where the British Army had been fighting a long campaign against nationalist guerrillas. It was a dry-mouthed Charlton who phoned Old Trafford to explain the calamitous situation. He was told not to worry: 'We are certain your orders are to travel to Shropshire, not Malaya. It will be sorted out.' The next day, he was instructed to take the train to Shrewsbury.

Duncan Edwards was already in the services. He'd got his call-up the year before and had travelled to London in the back of an army truck with Bill Foulkes. Foulkes had gone one way on arrival and Edwards had gone the other – to RAOC Donnington, in fact, near Shrewsbury.

'He took charge of me the moment I arrived at camp,'

Charlton later remembered. 'He had my billet arranged and everything. When he showed me to the billet, he noticed there was a spring sticking out of the bed. "We can't have that," he said. It was a great big iron bed, but he hoisted it over his shoulder, mattress, frame and all, and went off in search of a better one for me.'

In 1957, United retained the Championship title they'd won the previous season. Edwards played in most first-team matches, Charlton in a dozen or so of them. At the same time they were part of a British Army side so stuffed with quality players it would have beaten most teams in the First Division. Edwards was also putting in regular appearances for England. In one twelve-month period, he played nearly a hundred games for United, England and the Army. 'For Duncan', Charlton would write, 'there was no such thing as an unimportant match. He gave one hundred per cent in the lot. I think that supplies the key to his genius.

'I don't say he always intended to [give as much as he did]. There were probably small-time Army games when he thought he would have a quiet cruise through – just keep out of trouble and not over-tire himself for the next international or League match. But, once the game started, everything else went out of his mind. He ran and tackled and surged through as if his reputation depended on it. Whether it was Wembley or on a bumpy pitch behind the barracks, he became immersed in it.

'How to describe him? He had the sort of build a boxer pines for . . . He was a hard, tough man in the tackle – tougher than Tottenham's Dave Mackay . . . With it, he was as shrewd as Danny Blanchflower [Jackie's elder brother], an intelligent player, but more definite than the Irishman. He liked to be winning or saving matches. He had a shot that could burst through the best goalkeeper's hands yet, when the pressure was on in his own goalmouth, he would be back there battling away.

'He had the sort of speed which made that possible and ensured that he was never caught out of position. One minute he would be clearing off his line, the next surging through at the other end.'

Charlton and Edwards were still close enough to the war in 1956 to think of each other in a way which even then was on the verge of becoming outmoded and soon would be extinct: they were 'comrades'.

When he was unsure whether he ever wanted to play again, in the week or so after Duncan Edwards's death, Charlton went to see his GP in Ashington to have the few stitches over his eye that had been put in at the Rechts der Isar hospital in Munich removed. The stitches were just a pretext, really; Charlton's mother hoped the family doctor might be able to find the words none of them had been able to, which would make Bobby want to pick up his life and go back and play football again.

The word the doctor came up with was 'comrades'. He took out his stitches and told him how it was in the war, pilots having their friends shot down and having to go up again next day. He told him he had been in the RAF and had seen his friends shot down repeatedly, but there was no alternative but to carry on. He spoke not only as a veteran of the war but as somebody whose practice was at the heart of a mining community where crippling injury was an everyday occurrence and death could – and did – happen on any shift. 'Sitting at home reading, or quietly in his place at the tea-table,' Norman Harris writes, 'Bobby saw his father come in most nights not only black but also wet, from working in water up to his neck. Occasionally he heard his father mention that someone that day had got caught between the trucks and been killed. He said it in a sorry, matter-of-fact sort of way, as if it was part of the job.'

Matt Busby, the product of a hard mining background himself, had said in a message from his hospital bed in Munich that the club must go on.

'I expect to see you at Wembley,' was the Ashington doctor's parting shot. And that's what happened. With their patched-together side reconstructed around the nucleus of Bobby Charlton, Manchester United played Bolton Wanderers in the 1958 Cup Final, only twelve weeks after Munich. But the charge of popular sentiment which had carried them to unlikely, emotionally fevered wins in the earlier rounds wasn't enough. They were spent by then, and lost 2–0.

With its lofty calm and English tea-room gentility, Mrs Watson's double residence at Birch Avenue (so different from the tree-named streets on the Priory estate) was the realization of the middle-class ideal of respectability. All the players' mothers approved. Just as the quiet urbanity of Mr Busby fitted their image of a 'real' gentleman, so Mrs Watson, both in her person and in her equably run guest house, was a model of conservatism, order and stability.

The spiritual home of the Busby Babes, though – and, as luck would have it, through the miracle of television it was to become the surrogate home of Britain's uprooted, declassed post-war generations – lay a mile or two to the north of Ma Watson's, in a more traditional, far from gentrified part of Manchester.

In point of fact, Archie Street wasn't in Manchester at all. It was in Salford, which is close enough in geographical terms to be thought of as a district or suburb of its dominant neighbour but tough enough in terms of nous and self-identity to have survived as a separate, free-standing civic entity.

Archie Street was in Ordsall by the docks, in an area dominated by a gasworks, a coal depot and the gothic, liver-coloured brick of the vast Ordsall slaughterhouse. This wasn't 'Lowry-like'; this was *echt*-Lowry: narrow back-to-back rows of workers' terraces set down in the shadow of the mills and factories where generations of Archie Street residents had been put to work 'to serve under the chimney', as they used to say. It was a streetscape whose every lamp post and coal house became familiar to millions of viewers of the new Independent Television station when the cobbled street where the tykeish little player, Eddie Colman, his mum, Liz, and his dad, Dick, lived was chosen for the opening credit sequence of ITV's flagship early-evening serial, *Coronation Street*.

Eddie Colman was 'the flash little townie', in Bobby Charlton's words. Born and brought up in the two-up, two-down in Archie Street where he still lived, he had what we would now think of as 'street smarts' but what his neighbours in those days called 'brass balls'. He was the first person Charlton ever saw in a pair of drainpipe jeans. Eddie prided himself on being the most 'forward dresser' among a group of players who thought that wearing a duffel coat instead of the standard gabardine mac was only asking for ridicule.

Known when he was a kid for being a bit of a villain, he got himself a reputation among the other Babes for being a 'character'. You could always rely on Eddie to get up at the front of the team bus to lead a sing-song. And he never needed much persuasion to dive in and make the running with a couple of girls when Duncan or Bobby or some of the others were too shy to break the ice. David Pegg was another one who was always quick off the mark in that department, and on Saturday nights at the Plaza ballroom, run in those days by Jimmy Savile, or at the Continental, run by 'Mr World', the organizer of the Miss World pageants Eric Morley, Dave and Eddie were happy to 'carry' 'Big Dunc' and Bobby, who were shy with the girls and wouldn't dance and, unless they were pushed, would stay on the edge all night, just standing there looking.

Eddie's house in Archie Street was where Saturday nights often started. There was a little off-licence on the corner and they used to sit in the parlour with Eddie's mum and dad, who'd send down for a jug of beer. Sometimes Eddie's grandad from a couple of streets away would come in and get them started on jokes. Four feet nothing and a complete original. It ran in the family.

'I was very close to Eddie,' Bobby Charlton has said. 'We were all close at that time. At Christmas I would stay with him. We'd play in the morning, then go back to Archie Street for the turkey. We'd have our dinner and then every house in the street would have the doors open. People would be in and out, down to the off-licence for jugs of beer, a real party. Eddie would say, "You've got to hear my Uncle Billy singing, he wants to give you a song, he's the best singer in the world." So Uncle Billy would sing, it was hilarious and non-stop. We'd have a match the next day, so we'd try and get to bed at twelve o'clock. But it was impossible to sleep. Someone was always coming up the stairs saying, "Grandad's here," or whoever.

'I loved Eddie. He'd strut, always laughing, always cool. A Salford lad.'

In the 1980s, Salford Lads' Club (motto: 'To brighten young lives, and make good citizens') would become iconified in a modern, ironic way when The Smiths posed in the street outside it for the picture on the cover of their album *The Queen Is Dead*.

Eddie, the son of Dickie Colman, who was presented with a pair of heavy working boots and a new suit for scoring three goals in the Salford Unemployed Cup Final at Old Trafford in 1933, was an ordinary member of Salford Lads'. Although never taller than five feet seven, he would be remembered as a brilliant basketball player. He was part of the furniture at the club and would often stop by with Bobby or Duncan and other teammates after a United home game. Everybody associated with the club liked him immensely. In Jimmy Murphy's opinion, Colman and Edwards were the best winghalf, or to use the modern terminology, midfield pair seen for many years. The long and the short of it, the one famous for his speed and power, the other for his dinking agility and being able to ghost past defenders, they shared an understanding with each other which struck people as uncanny.

On the morning of the day he was leaving for Yugoslavia, convinced he was taking a step into the unknown by venturing beyond the Iron Curtain, Eddie's mum made him up a parcel containing apples and oranges and a small packet of loose tea. Foreign travel in those days was still an event: Jimmy Savile, always in the vanguard of a trend, used to put a big twelve feet by twelve feet sign up outside the Plaza advertising the fact that he was holidaying on the continent: 'Jimmy Savile is going to the south of France, leaving your entertainment in the very capable hands of his good friends.'

Warned by more experienced players who had already been there of the horrors that could turn up on your plate in the Eastern bloc countries, Bobby Charlton had packed his bag for Belgrade with sweets and chocolates and several packets of biscuits. (The hotel they stayed in turned out to be modern, the catering reasonable; he gave the biscuits and sweets to the cleaner.) Eddie's brown paper bag with some pieces of fruit and the newspaper-twist of tea still in it would turn up among the wreckage at Munich. As a gimmick, Eric Morley of the Continental used to present flat caps with the person's name inscribed inside to mark a certain number of visits to his place. Eddie used to wear his cap, and there it was in the wreckage, together with the red and white Manchester United scarf he used to wear.

On the night of the disaster, Salford Lads' Club opened its doors to mourning supporters, who found it a comfort to know they could go there and find the kind of community feeling which soon would draw viewers to *Coronation Street* in their millions, just as it was disappearing from the real world.

The legend of the holy drinker #11

In October 2003, Best sold his 1968 European Footballer of the Year trophy at auction. It consisted of a small metal replica football on a wooden stand. He put a second trophy, featuring a six-inch-high nickel-plated figure of a footballer on an ebonized plinth, which he got for being voted British Footballer of the Year 1968, into the same sale.

They didn't look much when you saw them; they were a couple of steps up from the painted plastic trophies with little figurines of darts players and golfers on the top that you find

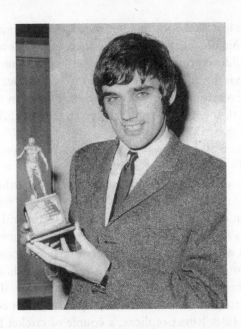

on seafronts up and down the country. They would have had scrap value without Best's name and untarnished, indisputable genius attached to them. But they were the only things of any value from a career that ended when he was twenty-seven that were still in his possession. After letting them lie around half-forgotten in various cellars and attics for over thirty years, the trophies had slipped into a sort of limbo that carried echoes of the strange place Best himself had been since his great glory days blurred into a memory, living always with one foot in oblivion and the other in immortality.

Best was as careless with the things his talent had brought him as he was with his body. While the strips that were actually worn by the other heroes of the club can be seen in the Manchester United museum at Old Trafford, Best's showcase contains a bronze bust that used to adorn the playboy-modernist house he had built in Bramhall and a pair of side-lacing boots 'of the style worn by' George Best. The real things, like all his belongings, have been dispersed, scattered to the wind in one of the lost weekends that, extended, overlapping, came to make up his life. 'This is really all there is,' Best's agent Phil Hughes told me around the time of the Bonhams auction. 'All the rest has been stolen or burgled or given away or just walked. Everything. Contracts, clothes, European Cup winner's medal, the lot. Bled dry. Picked to the bone. After this, there is no more.'

'Of course all life is a process of breaking down,' F. Scott Fitzgerald's story 'The Crackup' famously begins. It was easy to be reminded of this as the lots in Bonhams' sporting memorabilia sale opened for viewing for the first time at the Chester showroom on a biting fresh Saturday in October. Dead and sometimes forgotten and invariably over-the-hill men's boots and shirts went on display alongside prints and drawings and crates of programmes and a signed litre bottle of whisky (slight evaporation) brewed for Sir Matt Busby's testimonial in 1989. The Best trophies occupied a display case which contained some old Jules Rimet replicas, a couple of cricket balls and some other stuff. I was allowed to handle lots 153 and 154 under the supervision of Bob, one of the security staff at Bonhams. 'You're looking at three hundred grand there,' Bob said. 'Some people would rather have a Georgian terraced house, like.'

I asked Dan, Bob's boss, who he thought might buy them; whether he'd had any nibbles. 'You've only got to look at who's in the stands at football grounds these days,' he said. 'You get film stars and pop idols watching. Important people from the law. Big business. I'll say no more than that. Certain pension funds are investing in all sorts of things. The flat cap has gone and the prawn sandwich has come in, so to speak.'

Then we contemplated the trophies for a while in silence. Bob was the first to speak.

'It's a hero's trophy,' he said, polishing the little figurine's noggin with his jacket cuff. 'It's the fruit and rewards of his efforts. We've all witnessed him, haven't we? We haven't had to wait for some jacked-up critic to tell us why he's good. "Oh, look at the brush strokes on him, the character and depth of colour," and similar-like shite. Picasso never had to run around with 100,000 yelling for his blood. We can't all be twinkletoes, but you want to *live* George. That's the beauty and value of his stuff.'

Best had said he intended to use the money to buy a place where he, his soon to be ex-wife Alex, his son Calum and other family and friends could go and relax in the sun. The trophies represented a profound emotional link with Matt Busby and the players who died at Munich. Best had made it clear there was only one place he wanted to see these mementoes of his *annus mirabilis* of 1968 end up. 'It's a money-making machine at Manchester United,' Hughes said. 'They're the richest club in the world. And even the miserable bean-counters who know to the nearest penny what's going in and out should be saying we want this stuff and will buy it at any fucking cost. No two ways about it, it should be there.'

On the day, United weren't in the bidding. The European Footballer of the Year award went for £167,000. The other lot failed to find a buyer.

Five

The Duncan Edwards

Beside the font there's a tray containing jars of home-made marmalade and jam and quince jelly, dated and hand-labelled in a way that has been familiar in England for generations. The church kneelers and samplers have been hand-embroidered by parishioners and, to complete the peaceful, pastoral picture, Father Geoff – warm, welcoming, his cheeks plump and rosy, his silver hair worn in a schoolboy fringe – has on a pair of open-toed Jesus sandals. It is a summer afternoon and Father Geoff is wearing a grey, short-sleeved vicar's shirt with his dog collar. On his wrist there's a white 'Peacethroughunderstanding' charity bracelet.

The atmosphere inside St Francis's is benign. It could still be the rural parish it once was, almost within living memory, when it was woodland all across the Priory where the big council estate spills like paint and the surrounding green spaces were true nature rather than, as now, a 'green-lung' nature reserve.

The church itself is a solid red-brick building, plain apart from some Arts and Crafts-type detail around the porch. It is hemmed in by monotonous streets of the Depression-era housing built for what were then referred to as families of the 'working poor'. Duncan Edwards was buried from St Francis's on 26 February 1958, when 50,000 people lined the route and the curtains of every house on the Priory were pulled shut as a mark of respect.

Crowds gathered again three years later to see Matt Busby, Bobby Charlton and all the survivors of Munich attend the service of dedication of the Duncan Edwards windows, led by the Bishop of Worcester. Prayers were offered, lessons read:

'The light of the City was like unto a stone most precious / Even like a jasper stone, clear as crystal.' Unveiling the windows, Matt Busby said: 'Behold, God himself is with us for our captain,' a text from Chronicles which was incorporated as a scrolled caption in the glass. The service was concluded with 'Abide with Me', the football hymn.

National life, George Orwell wrote in 1940, was 'somehow bound up with solid breakfasts and gloomy Sundays, smoky towns and winding roads, green fields and red pillar boxes', a continuity stretching 'into the future and the past'. He also saw the British as a remarkably pragmatic, polite, law-abiding people, filled with a deep longing for the rural idyll that they had lost.

Orwell, of course, was writing in the first year of the war and at the end of twenty years of rule by what history has come to regard as 'the respectable tendency'. Stanley Baldwin was the pivotal political figure of these years, and Francis Brett Young, a now forgotten and deeply unfashionable novelist, was a significant literary force. Both Baldwin and Brett Young were Black Countrymen – almost up to the time he became Prime Minister, Baldwin was an ironmaster, proprietor of the Baldwin ironworks – and also Worcestershire neighbours, near contemporaries and friends.

Baldwin was one of the last representatives of a world whose best values, he believed, were nurtured by an atmosphere of tranquillity rather than excitement. 'He was at heart a Quietist,' Brett Young wrote after Baldwin's death. 'His greatest asset . . . was his power of identifying himself with that part of the nature of masses and individuals which can only be described as their essential "Englishness".' Central to this were the virtues of plainness and ordinariness and decent obscurity. 'I am', Baldwin once told his Worcester neighbours, 'just one of yourselves, who has been called to special work for the country at this time.'

Throughout his years of power and pre-eminence, David Cannadine has written, 'Baldwin went to great trouble to stress his unexceptional averageness and reassuring plainness by turning self-deprecation into a minor art form . . . [He] presented himslf as a "typical Englishman", who made no claim to any special skills, who lacked the temperament to seek, and the talent to win, those "glittering prizes" . . . His wholesome ordinariness gave him unrivalled moral authority.' This was reflected in his appearance which, unlike his political contemporaries, 'was essentially postwar, seeking to blur rather than reinforce class divisions, and expressing ordinary plainness rather than privileged individuality'.

Baldwin stood down from power in 1937, the year after Duncan Edwards was born. But twenty years later, Edwards seemed to have a pronounced Baldwinian, 'oos is ownly fowks', Black Country imperturbability about him. In the week after his first League game for Manchester United at Easter 1953, his old headmaster from the secondary modern saw him back in Dudley and still having a kickabout in the street with kids he had been at school with. (A group of his teachers took to following him about the country as his eminence increased, and after matches he would always address them as 'Sir'.)

After he met a girl called Mollie Leach at the Derby Street Ice House, a skating rink in Manchester, Duncan disappeared off the social radar. Mollie wasn't one of 'the vivid, coarse girls' that reporters on the United beat wrote about as having to be held off by policemen when the players were getting in and out of the team coach: 'Mollie was a nice girl, very nice, but a bit up-market for us,' Edwards's friend Gordon Clayton said. 'Not what you might call a footballer's girl.'

Duncan was a famous face by then; it was difficult to go out. Now he could go round to Mollie's and sit with her. That's what he loved to do. 'As with any other sport that is your life, you can live too close to it,' he said. 'Not only are you training and playing all the time but the talk wherever you go is of football.' Watching the planes take off and land at Ringway airport was another way he found to relax.

Arthur Hopcraft interviewed Edwards around this time. 'He could have been a young miner freshly scrubbed for a night at the Labour Club dance,' he wrote. 'He did not look important, in the celebrated sense; he looked as if he mattered, and belonged, to his family and his friends. The anonymity of style was true to his generation and his kind.'

'He was a most model servant,' Harold Hardman, the Manchester United chairman, said after the crash.

None of this dogged and self-effacing ordinariness prepares a visitor for the experience of seeing Edwards translated into a church setting, depicted in stained glass the way that heroes of the middle ages and saints in gilded tabernacles normally are.

The black granite of his grave absorbs light; sucks light into itself. The portrait of Edwards etched into the tall headstone – ball raised above his head, arms outstretched behind it, taking a throw-in – does an odd little strobe or flutter, depending on how the light strikes it, creating a high-contrast photographic negative – a peculiarly jittery white-on-black negative image.

Simple daylight pours clearly and unrefractively through the rectangles and quadrants of glass which make up the paired images of Edwards – one in a white England shirt, the other in red United strip – in the stained-glass windows. He is shown kneeling in both panels, with the scrolled 'God is with us for our captain' banner running across his chest in the left-hand one, and a banner reading 'Though there be many members, yet is there one body' in the other. In addition to the coats of arms of Manchester and Munich, the design incorporates the insignia of Brentford and Crystal Palace, the only clubs who donated money towards the £300 it cost to have the windows designed and put in place in 1961.

The church takes its name from St Francis of Assisi, and the windows are in a recess close to the main door known as the Assisi chapel. The image of a tiny wren in one of the panels is an acknowledgement not only of the financial contribution made by members of the Wren's Nest Bowling Club but also of the fact that St Francis preaching to the birds is a favourite painter's subject. A full-length figure of the saint hovers above Edwards in the left-hand window; St George-with-sword is shown in the right. 'These windows should keep the name of Duncan Edwards alive for ever,' Matt Busby said at the service of dedication, 'and shine as a monument and example to the youth of Dudley and England.'

United's third match after Munich, which also marked Bobby Charlton's return to the game, was an FA Cup tie against the 'Baggies' in West Bromwich, almost on Duncan Edwards's doorstep. It took place less than a week after his funeral, and fans in their hundreds brought wreaths to lay on the grave. 'It's a touching thought that so many of them should make the pilgrimage,' the *Dudley Herald* noted afterwards in an editorial. 'But it's equally touching in its sadness that so much damage has been caused to surrounding graves by the sheer thoughtless trampling of the masses. Nearby graves have been trodden down and headstones have been flattened with complete disregard for the feelings of relatives of people buried there.'

The trampling of graves is no longer a problem (although the football-shaped granite flower-holder from Edwards's grave was stolen some years ago, only to be returned, following appeals by his mother, a couple of months later). Local residents haven't had recourse to the bumper sticker sometimes seen in other popular tourist ports-of-call: 'Welcome to X. Now go home.' But every season sees a steady stream of visitors to the cemetery and the Leisure Centre and the stained-glass windows at St Francis's church.

In 2002, in order to take advantage of this untapped trade, the owners of a pub on the Priory estate decided to change its name from The Wren's Nest to The Duncan Edwards. A case could be made for a genuine connection: The Wren's Nest was a quarter of a mile from Elm Road, where Edwards had grown up; he used to kick a ball around in the car park of the pub when he was a boy, and his father was bought the odd pint of mild-and-bitter in the public bar at the Wren by the scouts from Bolton Wanderers and the other clubs who were keen to get Duncan's signature.

But The Duncan Edwards is such a grimly accurate reflection of the contemporary football culture of roasting and dogging and squalid drunken sex that it would have been more appropriate to rename it The Lee Bowyer or The Wayne Rooney ('He's fat, he's scouse, he's gonna rob yer house,' 'He'd rather shag your granny than Colleen') or (the best alternative, given his local connections) The Stan Collymore, after the serial wife-beater and obsessive dogging enthusiast from Walsall (favourite spot for engaging in outdoor sex with strangers: Cannock Chase, the very place where the barking disciplinarian Stan Cullis used to put young Wolves players through their pre-season paces to see who was still standing at the end. It was the Cullises that Germaine Greer had in mind in 2003 when she wrote that 'the champions of team sports as essential tools in building a strong, healthy, integrated, clean-minded society have been swept off their perch by an unprecedented torrent of sleaze from the locker room. This unsavoury stream bids fair to run and run').

George Best never made any secret of his fondness for rough pubs. They were particularly handy when he was 'going on the missing list', as he frequently did: 'I used to go to some real dives – the sort normal people didn't even know existed.' He had his scalp lacerated by a pint pot in one; he was beaten up by a gang of men running in off the street in another. The Duncan Edwards in Dudley would have been Best's kind of place.

To walk the fifty yards from the Assisi chapel and St Francis's church – Duncan Edwards *in excelsis* – to the point on Priory Road where The Duncan Edwards stands is to experience a kind of fast-forwarded time shift. It is to be catapulted out of a world of Orwellian Englishness characterized by decency and civility and pots of home-made jam into an inner-city England all too obviously blighted by street crime and vandalism and drug abuse. History in the microwave.

The menacing atmosphere begins on the forecourt outside the pub, where a gang of a dozen or so youths – sweatpants and baggy jeans, face studs and heavy jewellery, several Burberry-check baseball caps, all of them skinny, white, sullenly ferret-faced – mill around outside a small shanty-like structure that has been tacked on to the side of the main building. This is a betting shop, it turns out, but there is no way of telling that from the windowless, fortress-like, plate-metal facade, which has been daubed with slogans and covered in graffiti.

Inside, the three or four men at the bar look as oily and grimy – scabbed and stubbled faces, matted hair – as if they had just wandered in from the old Dudley of Dickens-world.

They are drinking Magners Irish cider; a big zinc dustbin conveniently close by them is filled with their empties and also scraps of domestic refuse: grease and grey cigarette ash coat the bottles. A little girl in a grubby pink velour outfit with a headband covered in flashing pink fairy lights sits picking at a plate of chips and patty of industrial burger; with her is a woman who might be her grandmother, Superkings and lighter clamped protectively in one hand, pint of Star in the other.

But holding centre stage here is a group of three men and two women who converge in a skanky unisex style of tattoos and piercings, gnawed-down nails, red-rimmed eyes and a heavy embellishment of sovereign rings and brass and gold jewellery.

'Boysie, down!' a woman's voice rasps from out of the bubbling, toxic plume of blue smoke that engulfs the table. Boysie is a Queen Anne-legged, brindle Staffie in brasses and full leather chest-harness whose nose has been drawn to something in the bin. 'Nah, let the poor coont 'ave it,' one of the men says from the bar, as the dog legs it with part of a chicken carcass to the far end of the room. 'Cor do 'um no 'arm.'

It's a big room, with a high pitched ceiling and bare, black, creosote-like floor. *The Weakest Link* is on the telly; George Michael on the jukebox. Despite its name, there's not a lot for tourists on the Duncan Edwards trail to see, just a few faded photocopied pictures here and there. Much more conspicuous is the gallery of Polaroids on the wall next to the bar showing male customers stripped to their underpants in the company of one of the girls from Class Strippergrams of Dudley. Next to each photograph is a mock-official-looking piece of paper: 'This is to certify that X has been rewarded with Miss Whiplash/a Wicked Schoolgirl/a Policewoman strip-o-gram on the occasion of his X birthday.'

'We get on proper style, down't oos?' one of Boysie's group says. 'Now can I ask yow a question? What's your first name?'

'Tracy.'

'What's the dearest reeng on moy hand, Trocey?'

85

'There's a shop opening in Dudley next week, an' I tell you what, the biggest, goldest bracelets for evah . . .'

'Oy'll have a pish.'

A sign common in many of the pub toilets in Dudley reads: 'In the interests of security and customer safety smoke detectors have been installed. Also CCTV cameras recording the date and time of all activity.'

The other woman in the rowdy group who isn't Tracy is suddenly in tears. 'What d'you mean I'm a cheap-faced cheap cunt?'

'Down' worry 'boud it.'

'When you've got fuck-all, they down't boy you a drink. Fook 'em!'

The channel has been flipped to Sky Sports News. Hanging between the neon-hyper 'Grand Blaster Cash' and 'I'm Jackpot . . . Get Me Out of Here!' gaming machines is a photocopy of a picture of Gladstone Edwards bending to lay flowers at his son's grave which has slipped slantwise several inches out of the bottom of the frame.

'These memorials commemorate not only Duncan Edwards's football but also the simple decency of the man,' Arthur Hopcraft wrote forty years ago, when the church windows and the grave were both still less than a decade old. 'He represented thousands in their wish for courage, acclaim and rare talent, and he had all three without swagger. The hero is the creature other people would like to be. Edwards was such a man, and he enabled people to respect themselves more.'

Boysie has polished off his carcass and is back sniffing around the bin looking for something else to scavenge. 'Remember the bottle of wine you brought round for me, Dave?' one of the men says. 'See, he remembers, look. Twenty fookin' yeer.'

'Where's she gone? Yer mate? That yoong bird?' Dave says to Tracy.

'That young bird? That's my baby,' Tracy says. 'My daughter.'

*

86

The Duncan Edwards closed down suddenly just before Christmas 2005. The doors and windows were boarded up and it quickly became a target, according to the *Black Country Bugle*, 'for vandals, arsonists and unruly youths'. Under the headline 'Eyesore is an utter disgrace', the paper reported that 'Raging residents are calling on brewery bosses to remove the name of the legendary Duncan Edwards from a derelict pub – branding it "disgraceful" and "disrespectful".' It quoted ward councillor Margaret Aston: 'Since the pub closed we've had serious problems with antisocial behaviour and there have been at least two attempted arson attacks this month. Unless something is done urgently with the site it will become nothing other than a drugs' den.'

The chairman of local residents' group Friends of Priory Park, Janet Alderman-Rowe, was particularly concerned about a £100,000 National Lottery-funded football facility for young people which was about to open directly opposite the pub, just after the forty-eighth anniversary of the Munich disaster, in February 2006. The guest of honour at the Grand Opening Gala of the new games area, dedicated to the memory of Duncan Edwards, was to be his former teammate and great friend Sir Bobby Charlton.

'Duncan Edwards is an icon in Dudley and his memory is very vivid on the estate,' Mrs Alderman-Rowe told the *Bugle*. 'If [his name] is not removed [from outside the pub] it will be very embarrassing when Sir Bobby drives down Priory Road and sees it.'

Sees it and notes it for what it was very probably intended to be: an act of revenge on the hero figure who, with the opening of the new games area, was having another monument to his achievements placed at the centre of their crappy lives. 'Transforming Your Space' the project was called. Their appropriation of The Duncan Edwards, both before and after the brewery finally threw in the towel, was a way of taking it and making it their space, to fuck up if and when – a rebuke to the great man's great looks, his larger-than-lifeness, his glory, their sense of his having been exempted by his heroic role from the self-doubt that was the basic condition of their struggling existences.

The legend of the holy drinker #30

It was typical of the contradictions that riddled his character that, when he finally moved into his own 'bachelor pad' at the age of twenty-three, having said he didn't want to clutter it up with football pictures and trophies and embalmed caps and jerseys the way the cardigan-and-slippers players of the old school did, Best chose as the colour scheme for his modernist-playboy mansion in Bramhall, a 'desirable' suburb in southern Manchester, the team colours which he said also happened to be his own favourite colours: red and white. Red and white mosaic tiles surrounded the plunge bath ('large enough and deep enough to warrant an attendant', it was reported) off the master bedroom ('where he now does most of his best work'). He placed the armchairs and sofas of an emphatic red leather suite against the plain white walls of the spacious L-shaped open-plan lounge.

It was also typical that, at a time in his life when all the adulation and non-stop attention were starting to weary him, he decided to disappear in plain sight, into a modern, custom-built, brutalist mansion whose clear-headed design and pure geometry of form threw into stark relief the disorderly actuality of his life. The house's main feature was a pair of show-room-sized picture windows raised several feet above ground level to ensure that every tourist snapper and passing motorist could see straight in.

The papers had a field day, and it had its effect. 'Sunday trippers in their hundreds turned up yesterday to see the house that George Best built,' the *Daily Mirror* reported in September 1969. 'The visitors peeped through the windows, gazed into the fishpond, tramped around the garden and climbed the

outside verandah stairs to get a closer look. And in the end most of them reached the same embarrassing conclusion about the white tiled residence in Blossom Lane, Bramhall, Cheshire. It reminded them of a loo.'

The house's novelty as a sightseeing destination never wore off. Busloads came from all over England. Crowds swarmed around the owner if he tried to go to the shop. Entire families sat in cars in the field opposite for hour after hour and gawped. Matches flared, cameras flashed; one man put an armchair on Best's front lawn and never took it away. 'If I go out on a Sunday,' Best complained, 'I can never get back in. I have to ask them to move their bloody cars from the approach to my house.'

It was an early example of a phenomenon which grew increasingly commonplace as the century drew to a close and the new millennium approached: adulation as an aggressive act. 'It is painfully obvious to us that our communications with our celebrated favourites is all one way,' the American essayist Richard Schickel has written. 'They send (and send and send) while all we do is receive (and receive and receive). They do not know we exist as individuals; they see us only as the components of the mass, the audience. And that is frustrating. In the dark nights of our soul it makes us feel bad . . .

'This new relation is based on an illusion of intimacy . . . Thanks to television and the rest of the media, we know them, or think we do. In many respects we are more profoundly involved with their fates than we are with those of most of the people we know personally. They command enormous amounts of our psychic energy and attention . . . No wonder the relationship between the modern performer and his following is so volatile, so marked by paranoia. The star has a secret – lots of them, actually. And the crowd suspects he might have. And so it must test him, by offering the friendliness he appears to invite. It is a wonder this relationship is not marked by more violence.'

By 1969, Best had crossed over to a level of celebrity no sportsman in Britain had ever experienced before, and it was a lonely place. In becoming 'the way-out winger with a wardrobe of mod gear as vast as a pop star's', the dolly birds' favourite, the housewives' choice, he had moved away from his original football fan base. The great country singer Waylon Jennings was following a similar trajectory at around the same time, swapping respectable record sales and a small but devoted following for mass-market, mainstream success and could speak eloquently about the stresses it brought in a way that Best was unable – certainly unwilling – to do.

'They think you just get up there and sing your songs,' Waylon said. 'They think it's just a one-way deal, but it's not like that at all. Because you start out playing for people that are just like you. That's the only place you can. You play for people who come from where you come from. They seek you out in little clubs because they understand what you're doing, so you feel like you're doing it for them. And if you go wrong in these clubs, you know it immediately. And maybe you want to go wrong. That's your option, but you know it when you do it. Then one day, you're not playing for people like you any more. You look out there, and you're playing for people who want to be like you, and you can't trust these people. Because to them, whatever you do, that's you, and that's cool. Which would be okay except! – even though all these people want to be like you, you don't know who you are any more, because it was the people in those little clubs that gave you that understanding in the first place. God knows where they are tonight. Sitting at home, probably. Pissed off at me. Listening to Willie Nelson records.'

So what do you do? Waylon was asked.

'Right now, hoss,' he said, 'it's completely out of my hands. I'm looking at those people out there, but I don't know what I'm seeing. And they're watching me too. But they don't know what they're looking at. My best guess is that they'll keep on loving me till they start hating me, or their Waylon duds wear out. Because they already hate me a little, just because I'm me and they're them. That's why they always go on about how talented you are. Because they hate you. Because if they had this talent, they would be you. The fact that you've worked like a dog, lived like a horse thief, and broke your mama's heart to do whatever you do, that don't mean diddly-squat. To them, it's talent. Supposedly, you got it and, supposedly, they don't. So eventually you're bound to disappoint them.

'My real people, they get jealous because their girlfriend thinks I'm cute and try to kick my butt. They get envious because singing pays better than roofing and try to kick my butt. But, basically, they understand I do this job for them – that I'm up on stage with my Telecaster, sweatin' in the lights, coughing in the smoke, and trying to hear the monitor – that they're sitting out there all cool and comfortable with a bottle of beer and a bowl of peanuts. So when all this blows up, I'll just go back and do that, find out if I'm still me.'

Best called the house 'Che Sera' after the *News of the World* ran a competition among its readers to come up with a name. (He rejected others such as 'Left-wing', 'Off-side', 'Soccer Haven' and 'Goal Holme' on the grounds that they reminded him too much of work.) 'Che Sera'. 'What will be'.

The building was constructed on two levels, with the main living area on the first floor. The ground floor had a two-car garage, a billiards room and a bedroom and bathroom for the resident housekeeper. Upstairs was the main living room, described by Best as 'the second most important room in the house'; a bar ran the length of one wall, with pumps to bring draught beer up from the wine cellar next to the garage. The papers got very excited by the fact that he could lie in bed and open and close the curtains, dim the lights and open the garage doors at the flick of a switch. He could flick another switch and the television would disappear up the Scandinavian-style chimney.

The house-warming party was paid for by the *Daily Express* in return for exclusive rights. Richard Burton and Elizabeth Taylor said they couldn't make it, as did Tony Curtis and Pierre Trudeau, the Canadian 'playboy' prime minister. The British Prime Minister, Harold Wilson, sent a telegram of congratulation on behalf of himself and his wife. Tommy Trinder, the Fulham FC chairman and comedian, did arrive, along with Misses United Kingdom and Great Britain, and Kenny Lynch. Three security men controlled the doors and policemen were on duty on the narrow country roads to control crowds and traffic.

The domestic appliances, much of the furniture and all the electronic boys' toys had been donated by their designers and manufacturers on the understanding that they would become hot and happening by association. But pretty soon, in addition to feeling resentment about the relationship of false intimacy he was being forced into with the rubberneckers, the relentless clutching at connection – 'It got so I wouldn't answer the phone. When the doorbell rang I used to stay quiet and pretend I wasn't in, I used to hide behind the curtains,' he said – George was bored.

'The sunken bath and the wine cellar cannot compensate for George Best's nagging feeling of boredom,' a profile-writer for the *Daily Sketch* wrote when Best had been in the house for only a few months. 'He is fed up with his car, a Lotus Europa, so he's changing that. He's fed up with choosing clothes for his shops, so he doesn't do that any more. He's fed up with the rigours of keeping in training but he goes along with them – with the exception of the occasional fall from grace. "I can get almost anything done that I want," he says. "But I sometimes think I would like to be an ordinary bloke. If I were, I'd probably be bored with that, too."'

The remote for the gadgets went on the blink, with the TV yo-yo-ing up and down the chimney and the curtains opening and closing of their own volition. The pleasures of operating the footrest on his new designer armchair wore thin. The house, envisaged as a place that he could retreat to and pull down the shutters, had become an advertisement of his mysterious otherness and his difference, and it seems to have spooked even him.

Outwardly, Georgie the tabloid tupper gave the appearance of being totally in tune with the times. ('He has to be a great footballer', a disbelieving teammate once commented to a reporter, 'to get away with that haircut and that outfit.') Never very far below the surface, though, was Belfast George, who was a traditionalist at heart and, even while he was still a teenager, had established a basic style and routine of living which he would follow, with very few signs of impetuosity or variation, for the next forty years: the bird, the boozer, the puzzle book and the gee-gees, and then the inevitable alcoholic sprees and five-day benders which would go on earning him a reputation for chronic flakiness and unreliability long after they had cost him his career.

'To be modern is to experience personal and social life as a maelstrom,' Marshall Berman wrote. 'To be a modernist is to make oneself somehow at home in the maelstrom, to make its rhythms one's own.' George's adherence to a familiar routine and the rigidity of his habits marked him out as being, like most footballers, a natural conservative. He liked the homely and familiar rather than the futuristic, hard-edged environment which he thought he wanted, had asked for and had been given. But it was a design driven by the idea of bringing the outside in, when what he wanted above everything was to keep the outside at bay. The world was already too much with him without waking up to find it peering into his kitchen, his bedroom and his toilet.

Before long he was back in his single bed in his upstairs room at Mrs Fullaway's, with Kim the spaniel hogging the armchair in front of the television, the landlady waking him every morning with the intimate nose-tickle he hated, and a Ferrari parked outside in the street.

As a single man, even one earning £50,000 a year and pursuing a life appropriate to his position as football's first bona fide, media-ordained, go-go age celebrity, he wasn't supposed to be living on his own anyway: like all Manchester United players, he was bound by contract to live in digs until he was married. But the club, under the faltering management of Wilf McGuinness by then, Busby's annointed successor, had done what they always seemed to end up doing with Bestie, and turned a blind eye.

Not that, in the end, it mattered. 'Che Sera' went on standing on its plot in the Cheshire countryside, a monument to football's new money, its glinting bleak geometry a visual affront to its stockbroker neighbours. Lights came on and went off at regular intervals set by a timer, but there was never any traffic on the stainless-steel and Sicilian marble staircase, nobody moving behind the tinted curtain windows, contented and finally at home in their place in the world.

'Architecture is a stage set where we need to be at ease in order to perform,' J. G. Ballard has written. 'Fearing ourselves, we need our illusions to protect us ... Modernism lacked mystery and emotion, was a little too frank about the limits of human nature and never prepared us for our eventual end.'

'Instead of having the rehabilitative effect that his advisers intended, the house undoubtedly emphasized his predicament and increased his frustration and anguish,' 'Che Sera' visitor and Best's friend from those days Michael Parkinson commented. 'No single episode in his life so illustrates the predicament he was in . . . From the moment he went to live there he began his rapid descent downhill.'

Six

*He wanted to have been born something more than a physical
wonder. As if for one person that isn't gift enough . . . The
responsibility of the school hero follows him through life.
Noblesse oblige. You're the hero, so then you have to behave in
a certain way – there is a prescription for it. You have to be
modest, you have to be forbearing, you have to be deferential,
you have to be understanding . . .*

*How could he, with all his carefully calibrated goodness,
have known that the stakes of living obediently were so high?
Obedience is embraced to lower the stakes. A beautiful wife. A
beautiful house . . . This is how successful people live. They're
good citizens. They feel lucky. They feel grateful. God is smiling down on them. There are problems, they adjust. And then
everything changes and it becomes impossible. Nothing is smiling down on anybody. And who can adjust then? Here is someone not set up for life's working out poorly, let alone for the
impossible. But who is set up for the impossible that's going to
happen? Who is set up for tragedy and the incomprehensibility
of suffering? Nobody. The tragedy of the man not set up for
tragedy – that is every man's tragedy.*

Philip Roth, *American Pastoral*

Duncan Edwards's fastidiousness was offended by the conditions at United's training ground at the Cliff in the Lower
Broughton area of Salford. It was a dump. For all its reputation as one of the great glamour clubs of the era, the facilities
that United laid on for teams at all levels, from the youth side
up, were basic at best. (For a long time after the abolition of
the maximum wage in 1961, Manchester United would trail
some way behind the First Division's big payers.)

The post-war reconstruction of Old Trafford had concentrated on facilities for the paying public rather than the players. Even that wasn't state of the art: the main stand was constructed out of tubular steel and scrap metal, and the Stretford End remained uncovered and open to the elements until 1959. But even new arrivals who had only been used to the facilities provided by school and boys' club sides were surprised by the primitive training arrangements in place at one of the most storied grounds not only in the football league but in Europe.

The gym was a dingy space, spartanly equipped with wall bars and squares of dusty mat and a few footballs hanging from the roof on ropes. The main area for exercise was an old piece of spare land at the back of the ground for practice matches. Often twenty-a-side and involving players of all ages and levels of experience, these took place on a rock-hard, cinder-gritted surface which was squeezed in-between the concrete wall of the grandstand and the wooden fence along the railway line where the crowd used to queue on match days. These kickabouts 'round the back', involving the pros and the hopefuls whose ambition was to displace them, had a reputa-

tion for being brutal. The apprentices had to be prepared to get clattered and to give as good as they got. It could be bloody.

But the place where the club's penny-pinching was most in evidence was at the main training ground, the Cliff. In the mid-fifties, Edwards, Charlton, David Pegg and the rest of Busby's Babes would travel to Lower Broughton by corporation bus, changing buses in the city centre. Once there they would kit themselves out from a pile of heavy woollen sweaters and blood- and mud-encrusted tracksuit bottoms that would have been tipped out on to a long table. Noel Cantwell arrived at United on a £30,000 transfer from West Ham in 1960: 'At West Ham we'd had modern training gear. But at Old Trafford it was all great big old sweaters and socks full of holes. We were given boots in training that were like cut-off wellingtons. It would remind you of being in prison.'

'Looking back it was bloody awful,' Wilf McGuinness has said. 'The floodlights [at the Cliff] were dreadful, you could hardly see. The training kit was the worst imaginable. It was never washed . . . Afterwards you'd get in the bath – forty of you – it was black within two minutes. When you got out you'd have to have a cold shower to get the muck off. Many's the time I remember standing there shivering, looking for a towel, practically in tears after a bollocking Jimmy had given me.'

Even by the time of Denis Law's arrival at the club from Italy in 1962, the ethos was still one of counting the pennies and encouraging frugality. 'We were lucky if we had five balls for the whole team,' Law remembered. 'When we came in for training, they slung a pile of old jerseys on the table and you had to sort through it like at a jumble sale. On a good day you might get one which only had a big hole in the sleeve, and a decaying tracksuit to go with it. If you wanted a pair of boots, they looked at you as if you were asking for the moon. If you wanted a second pair of boots, forget it. The facilities were more fit for horses than for men.'

Lower Broughton is the part of Salford where the playwright and film director Mike Leigh grew up. 'Visiting the area', Leigh's biographer Michael Coveney has written, 'it becomes clear that everything in his work that involves net curtains, bleak moments, dead afternoons, peculiar relatives and the daily, grinding sadness of people's lives comes from this suburban patch of Salford, with its quiet streets of Edwardian villas, 1930s estates, leafy lanes and bland (or suffocating?) respectability.'

Throughout the 1950s, the quiet would occasionally be broken by the crowds at the Castle Irwell racecourse, which fitted perfectly inside a loop on the other side of the Irwell river from the Cliff. On training days the quiet would be disturbed by autograph hunters and reporters and the sound of Jimmy Murphy pounding up and down the touchline, bawling the young players out. 'Keep it moving, keep it simple! . . . The ball is made round to go round! . . . Make yourself available! Be there for the man on the ball, in case he wants to use you! . . . Get out of his fucking way quick, Billy son!'

Eddie Colman would make the journey from Archie Street every morning on foot. After his twenty-first birthday in 1957, Duncan Edwards started to travel in on the racing bike that Mr Busby had given him permission to buy, although Roger Byrne, the captain, had a small endorsement deal with Raleigh. This, plus what he got paid for his column in the *Manchester Evening News*, pushed Byrne's earnings above the £15 a week that the rest of the first team were on (which was about £9 a week above the average wage).

A player's basic pay could be bumped up by a win bonus of £2 and a 'signing-on fee' of £10. Byrne's salary for 1957, for example, comprised a basic wage of £744 from the club, plus league match bonuses of £72, talent money of £45, European Cup bonuses of £60 and an 'accrued benefit sum' of £150. He got married in June 1957, the same month as Jean and Jackie Blanchflower, and Byrne and his wife Joy found themselves on honeymoon in Jersey with the Blanchflowers and most of the United team. Roger played football and cricket the whole fortnight.

The Byrnes had a club house in upmarket Urmston and, like many young couples in their income bracket, they were the owners of a Morris Minor. (Being single men, David Pegg, Bobby Charlton and Tommy Taylor all had sportier Vauxhall Victors that they would go for a spin in, as the expression then was – across the Pennines, up on the moors – in convoy together.) Because he was the captain, slightly older and married, and because he had extra income to dispose of, Roger Byrne was always welcome at the Manchester club which was one of the Boss's favourite haunts.

In his biography of Matt Busby, Eamon Dunphy makes it very clear that he was not the puritan, even sanctimonious, soul that some of the hagiographers tried to make him out to be. Busby liked a drink and a laugh and a flutter, and he liked to do all these things in rather gamier company, and in slightly racier surroundings, than his Father of Manchester image sometimes suggested.

For the whole of his long career at United, Busby, his wife Jean, their son Sandy and daughter Sheena lived in the same modest house on Wilbraham Road in Chorlton, close to Old Trafford and only a few streets away from the council-house digs of Mary Fullaway. (As a youth-team player, George Best used to try and disappear into the queue at the bus stop in the mornings if he saw the Boss's Jag approaching. Mr Busby had stopped and given him a lift once, but he had been so shy and tongue-tied, so overwhelmed by the cream leather and the cherry-maple dash, the exotic odour of cologne and rubbing tobacco that, cheeks and ears on fire just remembering, it was an experience he was never in any hurry to put himself through again.) Busby's urbanity, the quality about him that everybody who met him was instantly impressed by, was something he wore lightly. Gentlemen stroked with the bat, but players sweated with the ball. He was the product of a pitmen's terrace in a mining village in Lanarkshire, but there was never any doubt that Busby was a gentleman. Jimmy Murphy, his loyal assistant, a sixty-cigarettes-a-day man and a non-driver, was sergeants' mess rather than officer-club material; Busby and Murphy were never seen socializing together. Busby would arrange for a couple of crates of beer to be in the home-team dressing room immediately after the game, but it would be Jimmy rather than the Boss who would stay drinking with the players. The Boss's friends tended to be, by and large, non-football and represented a different side of Manchester life.

A family-man Catholic himself, in his social life Busby was drawn to what Dunphy calls 'roguish types': 'Ideas about respectability were not formed as rigidly in Manchester as elsewhere. Almost everyone had a past of kinds, old money was rare. There was no aristocracy, except of those who made things or sold them or otherwise excelled, even if it was only at the art of living . . . [Busby] was no playboy, but he loved characters whose spirits were freer than his own. [He] loved Manchester, its looseness, its *joie de vivre*, its tolerance. Matt didn't play but he liked to spectate, to be in the company of larger-than-life characters in his leisure time . . . He didn't want to be the life and soul of the party, yet he enjoyed the company of self-made men, the better if they were amusing, a touch extravagant by nature, untainted by pretension . . . He loved the banter, the light undemanding hail-fellow-well-met-ship of dog-track, pub or party.'

Busby's salary was huge even by today's standards, and he liked mixing with men who had money and knew how to spend it. These included Johnny Foy, a Manchester bookmaker; Tommy Appleby, the manager of Manchester Opera House, who would comp them the best seats and take them backstage after shows to introduce Jean Busby to the stars; Eric Richardson, who was in the carpet trade; Willie Satinoff, whose family owned a Manchester clothing company; and, most famously, Louis Edwards, head of a flourishing wholesale butchering business, who Busby would steer towards becoming a director, and eventually chairman and majority shareholder, of Manchester United.

But Busby's closest friend, and probably the most roguish

and larger-than-life of the lot, was Paddy McGrath. Out on the town together, Matt and Paddy, both of them handsome, well-built, dapper in their Crombies and snap-brim trilbies, were a kind of Rat Pack of two. The Irish writer John McGahern, who knew nothing about football or Manchester United, once recalled seeing Busby in the elegant old Russell Hotel in Dublin around this time. 'This incredibly imposing man walked in off the street. He was an extraordinary presence, like a great politician or theatrical figure. Who is that, we all wondered?'

Busby had been introduced to McGrath by the former Scottish international Jack Dodds in Blackpool immediately after the war. McGrath came from Collyhurst, a tough, Irish Catholic area of Manchester famous for breeding great boxers and footballers. Nobby Stiles came from Collyhurst and, although he was small and scrawny when he joined Manchester United in the late fifties, Jimmy Murphy used to tell people, 'Don't worry about Nobby. He can take care of himself. He's a Collyhurst lad.' Louis Rocca, United's chief scout who had been responsible for bringing Busby to United in the closing months of the war, also came from Collyhurst and was a friend of McGrath's, who had gone to school with Charlie Stiles, Nobby's undertaker dad, at the famous St Pat's.

After a period earning his living as a prizefighter in fairground boxing booths and working on distribution for the *Daily Mirror*, McGrath had moved to Blackpool in 1939. He was a physical-training instructor with the RAF at an embarkation centre outside the town and was often able to help Rocca out by letting him have whatever professionals they had in the camp as part of the effort to keep United going during the war. He started an ice-cream business, then sold it and went into candy floss and rock.

'Blackpool was at its peak during the war,' McGrath said. 'Those were great years. Apart from the fellers in Burma and elsewhere who were suffering, if you were home on leave every pub was like New Year's Eve because everyone thought I'm not stopping in. There was no television, only a few wirelesses, and there were so many girls whose husbands were away. It's only natural. It's physical. And a lot of girls who wanted to remain faithful nobody would take them out. After two or three dates they would be dropped. So a lot of women had to go crooked. There was so much life.'

McGrath's Blackpool connections were to remain vital to United. He was instrumental in getting the Blackpool inside forward Ernie Taylor to sign for Jimmy Murphy when he was trying to scrape a team together in the days and weeks after Munich. He also influenced the decision to take the players away from the strained, emotionally overheated atmosphere at Old Trafford and put them into the Norbreck Hydro hotel on the Blackpool promenade for what was left of the 1957–58 season. But, in 1954, McGrath moved back to Manchester to open what was to become a city institution, the Cromford Club off Market Street in the central shopping area.

The Cromford was a private members' club which almost from the day of its opening became a favourite meeting place for sportsmen, particularly footballers and boxers. There was roulette and blackjack, a floor show, sophisticated decor, a nice meal to be had. They used to have the big race call-overs and often held weigh-ins for the boxing at Belle Vue. Rakish characters, charming and slightly iffy, were the staple. Being members-only meant there weren't too many civilian customers – 'Billies' in the argot of the dressing room. Billy Bunters. Punters. Jean and Matt Busby met up with Muriel and Louis Edwards, Johnny Foy, the Satinoffs. The players often went in for lunch during the week and at weekends would gather with their wives and girlfriends. Roger Byrne and Johnny Doherty held their wedding receptions at the Cromford.

Later, in the 1960s, Paddy McGrath would up the stakes and open Playboy of Manchester. But if the Cromford had a model in the fifties it was the famous Stork Club in New York. The Stork – 'Entices the well knowns from all divisions nightly' – had hit its peak in the 1930s. It was the haunt of the legendary gossip columnist Walter Winchell, reviled and read coast-to-coast for his snide asides and his acid tongue. The Cromford couldn't boast a journalist of his stature among its members, but Manchester was still a major publishing centre in the 1950s. All the national daily papers had offices there, and McGrath's Cromford Club was one of the places reporters on the United beat could rely on for picking up stories.

These weren't scandal stories, of course, as we know them today, revolving around revelations about sex and drugs and corruption. They were human-interest stories about which players had been visiting children in hospital and whose wife was 'infanticipating', and snippets of team news about who was rumoured to be being left out of Saturday's home game and who had spent half an hour on the physio's table being treated for a minor strain.

(Mrs Watson's was another useful provider of this kind of trivia and, just as with the lodgers, she had her favourites among the football hacks: she had a soft spot, for instance, for George Follows of the *News Chronicle* and later the *Daily Herald*, and for a while he moved into Birch Avenue to be closer to the source, as one of her paying guests. This must have led to some awkward silences at the breakfast table. In his book, Duncan Edwards recalls an occasion when Follows of the *Herald* gave him a glowing write-up, only to take it all back in print a couple of matches later, when he'd had a stinker.

'Criticism has strange effects on a player,' Edwards writes. 'Some wilt under it and lose confidence. They react almost as if they have been stabbed in the back. With me it's different. Criticize me and I will go all the harder to make you eat your words. It stings my pride, and once I consider I have made an adequate reply in the shape of a good performance, I lose any animosity towards the writer.

'A few weeks [after George Follows' second article], as I went into the ground I saw placards outside proclaiming that Mr Follows was present again. I thought to myself: "I'll show him something. He will never have seen the likes of this." So I went out and played probably the best game I have ever played in my life. After that I was content again.')

Something that most of the football writers based in Manchester had in common was that they had seen service in the war, had witnessed the devastation it had caused and lost family and friends. They belonged to the same generation as Jimmy Murphy and Matt Busby and, like them, had lived long enough to have developed eccentricities in how they behaved and what they wore. Henry Rose of the *Daily Express*, for example, acknowledged even by his competitors as the doyen of northern sportswriters, wore his cap at what a colleague described as 'a jaunty, defiant, impudent angle' and teamed it at all times with a Howitzer Havana cigar; Archie Ledbrooke of the *Daily Mirror* was a donnish sort of journalist, tall, bald, aloof, remote; Eric Thompson of the *Daily Mail* ('the J. B. Priestley of Manchester journalism') wore horn-rimmed spectacles and illustrated his own stories; Donny Davies, 'Old International' of what was then still the *Manchester Guardian*, wore a cloth cap and plus fours and carried his personal rug with him everywhere, in all weathers.

They all shared a belief in the muscular Christian values of physical culture (strong mind in strong body, etc.) and, maybe as a gesture of defiance against the brittle superficiality of the new world that was starting to come into being in 1957 – American comics, denim, rock'n'roll – nearly all smoked solid briar pipes. In the byline pictures that appeared over their articles, every writer was shown wearing a collar and tie, a short-back-and-sides haircut and a three-piece suit; they were virtually all nursing pipes. Alf Clarke of the *Manchester Evening Chronicle*'s slogan 'Behind the Soccer Scenes with Alf Clarke' was framed in a puff of dense, reassuringly masculine black smoke.

Busby was particularly close to Clarke and his opposite number, Tom Jackson of the *Manchester Evening News*. This was inevitable, given the nature of the relationship between a local newspaper and the city's leading clubs: it was as much in

Busby's interests to keep the reporters sweet as it was in Jackson's and Clarke's not to write anything that could in any way be construed as rocking the Old Trafford boat.

Not that the chances of this happening were ever very high. Jackson and Clarke had been covering United for a quarter of a century in 1957, authored 'Casual Comments' and 'United Topics' in the club programme and, no less than the manager, players, directors and supporters of the club, were Red all the way through. Unlike the writers for the national papers, and even given the fact their own papers were also bought by Manchester City fans, they made no pretence at objective reporting. 'There's only one team in this city,' Clarke, a pre-war amateur with United, used to say, 'and you can't write enough about them.' He and Jackson were constantly duking it out for snippets of gossip, tiny 'exclusives', crumbs from the table. Busby, needless to say, had learned how to play them like a violin.

Another reporter he never expected to kick up rough was Frank Swift, 'Big Swifty', known as 'the first showman goal-keeper', who had played in the same Manchester City side as Busby and was a teammate when City won the FA Cup in 1934. The son of a family plying fishing boats from Blackpool, Swift had been a member of the British Army team that Busby managed during the war, and in retirement had signed up to do a column for the *News of the World*.

The only irritant in the press pack who followed United was a writer who rivalled even some of the players in local fame. Henry Rose was a showman reporter – 'many even believe he goes out of his way deliberately to cause commotion', it was rumoured – who took particular pleasure in making his London rivals look on in awe and envy at the celebrity he enjoyed around Old Trafford. 'Henry Rose is Here!' the *Express* placards proclaimed before every game. And, just in case his arrival went unnoticed, he sometimes took the trouble to arrange his own paging at the stadium and in hotels, just to announce his presence.

Rose's views – for instance on what he regarded as the over-estimated talents of Tommy Taylor – occasionally rubbed Busby up the wrong way. But it is a sign of his sophistication in the black arts of press and public relations that, when Rose celebrated his twenty-fifth year at the *Daily Express*, Busby turned up as a guest at the party. Two weeks later, Rose, along with Archie Ledbrooke, Eric Thompson, Don Davies, Alf Clarke, Tom Jackson, Frank Swift and George Follows, would be killed at Munich. Of the nine British journalists who had covered the match in Belgrade, only Frank Taylor of the *News Chronicle* survived.

The annual Press Ball had been due to be held at the Plaza ballroom on the night of the crash. Jimmy Savile put a sign saying 'Press Ball cancelled' up outside, then locked the doors and sat around with his staff listening to reports as they came through on the radio. There were trestle tables full of food, and tinselly decorations. They had to put the radio in the middle of the floor before they could get it to work properly – something to do with the aerial.

On the morning of Henry Rose's funeral, a fleet of taxis arrived at the *Express* offices in Great Ancoats Street. Manchester's taxi drivers had volunteered transport free for anyone who wanted to be at the funeral. Rose was a Jew; head coverings had to be worn. Homburgs, bowlers, caps, trilbies, berets, headscarves, fedoras, people in unaccustomed head-gear, hardbitten newspapermen as cold-looking as cod in the face of the most blood-curdling stories now weeping, joined the six-mile queue to Southern Cemetery.

The Press Club and Paddy McGrath's Cromford Club filled up every night in the weeks after the disaster. People wanted to stay and drink; it seemed like they didn't want to go home. There was a melancholic Frank Sinatra atmosphere – the early Capitol Sinatra of *In the Wee Small Hours* and *No One Cares*. People got home at four or five, even later, and met the milk-man.

In his mother's house in Beatrice Street, the colliery row in

Ashington, Bobby Charlton was playing the same songs. 'He knew of the special meaning in Sinatra's songs, that the man had been down and got himself up,' Norman Harris wrote, 'and when he sang in the vein of "Only the Lonely" he made it sound so believable. Bobby bought all Sinatra's LP records, and Sinatra remained the one man he would have given anything to meet.'

By taking Manchester United into Europe, Busby had expanded the horizons of everybody connected with the club beyond Blackpool, Burnley, Bolton and Wolverhampton, and the usual cheerless winter round. Their first season in the European Cup had taken them to Anderlecht in Belgium, Borussia Dortmund in West Germany and twice to Spain – to Bilbao and then to Madrid, where Real, the holders, beat them in the semi-final. By early 1958, in their second season in Europe, they had already eliminated Shamrock Rovers in Dublin and Dukla Prague, and, in addition to their match reports, Alf Clarke, Tom Jackson and the travelling retinue of pressmen had been able to squeeze some decent human-interest mileage out of the food, the foreignness and the weather. (Ominously, before they could take off on the return journey home after the match in Bilbao, players, club officials and reporters had had to pitch in and help to clear layers of ice and snow off the wings of the plane.)

On 3 February 1958, United were due to fly to Yugoslavia to play the second leg of their European Cup quarter-final against Red Star Belgrade, having already beaten them 2–1 at home. Before that though, on the first, the Saturday, they had a vital League game against Arsenal in London.

United had won the First Division championship two years in a row, in 1956 and 1957 – in 1956 with a team whose average age was just over twenty. Busby had his eye on the treble. But in the 1957–58 season they had taken some time to find their form, and Wolverhampton Wanderers quickly set up a big lead. But now that was being whittled away. After the return match against Red Star in Belgrade, United were to meet Wolves at Old Trafford. First, though, there was the trip to Highbury for what, in the opinion of many of those in the stadium that Saturday, was the best match they had ever seen two English sides play.

Busby preached attacking football – he loved flair players. Consistently over the years he put together teams which dazzled. 'For men who work on the shop floor, the one highlight of their week is to go and watch football. Matt used to say you should give that man something he can't do himself, something exciting,' Bobby Charlton remembered. 'That's why Manchester United always play attacking football.'

'We were ruthless, you know,' Jimmy Murphy once said, 'and we had this dream. To do it perfectly. We'd win everything but with proper elegance. We'd play the sweetest football. We'd have great players. Poetic. Eleven grown men chasing a ball. Very poetic.'

Ruthless, properly elegant, poetic. Great young players playing the sweetest football. Contemporary reports suggest that United were all of these things in the match against Arsenal on the first of February 1958. Harry Gregg was in goal, Bill Foulkes and Roger Byrne were the fullbacks, with Eddie Colman, Mark Jones and Duncan Edwards supporting the front line of Kenny Morgans, Bobby Charlton, Tommy Taylor, Dennis Viollet and Albert Scanlon. The same team that would represent United four days later in Belgrade, and be largely obliterated at Munich.

More than 60,000 spectators packed into Highbury. It was United's first appearance in London that season; they were second in the League table behind Wolves and doing well in the European Cup. They were a side to be beaten.

United did everything perfectly, and scored three goals straight off. They took the lead within ten minutes with a thunderous shot from Edwards. Charlton made it 2–0 with a trademark blast that left the Arsenal keeper Jack Kelsey with no chance. Tommy Taylor added a third before half-time and it looked as though United had already done enough. But Arsenal came back at them and levelled the score at 4–4, before United came away again to win 5–4, with a second goal from Taylor.

'United that day were unbeatable,' Charlton said later. 'Four goals is a lot to concede, especially away from home, but I reckon that, whatever number had gone in our net, we would have passed it. I could feel it in the rhythm and power of the play. No English club side could have lived with us that day.'

'If there was one thing that distinguished Busby's youthful champions,' David Miller has written, 'it was that they had learned to change their pace; they now had the mark of a handful of great teams, that of being able to raise their game – suddenly, without warning, and to order, to get out of difficulty. This match against Arsenal saw them at the height of their powers.'

Standing in the Clock End at Highbury watching the game was a fifteen-year-old Tottenham supporter who had persuaded his father to do the unthinkable and go with him to the Arsenal. Except it was the already semi-legendary young England wing half that Terry Venables really wanted to see, and he wasn't disappointed. From that day on, asked to nominate his greatest/fastest/strongest/most skilled/most missed player, Venables has unfailingly put Duncan Edwards's name forward.

'When I was growing up, there was no televised football to speak of, and if you wanted to see a particular player or team, it meant going to one of their matches. It was February 1958, and United had just caused a stir by beating Bolton 7–2, and everyone was talking about Duncan Edwards. It was a day I will never forget, a lovely day out with my dad, standing behind the goal at the old Clock End at Highbury.

'It took Duncan Edwards less than ten minutes to show us what all the fuss was about. I remember I was a bit disappointed that United weren't at full strength. With the European Cup tie against Red Star Belgrade only four days away, Matt Busby rested his centre half, Jackie Blanchflower, the two wingers, David Pegg and Johnny Berry, and the clever, creative inside half, Liam [Billy] Whelan. It was still a hell of a team, with a forward line that included Bobby Charlton, Tommy Taylor and Dennis Viollet, supported from half back by Eddie Colman and the man I couldn't take my eyes off, Duncan Edwards.

'Jack Kelsey, a legend at Highbury, was in goal for Arsenal but, good as he was, he was beaten all the way when Duncan opened the scoring with a cracking shot. That was my moment. We had travelled in to see him and, with the latecomers still arriving, he had me turning to my dad with a "Did you see that?" look. Edwards had taken a pass from Viollet and strode forward like an unstoppable giant before shooting past Kelsey from twenty-five yards. There were eight more goals in a fantastic match, but Duncan's, and his overall performance, are all I really remember. Afterwards, I just couldn't get it out of my head how good United were.

'Duncan was marvellous. Everything he did comes back to me as if it was yesterday. Such strength, such poise. We are talking about a long time ago, but I can still see him, and that tremendous power of his, even now. He was only twenty-one, but already he had played for England eighteen times, and there were far fewer internationals played in those days. I was always Tottenham through and through, and it was not so much the Busby Babes as the Spurs double side [of 1961] that gave me a feeling for how I wanted to play the game, but I stood there that day thinking Edwards was a wonderful player, and that I wanted to play like him.

'United were the best around at the time, and he was their star man. I had heard tales of this real-life Roy of the Rovers a few years before. People at Chelsea spoke of a Youth Cup tie against United. Chelsea had an outstanding team that day, Jimmy Greaves and Peter Brabrook included, but the story goes that a storm broke during the game. Edwards scored two goals playing at centre forward, then when United turned round at half-time, and had the storm against them, they played him at centre half, and he won everything. He was blessed with an all-round ability no one had ever seen before. He had everything. He was potentially the greatest player I've seen.'

Very many years later, in the twilight of a career in which he had been both Tottenham skipper and manager, England coach, City high-roller, crime writer and TV pundit, Venables opened a nightclub in Kensington High Street in London called Scribes West which catered to the members of the many and varied circles he mixed in, who had all come to know him as an ebullient, larger-than-life character, everybody's mate. On Saturday nights, when he usually had Dennis Wise, Jody Morris, Gianfranco Zola and the rest of the Chelsea boys in, Terry would bring the evening to a close by taking the microphone and giving them his Sinatra. It was guaranteed to blow the roof off the place. This wasn't the downbeat Sinatra of the Cromford Club in the fifties. This was the upbeat Sinatra of strike-it-rich London in the nineties – the finger-popping Sinatra of shark-skin suits and hup-hup-hup; the 'Come Fly with Me' Sinatra of the Rat Pack and ring-a-ding-ding.

In his eye-line as Venables belted it out from Scribes's small stage was the portrait in oils of his hero that he had commissioned for the club – a picture of the Duncan he remembered from when he was fifteen and Edwards was twenty-one, heavily framed and picked out in a golden downlight which glowed through the fug of lazily spinning cigar and cigarette smoke.

While he was in London for the Arsenal match, one of Edwards's responsibilities – and he took all his responsibilities seriously – was to hand over to Mr William Luscombe of the publishers Stanley Paul the manuscript of the instructional manual that he had written without a ghost and tapped out with two fingers over many months on his Remington portable, either at the digs he shared with his old Midlands pal Gordon Clayton in Manchester, Mrs Watson having moved on by then, or at his fiancée Mollie Leach's house.

Tackle Soccer This Way was part of a series of sports books aimed primarily at young people which also included *Tackle Lawn Tennis . . .* by Angela Buxton and *Tackle Riding . . .* by Lt-Col. C. C. G. Hope. Although in his introduction to Edwards's book when it was published posthumously at the end of 1958 the publisher gave the assurance that 'We have not altered the book in any way; it remains exactly as he passed it over to us with almost boyish enthusiasm,' this doesn't appear likely. The pages are marked by an earnestness which doesn't seem in character; or maybe Edwards absorbed the writing styles of Lt-Col. Hope and Miss Buxton so conscientiously that he expunged any Black Country inflections entirely. He talks about himself and the lads at Mrs Watson's being 'a bunch of good fellows eating, drinking and playing together', managing to sound like Jennings of the first-remove or Bob Danvers-Walker, the famously cracked-leather voice of *Movietone News*, rather than big Doonc of Elm Rowd on the Priory in Doodlie.

'The responsibility on the sportsman is heavy,' he cautions. 'Boys often identify themselves with athletes and so try to model their behaviour and play upon them. Once he has attracted this hero worship he constantly has to conduct himself, both on and off the field, in a way that presents these youngsters with an example.'

Of his own playing position: 'My own idea of the top class wing-half is that he should defend and attack with equal competence, and that he should always remember that he is the nearest thing to perpetual motion the game will ever see. It is a position that will sap a man's strength both physically and mentally. Yet it is infinitely satisfying . . . Personally I am not enamoured of the dallying type of winger.'

And on the importance of treating triumph and disaster, those two impostors, just the same: 'Whatever precautions you take, the time is going to come when you will lose. Now I am not one of those people who believe that it doesn't matter whether you win or lose. I believe the object in starting a game of football is to win it. All the same, defeats will come, and when they do accept them as quietly and philosophically as I hope you do your victories. A great deal of fuss is made by people sniping at football about the high spirits among players when they score a goal. The fact that they might jump for joy, slap each other on the back and perhaps shake the hand of the scorer is seen as something to be sneered at. In reality these high jinks are just a spontaneous outburst climaxing a game that is hard on the nerves as well as the feet. A goal brings relief to the tension and the players are human enough to show it. I can see nothing criminal in that.'

The cover of *Tackle Soccer This Way* is a picture of Edwards in training with 'wing wizard' Stanley Matthews and the Wolves and England captain Billy Wright, who was Edwards's room-mate for internationals. Matthews was then already forty-two, a legend old enough to have received letters notifying him of his selection for England which began patronizingly 'Dear Matthews'. He still had another seven years of professional football left in him.

Edwards had been England's youngest-ever international at the age of eighteen, and in 1958 few were in any doubt that he was the team's captain-in-waiting. He would still have only been twenty-nine in 1966, and even Bobby Moore's friend Terry Venables believes it would have been Edwards instead of Moore captaining England in the World Cup that year: 'Perhaps Bobby would have got in the team in another position, because he was a great player, too, but you would never have picked Moore in front of Edwards. Duncan had the edge everywhere.'

'He was England's youngest player,' Matt Busby once said, 'and I have no doubt he would have lived to be the oldest.'

Bobby Charlton always looked forward to getting back to England when the team had been out of the country. United's summer tours of America were times that made him feel particularly homesick. The brashness of Americans is something he always found especially hard to take, and the attitudes and temper of their country were never to his liking.

'Paradise' is how he would always think of England in those long weeks he was away in New York, Philadelphia, St Louis and San Francisco.

'Paradise' is the word he also used to describe the world as he remembered it in the early years in Manchester, before anything had been won.

He was able to see Mr Busby and Duncan for a minute before leaving the Munich hospital for home. The Boss smiled and said, 'So you're going home, son?' Duncan recognized him, but not much more. Bobby could sense that Duncan was restless, that they were looking for him to be still and that he was trying to work out what was happening – why wouldn't they let him up?

Duncan had asked for his gold watch – the presentation watch which each of the team had been given in Madrid the year before – and a battered watch had been taken from the wreckage and strapped on his wrist.

Coming off the train at Liverpool Street station, Bobby was met by his mother and his brother. On the long drive up the A1 to Leeds he hardly spoke. Bobby and his mother continued their journey from Leeds to Newcastle by train, sharing the compartment with a sailor who slept the whole way.

The roads always seemed to be very little and winding after being away, and to pass by endlessly green fields. He had the same feeling when looking out of a train window after every journey overseas. His own country was the best in the world, and he would never want to live anywhere else except in England.

The legend of the holy drinker #1

'I have found a genius.' This is the telegram that Bob Bishop, Manchester United's chief scout in Northern Ireland, dashed off to Matt Busby after seeing Geordie Best of Cregagh Boys demolish his own highly rated, considerably older Boysland team single-handedly.

In football's mythology it ranks alongside the classic biopic moment when the Dudley schoolmaster writes urgently to a friend about Duncan Edwards, claiming that 'I have just seen a boy who will play for England before he is twenty-one', or when United's terrier scout Joe Armstrong turns to Cissie Charlton on the touchline of the Colliery Welfare ground in Ashington and tells her: 'One day your lad will play for England, missus.' Cue crane shot slowly pulling back to show a panorama of seven pitches shrouded in mist, eager fathers running up and down bellowing encouragement, whippet dogs leaping and barking, the colliery winding gear silhouetted against the sky. Cue voice-over: 'This is a story of simple working people – their hardship, their humours, but above all their heroism.'

Yet a question niggles: did Bob Bishop ever write that 'genius' telegram? Was it ever sent? If it was, it seems to have ended up on the midden heap at the bottom of history's dustbin.

And what about the boots that George was wearing on the fateful day that Bishop spotted his potential genius? His first grown-up football boots? What happened to them?

Even when the drink had taken hold, Best was always protective of his boots and placed them in the hands of the hairdresser and nightclub owner Malcolm 'Waggy' Wagner or the fur trader Danny Bursk or one of his other birding mates from Manchester for safe-keeping, like a boxer entrusting his fists to his trainer before a fight, like a snooker player's paranoia about his cue.

As a skivvy toiling in the tiny boot room at Old Trafford, George developed a technique to make the boots he had been given the responsibility for cleaning stand out. They belonged to the shovel-handed goalkeeper whose size the first time he'd seen him had made him bolt for home, the Ulsterman and Munich survivor Harry Gregg. The procedure was to (1) get all the surface cack off with a wire brush; (2) give them a good rubbing of dubbin; and (3) (and it was this that was the difference between acceptability and excellence) finish with a light glaze of Vaseline petroleum jelly for that man-of-the-match, boots-of-the-Gods, head-turning sheen.

Remember, these were the big old-fashioned boots of cork studs and reinforced toe-caps and hogsback pigskin leather. The heavy old boots that broke people's legs week in, week out in the Football League and that, according to a certain school of thought, were best broken in by pissing in them first to accelerate the softening-up process.

Large memory is recorded in books and small memory is all about little things: trivia, jokes, George's first boots that Dickie, his dad, who worked alternate day and night shifts as a turner at the Harland and Wolff shipyard in Belfast, and Ann, his mam, who worked on the production line at Gallagher's tobacco factory, had to 'go careful' for a while to be able to get him. This was after George had passed the eleven-plus and gone to a grammar school where they only played rugby, and then left after a short while to go to the secondary modern closer to home where football was the sport of choice and his footballing friends off the Cregagh were pupils.

To get to Grosvenor High Protestant School he had had to go through a Catholic neighbourhood wearing the blazer that identified him as a proddy dog. George always insisted this never played a part in his deciding to pack it in. Dickie Best, though, remains unconvinced: 'He'd go through with his badge clearly visible, and they'd throw stones and call him names. I think the journey to and from the grammar school bothered George more than he let on.'

He was skinny – 'a skinny little nowt' – and he believed he was unattractive to girls. The physique of a knitting needle/a match/a stick of rhubarb is the standard description from around that time. He was sparrow-legged, pigeon-chested. 'Look'tcha, you streak of piss,' the girls would call after him as he kicked a ball from Burren Way the couple of hundred yards to the field at the end of the road. Scouts from the big clubs would come to check him out and leave shaking their heads. 'What did they say?' George would ask Bud McFarlane, who ran the Cregagh Boys Club team. And McFarlane would have to tell him: 'They think you look like you've escaped from a refugee camp. They think you're too skinny.' The consensus was that he wouldn't be able to handle the physical side and perform against bigger and more experienced – dirtier, harder – players.

A key part of the folklore from the Cregagh Boys Club days (and it may have no more substance than the 'genius' telegram story) is that, after Mr McFarlane told him he was a bit weak on his left foot, he spent a week practising with a tennis ball using only his left foot, and then played in a match that Saturday wearing a canvas gutty on his right foot and a boot on his left and scored twelve of his team's twenty-one goals. It is testimony to the discipline and dedication Best was capable of in the early part of his life that when he was in his prime, irresistible and unstoppable, many people thought of him as a naturally left-footed player. 'George Best did not arrive on earth the complete player,' Michael Parkinson once noted. 'He made himself into a two-footed player, not in the sense that he was marvellous with one and adequate with the other, but to the point where he had forgotten which was his natural foot. This gave him all the options when it came to beating an opponent, but particularly in the box, where Best was one of the most certain finishers I ever saw.'

The foundation of his talent, everybody agreed, was his balance. This was the thing that Matt Busby was most struck by the first time he saw him play: 'I sort of detected it somehow in his manner, in his approach to the ball. It was uncanny. He had that tremendous balance for a boy. It was the way he seemed able to make the ball do what he wanted it to do. In all my experience in football I have never seen a player who could beat a man – or men – so close, and in so many ways. When men are on top of him and it seems impossible to do it, he still does it.'

'Here at Old Trafford', Sir Alex Ferguson once said, 'they reckon Bestie had double-jointed ankles. That it was a physical thing, an extreme flexibility there. [It explains how] he could do those 180-degree turns without going through a half-circle, simply by swivelling on his ankles. As well as devastating defenders, that helped him to avoid injuries because he was never really stationary for opponents to hurt him. He was always riding or spinning away from things.'

Few people have written better than Hugh McIlvanney about George Best; he writes with the conviction of personal acquaintance, and in 1969 he wrote this: 'His game is an amalgam of superb, almost supernatural, balance, unbreakable spirit, a delicacy of touch that stays true no matter how fast he moves, limitless ingenuity and ambition, and force out of all proportion to his physique. He carries on to the field a constant threat of the impossible.'

Adidas X-tra Ion Supernova Soft Ground. Puma Borussia. Nike Top Range Mercurial Vapor. Air Zoom Total 90. Adidas Predator Pulsion. Adidas Absolado. Nike Ultracell Vapor w/Traxion outsole and Supreltech micro-fibre inner sock. Mizuna Rivaldo Moulded. Stainless-steel cleats w/DuoFlex technology.

In the months after Manchester United won the European Cup in 1968, a local firm sold 250,000 pairs of its 'George Best' autographed boot. An informal ceremony took place in the sample-lined foyer of the boot-makers' factory to mark the occasion. 'This is the golden boot for the golden boy,' the middle-aged MD of the company said, making the presentation of a pair of lamé-like, slipper-style boots to an understandably uncomfortable-looking guest of honour.

'What is the material, Harvey?' a fellow director cut in, to cover Best's embarrassment. 'Classic kid,' was the answer. 'It's genuine golden kid.'

Hair tonic and chewing gum were among the other products that carried the Best name by then, and he was filmed making a tour of cosmetics and chewing-gum factories, smiling shyly and nodding, posing for pictures, doing his Charlie Bubbles of zoning out while trying to look engaged. 'The wax paper comes in on these reels, you see, goes round here . . .' The camera occasionally caught a desperate, animal panic on his face signalling it was the sort of situation which cried out for the intervention of a Denis Law or a Rodney Marsh, or the Jimmy Greaves who, in later years, was willing to be big-hearted Laurel to Best's tongue-tied, taciturn Hardy on the roadshow they toured around the country, as reliable as George was wayward, as cheekily cockerney as his sidekick was protestantly self-conscious.

In his book *Golden Goals*, Jackie Milburn remembered as a boy getting up on Christmas morning to find a new pair of football boots among his Christmas presents. They were the first pair of new boots he'd had; up until then he'd always worn hand-me-downs from the family next door. At 3.30 a.m. he put the new boots on and went out 'to find most of my friends, wearing their new boots, playing football by torchlight in the middle of the street'.

George finally got his boots around the time he signed up for the Cregagh Boys Club, when he was about thirteen. That Christmas a pair of shiny new leather boots was added to the shirt, shorts and socks he got for Christmas every year. He considered them beautiful. Like the ball he took to bed, they assumed a place of elevated importance in his life. He fed them and tended them and personalized them in a way that infused the boots with mystery, aura, magic, whatever it is that modern-day collectors of this kind of object are seeking and are prepared to devote considerable parts of their lives to tracking down. He oiled and dubbined them until the pebbled leather was smooth and supple. And then he developed the habit, after matches, of systematically inscribing the history of those early years on to them. After every game he dipped into a jar of whitening and along the sides of the boots wrote down the name of the opponents he had just played, plus the number of goals he had scored against them. And so the boots became not only imprinted with the life that had been lived inside them but also turned into an intimate diary of the sort that can often throw up clues that were absent or indecipherable in an individual's prickly, opaque or otherwise uncommunicative personality.

Everyone has a dead child inside them. Mementoes of childhood – a favourite toy, a shoe – are sometimes sent to the silversmiths to be preserved. The first schoolboy boots, which it was a stretch for them to buy, and into which George invested so much of himself, are a touching symbol of what Ann and Dickie Best lost when they put him into his first pair of long trousers and saw him off on a boat with a boy that he didn't know to make the night crossing to a place he had never been before.

'Now you mention it,' Dickie grew into the habit of saying, 'George has had them off me, and I never got them back.' For many years George sent all the trophies and medals that came to him, all the keepsakes and mementoes of a career that he was too busy living to be a curator of, straight home to Belfast to his mother. It was a way of staying in touch that he was able to do less and less in person. Ann Best didn't take a drink until she was into her forties. The family said she started drinking because of the unwanted attention that George's fame, later his notoriety, had brought. People pointed her out in shops. Her life ceased to be her own. Crowds gathered outside in the street when word got round that George was home, and so he hardly ever went. Mrs Fullaway dropped his mother a line every so often to tell her how George was going along. When his mother made her weekly call, it was usually Mrs Fullaway she got on the other end. The phone mounted on the wall by his bed in the small upstairs bedroom rang and rang. Of course, he didn't remember birthdays. All Ann knew of George increasingly was what she read in the papers. And what she read in the papers was less and less good. This or that girl; another drunken nightclub incident; a summons; a suspension from Manchester United; a crashed car. Studly George.

'It hurts me a lot when I listen to stories, especially outside, on buses and public transport, even in shops, where people don't know who I am,' his mother said. 'I have listened to people ridiculing him, they've called him all the names. On one occasion I was standing having a drink with a man, and he was actually ridiculing George to me, in a football conversation . . . So it takes a lot of biting your tongue, I can tell you that.'

Ann started to drink when Dickie was at work. He'd come home from work and find her and they'd have a row. He'd storm out to meet his friends at the social club they used to go to together, and she'd drink some more cheap wine and try and hide the bottles. A relative got a message through that his mother was going down fast and needed to see him, but still George didn't go. He was going down fast himself by then and staying drunk nearly all the time.

Slowly he started to take back things he had given in the past. 'George has had them off me, and I never got them back.' He told his friend and agent Phil Hughes that everything had been stolen or burgled or given away or just walked. That he had been bled dry. Picked to the bone. But it wasn't true. Some things had been sold. At a testimonial dinner organized by his friends Jimmy Tarbuck, Billy Connolly and Michael Parkinson he had auctioned off his medals, the shirt Pelé gave him, other mementoes. Then he took the £20,000 the sale had raised to the Playboy Club around the corner and blew the lot.

He had bought his mam and dad a fish-and-chip shop in Belfast, but Dickie had to sell it in order to stay at home and take care of his wife who, it had become clear by the time Best left United for the last time in January 1974, was drinking herself to death. George finally went home. His mother could only sit beside him, touching his arm or his hand and weeping. 'I would have liked to take them away from Belfast, but by this time I had no proper home of my own,' he said, ignoring the fact that his father had lived in the same house all his married life, near the same neighbours, and didn't want to be shifted. 'I was living the life of a gypsy, trailing from one place to the next in search of something I couldn't define. Eventually I left Manchester and went to America, putting myself even farther away from Belfast. But the newspaper stories kept my family misinformed of my activities, and for every good story there were ten to break my mother's heart.'

Ann Best died in October 1978. Dickie took her a cup of tea up one morning and she was dead. She was fifty-four. George and his then wife Angela, former personal trainer to the singer Cher who he had married in a *Sun* picture exclusive in Las Vegas earlier in the year, flew home from California for the funeral. He hadn't seen his mother for a long time, and he didn't want to see her body. He had been in Europe with Detroit Express, one of the tepid American soccer teams that were keeping him in drinking money, the month before, but he had made no attempt to get in touch. His mother knew about the tour and how near he had been to Belfast from seeing it mentioned in the paper. He had never seen a dead body and he had no desire to see his mother's.

In the vocabulary of psychoanalysis, the word 'phantom' is used for those family secrets whose pain is passed down from generation to generation without necessarily being made explicit in words. It would have been in character for Dickie, a tough-minded man under that affable exterior, a strong character with firm views about what is appropriate and right, to make a gesture whose purpose was to keep one last part of George from being interrogated or consumed. And the best way to do that would be to keep it close within the family. He could have put the boots into the casket with his wife. Or, if not then, he could have put them in the coffin with George when they brought him home to lie overnight in the quiet of his father's living room under the life-size, framed photographic portrait of himself from the sixties and the few remaining souvenirs, while the world beat in waves against the door and buzzed patiently overhead.

'I seen him going out of my life, into a country he knew nothing about,' Ann Best said in a documentary filmed in

1969, 'and I wondered what he would do. Because he was so shy and backward. So frail . . .'

'The first time I left Belfast, as the boat was pulling out and I could see my parents on the quayside, I didn't really think I was leaving home,' George said in the same film. 'It was a little adventure. I was going away for a couple of weeks' holiday; I didn't think I was going to make it, really. But then I came back, and as the scene repeated itself, I knew as we pulled out I was leaving home for a long time, and it made me a little sad.'

In the film, the camera lingers for a long time over his European Footballer of the Year trophy, which is sitting on the mantelpiece in Burren Way. 'After this', Phil Hughes would say when the small silver-gilt figure went under the hammer in 2003, 'there is nothing.'

His first boots have failed to materialize to date. The boots that he personalized and turned into a diary of the time he was just starting out on the road to himself. The plain fact is that, wherever they may be, whoever might have them, for now the boots have disappeared.

A postscript

Several weeks after writing this, I came across the following paragraph in *Joe DiMaggio: The Hero's Life*, by Richard Ben Cramer:

> *The treatment of Joe's relics was the surest sign of his new saintly status . . . Over the [family] funeral parlour in Newark, Geta and Bina Spatola were already saving Joe's wine-stained shirt . . . Soon the Spatola girls would receive the shoes Joe wore during the Sacred Streak – or as Geta insisted on calling them, 'The Spikes'. The two girls would have their coffin-maker fashion a beautiful encasement for The Spikes, which would then rest, in perpetuity, on rolled and tufted velvet, such as is seen in only the finest coffins. From time to time, over the years, the girls would bring out the velvet-lined encasement, so that Little Leaguers or*

*Legion ballplayers (who were playing for the Spatola
Funeral squad) could rub the spikes for good and godly
effect. But mostly The Spikes would remain in the reliquary
of the Spatola home – that was the closet, where the [Joe]
DiMaggio–[Dorothy] Arnold wedding cake was still perfect
in its tent of waxed paper.*

The legend of the holy drinker #19

For somebody with such a naturally quiet and shy disposition,
Best had a well-developed streak of exhibitionism. 'I always
saw myself as an entertainer,' is something he said repeatedly
throughout his life. 'It was my job to go out there and give
them a show.' And it's true that the sound of pre-match crowds
of 60,000 and more, the muffled thud of feet pounding on the
terraces above the dressing room, the chants, the anthems and
the tannoy announcements seemed to hold no fear for him.

Bobby Charlton was a wreck for days before a game.
'Fridays I used to dread . . . the day before the match . . . what
kind of game will I have? . . . will I do this? . . . will I get the
chance to do that? . . . It's a wonder I didn't go crazy. If we
were at Old Trafford I would go and sit up in the stand by
myself gazing at the pitch like some soothsayer peering into a
crystal ball for a message from the future. I would remember
moves that had failed or come off in the previous match. I
could see myself down there by that far touchline. And, if we
lost, I worried as hard on Sunday as I did on Friday. People
who didn't know me thought what a calm, quiet lad I was . . .'

Best's week, inevitably, had a rather different slant to it.
'Wednesday til Saturday is murder,' he said in 1966, when he was
still only twenty. 'I know I've got to stay off the town and get to
bed by 11. But it drives me nuts. I don't read. Well, only the
sports pages. The only thing that keeps me sane is remembering
that there'll be a party on Sunday and Monday and Tuesday.'

He spent the build-up to a game hanging round the players'

entrance chatting to friends, only going in to change at the last minute. Charlton and some of the more jumpy characters doused their nerves with a hit of ammonia or by taking a nip of scotch from the bottle Jimmy Murphy kept in the kit box before they ran out. George would get a sugar rush from half a bar of chocolate and a visceral one from the noise which grew steadily in volume the closer they got to the business end of the tunnel. He had a saying, which can still stand as a slogan for the period of which he was such a defining presence: 'Good things sound better loud.' Music or stadium crowds: he liked a bit of volume. The players made their entrance down a steep ramp on the halfway line at Old Trafford in those days, and Best admitted that, caught up in the mood of the crowd and the sense of excitement and anticipation, he sometimes had an erection by the time his feet made contact with the pitch.

'I noticed that when I touched the ball on the field you could hear this shrill noise in the crowd with all the birds screaming like at a Beatles concert,' he said, adding that this also aroused him. Less obviously, he got off on making monkeys of defenders like Chelsea's Ron 'Chopper' Harris and Bolton's Roy 'Chopper' Hartle and some of the other well-known hard-men 'stuffers' and 'destroyers' of the day with their hospital tackles.

'When I first started I didn't mind the hard men too much because it gave me the chance to rubbish them with my skill,' he once said. 'I'd go past them and they'd say, "Do that again and I'll break your fucking leg." And next time I'd do them again and they'd say, "Right, I fucking warned you." Next time I got the ball I'd stand on it and beckon them to me. I used to be like a bullfighter, taunting them, inviting them to charge me. They rarely got me. I was too quick. At moments like that, with the crowd cheering, I used to get the horn. Honestly. It used to arouse me, excite me. I felt the same way every time I walked on to the field at the start of a game.'

His exhibitionist tendencies extended beyond the field of play, when he would perform sex for his teammates' pleasure. When he was on Northern Ireland international tours, he would charge the other players fifty pence each to watch. The organizer of these evenings was a player who Best only ever identified as 'the Ferret'. It was the Ferret's responsibility to make sure that viewing conditions – the lighting and so on – were just so, and that the peepers had taken up position in the wardrobe or behind a curtain by the time Best got his unsuspecting partner up to the room. Most often, though, it was just the Ferret watching from a cupboard or a secret viewing place on his own. 'Sometimes when I couldn't get the bird into a room', Best said, 'I'd take her outside and I'd be making it up against a tree or in the undergrowth somewhere and I'd see the Ferret crawling on his hands and knees to a good spot, quiet as a mouse. He was always very quiet.

'One day he brought another player with him who ruined it for everyone by being a noisy crawler. Next morning I came downstairs and the Ferret had this player practising crawling across the hotel lounge. He was saying, "You'll never be a good ferret if you don't listen to me." The Ferret was a bit special.'

The legend of the holy drinker #24

The saloon's doors were ever open. And always and everywhere I found saloons, on highway and byway, up narrow alleys and on busy thoroughfares, bright-lighted and cheerful, warm in winter and in summer dark and cool. Yes, the saloon was a mighty fine place, and it was more than that . . .

In the saloons life was different. Men talked with great voices, laughed great laughs, and there was an atmosphere of greatness. Here was something more than common everyday where nothing happened. Terrible they might be, but then that only meant that they were terribly wonderful . . . Here life was always very live.

Jack London, *John Barleycorn*

One minute before opening time . . . A faint bustle of preparation in the other bars, but deep silence in the Saloon . . .

Bob switched on the lights in the Lounge (this was his routine) and went in and poked the fire into a crackling blaze ... He came back and encountered the governor lifting the flap of the bar, and coming out to unbolt the door ... He slid back the upper bolt; and he slid back the middle bolt ... A sharp click, a grunt of achievement and The Midnight Bell was open ... The public was at liberty to enter The Midnight Bell. No sudden eruption, no announcing sound, proclaimed the fact. Only the click of sliding bolts, and the steady burning of electric light behind a door which might be Pushed.

    Patrick Hamilton, *Twenty Thousand Streets Under the Sky*

The saloon opens at eight. Mike gives the floor a lick and a promise and throws on clean sawdust. He replenishes the free-lunch platters with cheese and onions and fills a bowl with cold, hard-boiled eggs, five cents each. Kelly shows up. The ale truck makes its delivery. Then, in the middle of the morning, the old men begin shuffling in. Kelly calls them 'the steadies'. The majority are retired labourers and small businessmen. They prefer McSorley's to their homes. A few live in the neighbourhood, but many come from a distance ... Only a few of the old men have enough interest in the present to read newspapers. These patrons sit up front, to get the light that comes through the grimy street windows. When they grow tired of reading, they stare for hours into the street. There is always something worth looking at on Seventh Street ...

*   It is possible to relax in McSorley's. For one thing, it is dark and gloomy, and repose comes easy in a gloomy place. Also, the barely audible heartbeatlike ticking of the old clocks is soothing. Also, there is a thick, musty smell that acts as a balm to jerky nerves; it is really a rich compound of the smells of pine sawdust, tap drippings, pipe tobacco, coal smoke and onions. A Bellevue intern once remarked that for some mental states the smell in McSorley's would be a lot*

more beneficial than psychoanalysis or sedative pills or prayer.

Joseph Mitchell, *McSorley's Wonderful Saloon*

It was the hour at last for the Pontefract Arms . . . While Henry fetched the drinks I went into the lavatory. The walls were scrawled with phrases: 'Damn you, landlord, and your breasty wife.' 'To all pimps and whores a merry syphilis and a happy gonorrhea.' I went quickly out again to the cheery paper streamers and the clink of glass. Sometimes I see myself reflected too closely in other men for comfort.

Graham Greene, *The End of the Affair*

I tried a number of places in Watertown before settling on the Parrot; though it was not exactly the cathedral I would have wished for, it was – like certain old limestone churches scattered throughout the north country – not without its quaint charms. It was ideally isolated on a hill above the city; . . . at the bar, the city could be thought of as a place remembered, and remembered as if from a great distance . . .

With the music stilled and the blinds thrown open allowing the golden autumn sunlight to diffuse and warm the room, I would stand at the bar and sip my Budweiser, my 'tapering-off' device; munch popcorn from wooden bowls; and in league with the bartender Freddy, whose allegiance to the Giants was only somewhat less feverish than mine, cheer my team home. Invariably and desperately I wished that the afternoon, the game, the light would never end.

Frederick Exley, *A Fan's Notes*

Everybody joined in the singing, drinking waterfalls of beer, emptying bottles of whisky, full of laughter and noise and a sense that I can only describe as joy. It was as if we'd all been looking for the same Great Good Place and created it here . . . I was soon one of the regulars, there every night, and sometimes every day. In the growing chaos of the Sixties, the [Lion's] Head became one of the metronomes of my life . . .

It was also the place in which everything was forgiven. Lose your job? Betrayed by your wife? Throw up on your shoes? Great: have a drink on us.

Pete Hamill, *A Drinking Life*

I'd always held to the romantic notion that we were hiding from life in Publicans. [But then I started to ask]: are we hiding from life or courting death? And what's the difference?

Many times that November I would look down the bar, at all the hollow-eyed and ashen faces, and I'd think maybe we were already dead. I'd think of Yeats: 'A drunkard is a dead man, / And all dead men are drunk.' I'd think of Lorca: 'Death / is coming in and leaving / the tavern, / death / leaving and coming in.' Was it a coincidence that two of my favourite poets depicted death as a barroom regular? Sometimes I would catch my own hollow-eyed and ashen reflection in one of the silver cash registers. My face was like the moon, pale and bloated, but unlike the moon I never left . . . Everything had changed . . . Publicans had devolved from a sanctuary to a prison, as sanctuaries so often do.

J. R. Moehringer, *The Tender Bar*

A horrible excitement was upon everybody and everything . . . It was the last five minutes of the evening, and they were drunk. And they were in every phase of drunkenness conceivable. They were talking drunk, and confidential drunk, and laughing drunk, and beautifully drunk, and leering drunk, and secretive drunk, and dignified drunk, and admittedly drunk, and fighting drunk, and even rolling drunk . . .

The governor began it. His voice was scarcely heard above the din. 'Now then, gentlemen, please!' he cried. 'Last orders, please!' . . . And now a kind of panic and babel fell upon the Midnight Bell. A searching draught swept in from the open door, and suddenly the governor lowered all the lights save one above the bar. At this a few realized that the game was up and left the place abruptly; others besieged Ella

madly for last orders. Some of the groups dispersed with
bawled farewells: others drew closer protectively, and
argued the louder and more earnestly for the assault that
was being made upon their happiness.
   'NOW then, gentlemen, please! LONG PAST TIME!'
   Patrick Hamilton, *Twenty Thousand Streets Under the Sky*

In the same way that he tended to be a loner rather than a con-
vivial drunk, Best always seemed to have a preference for pubs
over people. In the course of his life, a recognizable pattern
emerged of him finding a drinking place where he felt comfortable in his skin, and doggedly sticking with it. A place to be
alone with a drink. The simultaneous experience of intimacy
and distance. His own awareness of himself looking on. The
addict, strapping on his monumental thirst.

The legend of the holy drinker #8

The Brown Bull

He turned twenty-one in the Summer of Love of 1967. United
were the new League champions and their closed-season tour
that year took them to San Francisco, hub of the new stoned hip-
pie universe. The acid tests were happening – trippers scouring
their brainpans out with LSD. Happenings were happening –
people emptying buckets of blood over themselves, artists inviting strangers to snip off all their clothes with a pair of scissors,
crazies having themselves nailed to the roofs of Oldsmobiles.

On the night of his twenty-first, George's trusty radar took
him to a run-down, English-style boozer called the Edinburgh
Castle in the Market Street district of San Francisco, close to
the team hotel. There he and Dave Sadler, his room-mate from
Mrs Fullaway's, got tanked on beer and vodka-and-lemonades,
and soaked it up with fish and chips.

Only seven years later Best would be back in California,
playing for the likes of the Los Angeles Aztecs and the San Jose

Earthquakes, burnt-out, overweight, disillusioned, with both feet planted on the path to alcoholic oblivion.

But in the Summer of Love of 1967, Matt Busby was still in charge at Old Trafford, they were twelve months away from finally winning the European Cup, and – good-looking, fashionable, leisured and affluent – George Best was one of the most potent symbols of a decade dominated by a careless sense of vitality and youthful enterprise. He was on £160 a week, had a white 3.4-litre Jag, seventy shirts, a 15,000-strong fan club, an agent, three full-time secretaries dealing with his mail and half-shares in a booming fashion boutique. Constant excitement, action, fun, change and disposability were presented as the hallmarks of the Pop lifestyle of the sixties. And, by 1967, Best, the only footballer or representative of the sweaty arts among the movable feast of pop singers, film producers, models, fashion photographers, East End gangsters, painters and nightclub owners who filled the colour supplements, was seen as the embodiment of all of these.

There's some rare footage from around this time (rare because he didn't like to be seen dancing in public – 'Belfast men don't dance,' he said, 'at least not any that I know') which shows him shuffling among a crowd of dancers in a television studio, just in front of a stage on which the Rolling Stones are miming in a pointedly incompetent way to 'The Last Time': the whole golden boom is in the air, and Best doesn't look at all out of place among the lovely young creatures frugging expressionlessly as Mick Jagger pretends to muff the words and a saucer-eyed Brian Jones stares off beyond his peroxide fringe and the lighting gantry into outer space.

It is interesting that Best was never provincial. Manchester was, but he wasn't. He never got to know Belfast well; growing up, he hardly ever left the estate where he was born, and even as an adult was lost once he strayed from the Cregagh. But he never had a hick reputation. Unlike other footballers of the period who tried to get with it, he didn't end up the butt of anybody's jokes. Willie Morgan, for example, announced himself on arrival at Old Trafford at the beginning of the 1968 season as the new George Best, ignoring the fact that the real one still had tenure. Morgan's qualifications, in addition to his long hair and the tricky way he wanted to play, were a boutique he had opened on Keirby Walk in Burnley next door to a butcher's shop and his mother's opinion, given play in all the papers, that Georgie Best had copied her Willie's trendy Beatles look.

'The present-day player is what we would term in the film-star class,' the great Preston North End and England winger Tom Finney said in 1969. And outwardly Best had all the trappings: the car, the clothes, the girls, the boutiques, the newspaper columns, the modelling and merchandizing contracts. But underlying it all was an attractive lack of finish and sophistication. When England played West Germany in the 1966 World Cup final at Wembley, for example, Best rounded up his roommate from the digs David Sadler, his drinking pal and partner in the men's Edwardia boutique, the Manchester City player Mike Summerbee, and his fur-trader friend Danny Bursk, and the four of them piled into his new white Jaguar for the drive down to London, in the course of which Best was booked for the second time in three months for speeding. No invitations to any of the celebration parties were in the offing, so they gravitated towards the West End and drifted into a club on Shaftesbury Avenue called Tiffany's. Nothing came of it, and they ended up going back to the north London council flat belonging to Mrs Fullaway's sister, driving home to Manchester the next day.

Best had already given a demonstration of how close he still was to the background that had produced him a couple of months earlier, in March, when he had stepped off a plane from Lisbon wearing the floppy, Speedy Gonzalez, bobble-fringed tourist sombrero which was his souvenir of United's famous victory over the Portuguese champions Benfica in the quarter-finals of the 1966 European Cup. Repeated today, it would seem like a contrivance, a stunt dreamed up in a flashily appointed office in the hinterlands of Soho or Mayfair and choreographed step by step, photo op by photo op on the mobile. But then it still had the unfaked air of high-spirited spontaneity about it that had marked Best's performance against the Portuguese in a match which had decisively announced his arrival on the wider, European stage.

Before the game, the manager had given the only instructions he ever gave before they went out: to keep it simple, find another red shirt and express themselves, with the added, virtually unprecedented, caution on this occasion to keep it tight for the first twenty minutes until they got their opponents' measure. But United were already two up, both goals scored by George, when Dickie Best switched the radio on just a few minutes after kick-off, starting his night shift at Harland and Wolff.

It has always been Bobby Charlton's belief that the outside left is the loneliest man on the football field, not getting the ball half as often as his opposite number on the right. He had been a reluctant left-winger for both England and Manchester United – an outcast inside half looking for the smallest excuse to drift into the middle again. 'One of the earliest curiosities I noticed about the position,' Charlton said, 'was that, while I did less work, I felt more tired during a game. I came to the conclusion that this was because I had more time to think about it . . . I used to shout for the ball, wave my arms. It didn't make any difference. Sometimes twenty minutes would go by and I wouldn't get a kick. I wandered about inspecting the grass.' A textbook example, perhaps, of a player's personality being reflected in his style of play.

Best had played a game for the first team in September 1963, four months after his seventeenth birthday, but then had gone back to playing for the reserves and the youth teams in the Lancashire League. He was having Christmas at home in Belfast when he received a telegram telling him to fly back to Manchester immediately. On Boxing Day, Burnley had thrashed United 6–1 at Turf Moor. For the return fixture at

Old Trafford two days later, Best was put in at outside left, and Bobby Charlton moved inside. Best got his first senior goal in a 5–1 win and ran John Angus, the Burnley fullback, a player known for being hard and fast, ragged.

Playing alongside him in his first game, against West Bromwich Albion in September, Charlton hadn't been overly impressed by the boy wonder: 'In that match, Albion's full back, Graham Williams, knew the score, and went in hard from the start. Consequently George never had time to settle and show what he can really do. A couple of seasons of kicking around the junior leagues of Manchester might have given him the experience that would have made the vital difference.'

It was claimed after the Burnley game that the big defender Angus never fully recovered from the easy, ignominious way Best kept running at him and turning him inside out. The same was said of the Chelsea fullback Ken Shellito after a match at Stamford Bridge eight months later which was so memorable it introduced two new phrases into the football lexicon: 'mazy dribbles' and 'twisted blood'. The first was the Chelsea captain Terry Venables' description of what had made Best so special that night; the second was the United midfielder Pat Crerand's name for what Shellito – turned, dummied, nutmegged, passed so cruelly and so often – was suffering from by the end of the game. 'You could see in that game the complete range of his skills,' Crerand said. 'That's what made him so special, his range. He could do more things better than any player I have ever seen. He was a magnificent distributor of the ball, he could beat a man on either side using methods that no one had ever thought about, he could shoot, he could tackle, he was competitive and yet cool under pressure. What more could you want? I mean, what is the perfect player?'

After the whistle, both sets of supporters and the players from both teams, including Shellito, stood to cheer Best off. Mrs Fullaway's sister, who was at the ground, watched it all through a blur of tears. Reading the reports in the following morning's papers, which referred to his son's 'magic dexterity' and the coming of age of 'one of the greatest players the game has seen', among other things, Dickie Best also wept. 'The more I wonder when it all began, the more I keep coming back to that game,' George said.

He was still only nineteen, a year and a half later, in March 1966, when United beat Benfica in Lisbon in the quarter-final of the European Cup. The training staff at Old Trafford had been told from the beginning not to try and change his style; not to make him conform. Busby insisted that the only thing they could do for George was 'change nothing'.

'We knew that George was immature at times in his football, and even when he became an experienced player there were times when I wished he'd have passed to other players more often,' Jimmy Murphy said. 'He scored goals, made up his own moves, frequently out of nothing because of his fantastic skill with the ball, and if he had been forced to play to a rigid plan he might well have been a failure. So it was important to let him develop naturally as a boy. He held on to the ball too much, but that was his style. If George Best was starting out in football today, I wonder how he would have got on with the systems and whether it would have been so easy for him to reveal his genius to the world. I wonder how many George Bests are being destroyed at this very minute by coaches who fail to appreciate that a pennyworth of skill is worth a pound of theory any day.'

The day after the triumph at Lisbon he was splashed all over the front of the papers in his cheap sombrero. Geoffrey Green described United's performance in *The Times* as 'the most inspired, inspiring and controlled performance I have seen from any British side abroad in the past twenty years'. Best, he wrote, 'set a new, almost unexplored, beat. He seemed quite suddenly to be in love with the ball and the whole side followed his lead.' Even Bobby Charlton was quoted as saying he thought it was George's best game, 'largely because it wasn't a selfish performance': 'Sometimes it was all a bit unnecessary, but in the game against Benfica we saw him at his peak because he wasn't trying to be clever and torment people, he was just doing the best that he could. His control, his speed, his heading – his whole game was as good as anyone could get.'

The speculation was fevered: if United could be the first foreign team to beat Benfica at their home at the big bowl of the Stadium of Light, who was going to stop them becoming the first-ever British champions of Europe? The answer, unfortunately, came crushingly quickly. Best sustained a cartilage injury in an FA Cup match which was to trouble him for the rest of his career. Denis Law was hampered by a knee problem. United lost the first leg of the semi-final away to Partizan Belgrade. They won 1–0 at home, but it wasn't enough. They were out, and would have to set out to win the First Division championship all over again to requalify.

Matt Busby was distraught and, for a time, inconsolable. He had been at United for more than twenty years. He wanted to pack it in. The cost of the European campaign had been high. 'We'll never win it now,' he said.

Although Best had been at Old Trafford for five years in 1966, the word he had never heard uttered in that time was 'Munich'. There was a Munich clock and a football-pitch-shaped plaque dedicated to the memory of the players and club officials who had died that was fixed to the outside of the East stand. But there seemed to be an unwritten rule that nobody ever referred, even obliquely, to the events at Munich.

Busby was often still in considerable physical discomfort as a result of his injuries from the crash, but he was a stoic and didn't allow himself or anybody else to allude to them. Munich was never mentioned in the Busby household. The tone had been set on the Friday morning after the disaster. 'We were in the dressing room,' Wilf McGuinness remembered, 'and we all just sat there looking at each other. We didn't speak, say how sad it was or anything, we just stared at each other.'

After the journey north from Liverpool Street station with his mother and brother, Bobby Charlton never again spoke about what had happened at Munich. Jack never felt able to ask Bobby about the crash, fearing it might come across as ghoulish curiosity. 'Within the Manchester United team nobody was ever to discuss the Munich crash,' Norman Harris writes in his book *The Charlton Brothers*. 'If necessary, perhaps, to other people. But not to each other. Bobby especially was scarcely able, even after an ample passage of time, to discuss the subject without emotional distress. The same emotion was to show on other occasions, sometimes even surprising himself as if by ambush – occurring almost as a reflex action, like some sort of watershed necessary to retain personal equilibrium.'

When Best moved into Mrs Fullaway's in Aycliffe Avenue in Chorlton in the summer of 1961, United had just finished the

season at fifteenth in the table, their lowest position for a long time, and most of the survivors of Munich were gone. Jackie Blanchflower and Johnny Berry never played again after the crash. Kenny Morgans and Albert Scanlon left after less than a season, and Dennis Viollet had just been transferred to Stoke City that summer after scandalizing Busby with his clubbing and boozy nights on the tiles. To the young apprentices, the remaining Babes who were still around at Old Trafford – Bill Foulkes, Harry Gregg, Bobby Charlton and Wilf McGuinness (who had joined the training staff after having his playing career prematurely terminated by a serious leg injury) – seemed to have an indefinable aura or charisma: Best certainly felt this about Gregg, whose boots he had the responsibility of looking after.

Inevitably there was a connection – a sense of community – among those who had gone through the ordeal of Munich that the players and others who hadn't been around at the time couldn't share. There was an 'us' and 'them' atmosphere in the dressing room which became more noticeable as more players were brought in from outside. Young players from the reserves, like Mark Pearson and Alex Dawson, had been hot-housed after 1958 and, tragically for them, promoted beyond their abilities. Playing in the top division, their weaknesses had been fatally exposed. For the first time since joining as manager in 1945, Busby had to ask the board to put its cheque book on the table so he could go shopping in the transfer market. Denis Law was signed from Torino in 1962. Pat Crerand arrived from Celtic in February 1963 to help United in what was looking like a struggle against relegation. Maurice Setters, Noel Cantwell, John Connelly, David Herd and Alex Stepney were among other notable signings. There were immediate rumblings of discontent.

Setters and Cantwell, in particular, were dismayed by the lack of organized training and coaching and at being expected to join in the rough-house kickabouts on the piece of waste ground behind the Stretford End. Tactics were unheard of, team talks non-existent. Players were still being asked to rummage through the mud-caked rags tipped out on to the table every morning to find something to train in. You could read the morning paper through the skinny towels.

Factions started to form in the dressing room; alliances, gossip corners, cliques. 'A football club's soul is located in the dressing room,' Eamon Dunphy once wrote. 'The spirit emanating from this room will touch everyone, colour every aspect of club life. A dressing room changes day to day, hour to hour, the mood swinging from carefree to sombre depending on all kinds of things other than results. Jealousy and resentment are harboured here, alongside pride, fulfilment, and hope. Fear is also present, despair as well. Emotion is high in this unique workshop-cum-playground. Every man will have his day – good and bad – the wounds are bare for all to see.'

Dunphy had been part of the talented intake of fifteen-year-olds at Old Trafford in 1960, the year before Best, whom he was pitted against in the A and B teams for the inside-forward position. In those days, neither of them had any first-hand knowledge of the atmosphere inside the first-team dressing room or would even have been able to say with any certainty what it looked like. In common with the other boys of their age, they were in awe of the first-team players and barred from their parts of the club. Nobby Stiles signed amateur forms with United in 1957. 'We used to strip in the ballboys' room. Going in the first-team dressing room was a big deal,' Stiles remembered, many years after he had become one of the heroes of England's World Cup-winning side. 'I remember Mark Pearson and Alex Dawson getting hold of me one day. They wanted the first team's autographs. They were scared of going in there because the lads didn't like signing . . .

'Anyway I took Mark and Alex's books in and I went to Mark Jones and Duncan [Edwards]. They were gods in my eyes, so I said, "Will you sign this please," and Mark said, "Piss off." I knew if I went back to the ballboys' room without the autographs I'd get battered in there, so I said, "Please, Mark, sign it," and he told me to piss off again. And then he said, "Alright, give it here" . . . Eddie Colman was my idol. He used to wear a pork-pie hat. I would love to have been able to go up to him and [tell him what he meant], but I used to blush like anything when I'd meet him.'

George Best's accelerated progress from the beginning of 1964, when he became a first-team regular, erected a barrier between him and the players of his own age at the club who until then had been his closest friends and who shared a social life which revolved around the snooker hall local to Mrs Fullaway's and a bowling alley in Stretford. After matches, they went ten-pin bowling. That was their usual Saturday night. But after he established his place in the first team he was expected to hang around with the senior players and develop a taste for their more sophisticated ways. All the League side were older, most of them were married and Best couldn't see there was a place for him to fit in. The gap between them was so pronounced that at first he assumed they didn't like him and didn't want him to mix. Noel Cantwell, Denis Law and Paddy Crerand had got into the habit of going to an Italian restaurant for a meal with their wives on Saturday nights. It was always the same Italian restaurant, a place called Arturo's, across the road from the Ritz ballroom in Whitworth Street. And gradually George started looking in on his own for a few drinks, killing time until the real business of the evening started, never having anything to eat.

The Phil Moss Band, the resident outfit at the Ritz, had had a good reputation in the fifties, appearing on top BBC radio shows like *Swingalong* and *Ray Moore's Saturday Night Out*. The beat boom was in full flow by 1964, although Manchester could only boast Herman's Hermits and the Hollies (don't even mention Freddie and the Dreamers), while Liverpool had the Beatles and the Searchers and the whole, harder, youthza-poppin', 'rhythm'n'booze' Mersey scene. But a pepped-up Phil Moss Band were still going strong at the Ritz and after their last set, around midnight, their pianist, a little guy called Charlie, would nip over to Arturo's to bang out the old party favourites on a honky-tonk joanna while Paddy and Denis led a sing-along. This was always George's cue to slip away. He was starting to broaden his social circle by then, at clubs like the subterranean Le Phonographe and the Twisted Wheel.

He opened the first boutique in a riot of publicity a few days after the 'El Beatle' match against Benfica in 1966. His partner was a well-known Manchester rag-trader called Malcolm Mooney, who was later to become the owner of a high-end restaurant in Knutsford, the Belle Epoque. Compared to London, Manchester was a village. The businessmen, the foot-ballers, the show-business people, the professional gamblers . . . they all mixed and knew each other and provided the atmosphere for Manchester after dark. Mooney knew the crimper 'Waggy' Wagner, who knew the car dealer Hymie Wernick, who all the players got their smart wheels from, who knew Colin Burne, the owner of another nightclub, Reubens, who knew the wealthy Manchester bookmaker Gus Demmy's son Selwyn Demmy, who was famous for his Sunday teas where everybody came together to come down from the week-end and get acquainted with the latest leggy models in town, who had a reputation for being top-quality stuff.

Because of its village atmosphere there wasn't a chance of getting away with very much without somebody at the club, and therefore Matt Busby, hearing about it. That was partly why the *George Best Boutique* was in a shopping street in the blameless Cheshire suburbs, just beyond where the bush tele-graph normally reached. 'It was incredible,' Best told his friend Michael Parkinson, a familiar face on the Manchester scene himself in those days. 'I never had to do any work, take [girls] out for dinner or any of that crap. They'd ring me up or hang about in the boutique and straight upstairs. I had a flat above the shop. In fact, I think the only reason I opened a boutique in the first place was because it had a flat above it and it was a great knocking shop. Also it was a cover from the boss and the club. They liked to think I was living a pure life in my digs. Well I was, but I was leading another kind of life in that flat and the boss would have gone grey if he'd known what was happening.

'It's not good for an athlete to spend every afternoon fucking, every evening drinking and every morning thinking about fucking and drinking. But it didn't seem to matter then.'

When he opened more boutiques in the city centre, he used to get female journalists coming to interview him to report there so that the staff could look them over. 'If she was fair looking,' he said, 'they'd ring and tell me. If she was a drag I wouldn't bother. I could always tell the starfuckers,' he added, 'because just as they were going to climb into bed with me, they'd say, "I hope you don't think I'm doing this just because you're George Best."'

His accomplice in most of his extramural capers around this time was Mike Summerbee, who had signed for Manchester City from Swindon Town at the beginning of the 1965 season. The pair of them had joined forces after bumping into each other a few times at Le Phonographe shortly before it turned into the horsey-themed Blinkers ('Blinkers Special Nosebag' a large mirror-sign said over the bar). 'There wasn't much talk about football as I remember,' Summerbee once recalled. 'We had other things in common.'

Summerbee became Best's partner in the fashion business. And then they rented a flat together, in the suburbs again, in Crumpsall, for use at weekends. Threats, and warnings to stay away from other people's girlfriends, wives or daughters, were a regular hazard. Summerbee once described their routine: 'On Monday night we would go out, Tuesday night we used to go out, Wednesday night we went out, Thursday night we'd go out but get in early, and Friday nights we would keep it low-key because we had a game to play on Saturdays.' Some Fridays they went to watch Third Division football at Stockport County. Other times they spent Friday nights in Prestwich with Malcolm Wagner's family, drinking soft drinks and eating his mother's home-made matzo-dumpling soup and plaited bread. When Jack Rosenthal's play about Manchester Jewish life was put out by Granada television, the bar mitzvah boy of the title had a poster of Mike Summerbee pinned to the wall of his bedroom.

By 1966, George had a mop of hair thick enough to hide a crate of melons, as Frank Sinatra once complained about the Beatles. He also had an agent called Ken Stanley whose office – always a line guaranteed to raise a titter with Rodney Marsh, Alan Hudson, Terry Venables and their self-styled 'Clan' of London players on the razz at Tramp – was in Huddersfield. The industrial north of England was, and to some extent remains, the butt of southern players' jokes. 'Where are we – Brigadoon?' Jimmy Greaves is supposed to have said as the coach carrying the Tottenham Hotspur team began its descent from the top of Manchester Road into the cobbled streets of crumbling mills and back-to-back workers' terraces around Burnley in the early sixties.

But just as Stanley was nobody's fool – he was asked to negotiate all the contracts for the 1966 England World Cup party – so Best's attachment to a disreputable-looking Victorian pub on the wrong side of the river Irwell in Manchester's shadow city of Salford was maybe a declaration of his independence from the values that were in place in the 'soft' south. 'A hard-drinking pub in a hard-drinking town' was how he described the Brown Bull, which was wrapped around a corner under the railway bridge attached to Salford central station. It was run down and going to the wall when Best first wandered in, and quiet enough that customers could listen to the trains making the glasses rattle. 'During the night there were probably no more than ten people in there at one time,' Best said of his first visit, 'and none of them appeared very interested in George Best. It couldn't have been better. We knew we'd found our local.' Except, of course, it was soon one of the happeningest places in Manchester, solely on the strength of his sudden, stellar celebrity.

The Brown Bull was managed by a young American called Billy Barr, and he and George took to each other immediately. They soon arrived at a mutually beneficial arrangement: as long as George and the crowd who followed him were putting money in the till, Barr was prepared to stay open. If that meant keeping on serving until the morning buses started running, then he was willing to do it. The after-hours drinking was usually more hell-for-leather than anything that happened during normal licensing times.

The decor was nondescript until the painted portraits of Manchester United notables – Matt Busby, Denis Law, Bobby Charlton – went up; the big curved windows were panoramic, if mucky; the floor was covered in a sluiceable black composite, which was useful in light of the drinking games George and his friends were always inventing. 'Jacks' was one: you have a pack of cards and the first one dealt a jack has to order a drink. Anything he likes; straight or a mixture, and in any quantity. The next jack tastes it, and the third jack has to drink it down in one go. The fourth jack pays for it. And then they'd start all over again. People would come into the Bull and end up joining in. Other times there'd be arm-wrestling on the bar, picking up chairs by one leg, seeing who could do the most push-ups. Gunfights with soda syphons.

Saturdays were often cards nights, starting at midnight and playing – and drinking – right through. 'I've been in other places around the world where people are supposed to drink, but there's nothing to touch Manchester,' Best said. 'I've seen lads there go for days on end and still look as though they've only had one or two . . . I've drunk some poisonous mixtures like vodka, rum, scotch, gin and brandy in the same glass. A pint of it. Then I've gone in the loo, stuck my fingers down my throat and gone back and started again. I drank a pint of vodka one night as a bet. Straight down in one go just for the hell of it.'

He was in lodgings; he didn't have a home. The Brown Bull was his home. Billy Barr gave him a key to let himself in and to lock up when his friends had disgorged at whatever time on to Chapel Street. If George and his pals hadn't eaten, Barr would shout up to Leila to make them some steaks. Sometimes when George had guests round he would take care of the catering himself, as his sometime drinking partner and friend Hugh McIlvanney recalled: 'One night after a European Cup match at Old Trafford, a bunch of us gathered in the Brown Bull. No one had given much thought to dinner but, by the time the after-hours session was under way, hunger was a problem. At least it was until Best went round taking fish-and-chip orders from everyone in the bar, then disappeared. He returned half-an-hour later, not merely with all the orders accurately filled but with plates, knives and forks for everybody. The waiter seemed less like a superstar than the appealing boy who had worked small miracles with a tennis ball on the streets of the Cregagh housing estate in East Belfast.'

It was confirmation of a quality McIlvanney had noted on another occasion, in 1969, when Best was still only twenty-three: 'His maybe a whirlwind career, but no whirlwind ever had a stiller centre. Events and people wash over him and leave hardly a trace. There's a self-confident coolness about him that unnerves some men and fascinates most women. He seems to have a slower psychological pulse than the rest of us.'

It is a point Michael Parkinson had picked up on as well. 'He had the ability to be forever at the centre of things and yet remain private and remote,' he said. 'His appraisal of people around him remained cool and in the main shrewd.'

Parkinson was a Brown Bull regular. He was the producer of the local ITV news programme in the north-west in the mid-sixties, and the Granada studios from where *Scene at 6.30* was broadcast live were only a short walk away. Clive James, who succeeded Parkinson as the presenter of Granada's film review programme *Cinema*, once said the routes through the back streets to the Bull and the other pubs close to Granada's Quay Street studios were known as 'the Ho Chi

Minh trail': people nipping out for a sneaky drink or three thought they couldn't be observed from the main building, but they were wrong.

The first words spoken by an announcer when Granada launched in 1956 had been: 'From the North, this is Granada'. Its northernness was central to the station's identity and to the belief that being based in Manchester gave it a point of view which was different. 'Granada was at the epicentre of all that northern thing happening in the 1960s,' Parkinson has said, 'and George Best was at the centre of the epicentre.'

Shelagh Delaney had grown up in Salford, and Tony Richardson's 1961 film of her novel *A Taste of Honey* had been shot in streets close to the Brown Bull. (Salford Lads' Club, where Eddie Colman used to be a member, was also nearby.) *A Taste of Honey* was an example of the newly awakened – and intellectually fashionable – interest in working-class life which also accounted for the commissioning and the popularity of *Coronation Street*, Granada's flagship programme. Like the 'kitchen-sink' dramas which had prepared the ground for it, the *Street* was thought to represent authenticity, toughness and provincialism: the young actors of the period, such as Tom Courtenay and Albert Finney, also Salford-born, made a virtue of their humble origins. After centuries of stigma, it became okay, even desirable, in the 1960s to be provincial and northern.

'Improbable as it may now seem,' the historian Raphael Samuel has written, 'the North in the 1960s – anyway the early 1960s, when Harold Wilson made his appearance as the great iconoclast, the Mersey Sound first captured the nation's record players, and *Z Cars* put Liverpool in the front line of crime-busting – was definitely Mod, and on the side of radical change. It offered itself as an idiom for the degentrification of British public life. In place of an effete establishment it promised a new vitality, sweeping the dead wood from the boardrooms, and replacing hidebound administrators with ambitious young go-getters. Instead of the polite evasions of circumlocution and

147

periphrasis, it made a fetish of bluntness. In the sphere of town planning, the Northern cities were the sites of utopian redevelopment schemes, such as those of T. Dan Smith [in Newcastle], in which all things were made anew. Through the Lawrence revival and the Lady Chatterley trial Northernness was associated with the cause of sexual frankness . . . Socially, too, Northernness came to stand for a new and emancipatory openness . . . The Northern voice, as cultivated by the TV compère, was a classless one, an indigenous alternative to the starched accents of the Pathé newsreader and the BBC announcer. As projected by the Prime Minister [Harold Wilson] . . . it was also a gauge of authenticity.'

This could almost have stood as the prospectus for Granada when its founder, Sidney Bernstein, applied for the new ITV franchise in the North. ('If you look at a map of the concentration of population in the North and a rainfall map,' Bernstein said at the time, 'you will see that the North is an ideal place for television.') Having won the franchise, Granada attracted the kind of go-getters and iconoclasts who were to their generation of programme-makers what George Best was to the increasingly image-conscious world of football. Attracted by the glamour of success which he represented in an unprecedented way, and especially glamoured by finding it in such unlikely surroundings, Manchester's media world gravitated to the Brown Bull. It became a media hub. The best and the brightest from Granada and the *Manchester Guardian* were pulled into Best's orbit.

In addition to Parkinson, Clive James, Arthur Hopcraft and visiting star names from Fleet Street such as Jean Rook and McIlvanney, these included the writers Stan Barstow, Jim Allen and Jack Rosenthal, the presenter Bill Grundy, producer Johnny Hamp (responsible for *The Wheeltappers and Shunters Social Club* and *The Comedians*) and Oxbridge immigrants to 'Granadaland' and modern, snappy, classless 'people's television' like Michael Apted, Nick Elliot, Claudia Milne and producer of the weekly, left-leaning documentary programme

World in Action and future Director-General of the BBC John Birt. 'After [the show] we always used to go off and drink at the Brown Bull, which brought together a demi-monde of what I imagined to be the sub-criminal world of show business,' Birt once said. 'I remember somebody saying, "Come to a party. George Best is going to be there."'

Birt's first big job at Granada was as producer of a satirical entertainment series called *Nice Time*. The show's presenters were the disc jockey Kenny Everett and Germaine Greer, who was another after-hours Brown Bull habitué. In an affectionate piece published after his death, she wrote about Best's many attempts over many nights of 'assorted adventures' in the Bull (one involved most of the Manchester United team crowding silently into her room over the bar until the police had gone away) to tap her up:

'George was speaking. Even when my ears weren't drumming I had to struggle to understand his Belfast-speak, delivered as usual very fast from behind his teeth. What he was saying was, I worked out: "Why d'ye not fancy me?"

'"Not fancy you? Don't be ridiculous, George. Everybody fancies you."

'"So why not you?"

'"I do fancy you, George."

'"So why d'ye do nothing about it?" . . .

'"Because I'm not a fool, George. Every time you come in here you've got a different blonde on your arm."

'Possibly because George was paying for the drinks, his courtiers were seldom accompanied by women, but George invariably displayed his latest trophy. I recognized some of the women he brought in and I was surprised that the boy could set his sights so high, but even the classiest of them would not be seen twice in his company . . . One of my reasons for not entering into a flirtation with George was that, like other men I have known, George thought women were to be lied to, but if you were a mate, he was four-square . . .

'There are a few people who could tell you [his] thoughtfulness was typical of George, but not many of them are women. His pattern of emotional and physical abuse of the women who shared his bed, together with a strong but mostly notional attachment to his mother beside whom he is to be buried, is depressingly familiar.'

He used to talk about flying 'talent' in; paying to bring over girls he had met or been contacted by in Australia and other places on his travels and then sending them back after a couple of weeks when he grew bored. In 1969, a blonde asked him for his autograph during a pre-season tour of Denmark but disappeared before he could get her particulars. So ('You could say I fell in love with a pair of knockers') he wrote a letter addressed 'To my Danish dream girl' and gave it to a Danish reporter. There were a number of replies, but Eva Haraldsted was the one and Best had her shipped in. The Boss had been on at him to get shacked up with somebody and he thought he'd try it. But even before the media kerfuffle had died down he had got bored. What to do? By the simple expedient of sleeping with a woman reporter from one of the tabloids he broke the story that it was all over and curtains for Eva. She sued him for breach of promise – they had sort of become engaged – and he had to pay her £500. 'I liked that

journalist,' Best said. 'Every time she wanted a story she used to come and stay with me in Manchester.'

Billy Barr started to let rooms at the Brown Bull. Actors and others filming at Granada found the trip upstairs easier than going back to a hotel. 'There's a nice young lady in number four,' Billy would tell Bestie. 'Why don't you knock on her door and see if she fancies coming down for a drink?'

It was madness. It was non-stop. Around this time, Michael Parkinson met a woman – 'married, beautiful and quite intelligent' – who told him the following Best story: 'He had the most marvellous eyes and a shy boyish charm. I talked to him for a long time and entertained thoughts of seducing him. I wondered how I might go about it. We talked for about half an hour and all the time I fantasized an affair with him. All of a sudden a blonde girl came up to him. She said, "Hi, I'm Julie, would you like a quick fuck?" He said, "Certainly." He turned to me and said, "Excuse me," and went upstairs with her.'

(Best's eyes occasioned a great deal of discussion over the years. 'Now that the nation has seen in a thousand photographs those same eyes staring widely out of cavernous sockets, the only living things in George's wasted face,' Greer wrote, 'there can be no argument about their colour: deep, stormy ocean-blue. Many a drunk in many a pub from Enniskillen to Sydney has those heart-breaking Irish eyes.' Parkinson, however, was very definite about 'the violet eyes, with the long lashes'. 'He looked like Elizabeth Taylor around the eyes,' he once said. 'There was something very effeminate about that area of George.')

It must have occurred to some of the readers among the revellers at the Brown Bull that life had taken a bittersweet F. Scott Fitzgerald-like turn – the Fitzgerald who wrote about failure (if not the real thing, then a sense of failure) as the inevitable dark lining of success. '[We were embarked] on the greatest, gaudiest spree in history and there was going to be plenty to tell about it . . . [Yet] all the stories that came into my

head had a touch of disaster in them – the lovely young creatures in my novels went to ruin . . . In life these things hadn't
happened yet, but I was pretty sure living wasn't the reckless,
careless business these people thought – this generation just
younger than me.'

The debauch and bacchanal went into free fall when United
finally brought the European Cup home to Manchester, a
decade after Munich, in 1968.

They had won the FA Cup in 1963. It was their first major
trophy since the accident and, to mark the occasion, one of
the surgeons who had treated the injured at the Rechts der
Isar hospital had been invited over for the match at Wembley
and the celebration dinner afterwards at the Savoy. Shortly
before the dinner, however, Frank Kessel suffered a severe
nosebleed while he was changing at his hotel. Frank Taylor of
the *News Chronicle*, the only journalist to have survived the
crash and one of Professor Kessel's former patients, found he
had a vacant place next to him at the banquet. When he saw
a small, flushed, forlorn-looking man wandering around,
worriedly trying to read the place settings, Taylor beckoned
him over and told him he was welcome to take the empty seat
next to him.

Afterwards Taylor would remember the 'nervous-looking
gentleman' presenting him with his card and then putting the
card in his pocket and forgetting all about it. But this is a bit
like the judge at the Chatterley trial famously asking the jury
whether Lawrence's book was one 'you would wish your wife
or even your servant to read'. The chances of Dickie Best carrying a business card seem pretty unlikely. As do his cap-
doffing gratitude ('It's very kind of you to let me sit here, sir,
because I've never been in a swell place like this before') and
his Dickensian-sounding entreaty, as reported by Taylor, as he
passed the card over: 'That's my name, sir, if ever you can
help my son with his career, I would be very grateful.
Sometimes these young footballers listen to sports writers like
you.'

George had just turned seventeen at the time of Manchester United's FA Cup victory over Leicester in May 1963. (It was what Dickie Best was doing at the Savoy: it was a sop from the club for not inviting him to be there when George had settled professional terms on his birthday, three days earlier. Dickie had been brought in through a back entrance of the hotel. 'All the other kids' parents will want to come in', the scout Joe Armstrong told him, 'if they see you.') He had yet to make his debut appearance in the first team but he would be established as one of the stars of the side within a year, and his father, sometimes accompanied by his mother but usually alone, would try to get over to Manchester from Belfast for most of the big games. It wasn't easy, but he showed the same single-minded determination and tenacity of purpose which, years later, would see him step forward and take charge of all the key aspects of George's final days and his funeral. The dignity and lack of histrionics at the end were largely due to the restraining hand and iron will of Dickie Best.

When he was working nights, his usual routine after the regulation half shift on a Friday was to pick up his money from the wages office at the shipyard at 8.30 p.m., store his overalls in his locker and head for the boat, which was a fifteen-minute walk from Harland and Wolff. They'd dock in Liverpool at five o'clock on Saturday morning, then he'd catch the train to Manchester. He'd be back on the ferry by ten on Saturday night and in Belfast at seven the next morning. Then came a long walk to the nearest bus stop to get home. 'I found it hard going,' Dickie said, 'but it was worth it.'

Frank Taylor had forgotten all about his forgettable dinner companion at the Savoy by the time of United's European Cup triumph against Benfica at Wembley in 1968. He had just been told by Bobby Charlton's wife Norma that Bobby wouldn't be making it downstairs to the banquet in the Russell Hotel – every time he tried to make it to the bedroom door, she said, he fainted – when Taylor felt a tug at his sleeve. 'I looked hard,' he later wrote. 'Yes, I had seen the face before, but who he was

I couldn't say. To make things easier, I smiled back at him and said, "I know the face, old pal. But I have just forgotten the name." "I can't blame you," said the stranger. "We have met only once . . . I'm the fellow you kindly let sit at your table. I told you then, I hoped my son had signed for Manchester United and I hoped he would make a name for himself. Didn't he play well tonight . . ."

'I looked to where the stranger was pointing and saw George Best, a glass of champagne in his hand, chatting to a pretty girl. "That's my son . . . George Best."'

George was only one of many who never went to bed that

night. He didn't remember the banquet; he would never be able to remember the club they went on to afterwards, whom he left with or where he woke up.

Night after night, month after month, at the Brown Bull the party continued. When George was voted European Footballer of the Year at the end of 1968, it was cause for further celebration.

'For the next two years I had as much control over my own destiny as a convict over the cut of his clothes,' Fitzgerald wrote of his early adult life, a time which saw 'the improbable, the implausible, often the "impossible", come true'. 'The compensation of a very early success', he wrote, 'is a conviction that life is a romantic matter. In the best sense one stays young. When the primary objects of love and money could be taken for granted and a shaky eminence had lost its fascination, I had fair years to waste, years that I can't honestly regret, in seeking the eternal Carnival by the Sea.'

At the end of his career, before his early death from alcoholism, he would return repeatedly in his work to 'that all too short period when . . . the fulfilled future and the wistful past were mingled in a single gorgeous moment – when life was literally a dream'.

Billy Barr would go to bed and leave them to it.

George didn't want to go back to his glass box in Bramhall. Many mornings when he should have been training he would come to covered by somebody's topcoat on a bare mattress in the junk room at the Bull. Brooms and buckets, stacked wooden beer crates, a smell of ashtrays, and condensation on the window. Through a few clear inches of glass at the top of the window he could see people on the upper decks of buses on their way to work – the steady crawl of morning buses, jam-packed with seated and standing passengers.

'The nights spent at the Brown Bull probably did more harm to me as an athlete than any other single factor,' he said when it was all over. 'But I look back on them with more affection than I remember playing football in the mud and snow of a

cold January night. The Brown Bull recalls wonderful friend-
ships and one hell of a lot of laughs.'

Four years is what it had taken. The famous floodlit game at
Chelsea in 1964 was the beginning of the beginning. 1968 was
the beginning of the end. He was twenty-two.

Looking for a place to drink where he wouldn't be annoyed
by people driving him crazy.

Seven

We're the pride of all Europe, the cock of the North,
We hate all scousers and cockneys, of course. (And Leeds)
We are the Manchester boys, la, la, la.
  Manchester United terrace chant

Who's that dying on the runway?
Who's that lying in the snow?
It's Matt Busby and his boys
Making all the fucking noise
'Cause they couldn't get the aeroplane to go.
  Anti-United chant

At West Ham, Liverpool and Chelsea matches, and particularly at local derbies against Manchester City, it is often possible to witness a spectacle that, unlike the thousands-strong group hug of Emperor penguins waiting out the Antarctic winter or the snow leopard hunting to feed its young miles up in the Himalayas, has never been seen on television: hundreds of home supporters standing facing the enclosure where the Manchester United fans are penned and holding their arms out in the universally recognizable symbol of children playing at being planes. A whole stand of grinning supporters swaying in unison with their arms held rigid at shoulder height, making the schoolyard gesture for a plane about to crash land.

G-ALZU (known by the last two letters, pronounced in the phonetic alphabet as Zulu Uniform) was a forty-seven-seat Airspeed Ambassador, a type assigned the class name of 'Elizabethan' by British European Airways. It had been constructed in 1952 – a high-winged monoplane powered by two Bristol Centaurus 661 engines, with a tricycle undercarriage.

The port engine was fitted with a Peravia Recorder: this was a power-driven roll of waxed paper used to record, against a time base, data as to altitude, engine speed and manifold pressure.

According to the official record, the last message from charter flight B-line 609 Zulu Uniform starts 'with a howling-whistling noise and ends with a loud background noise after the message was broken off'.

On the flight deck Captain Thain and Captain Rayment had been told that the 'boost surging' they had experienced on the first two attempts at take-off was quite common at airports like Munich because of its altitude. At 3.03 p.m., 609 Zulu Uniform was rolling again. At the first of what would turn out to be multiple German and English official inquiries into the cause of the accident, Captain Thain described the next attempt at take-off:

'I told Captain Rayment that if we got boost surging again, I would control the throttles. Captain Rayment opened them to 28 inches with the brakes on. The engines were both steady so he released the brakes and we moved forward again. He continued to open the throttles and again I followed with my left hand until the levers were fully open. I tapped his hand and he moved it. He called "Full power" and I checked the dials and said: "Full power."'

Captain Thain again noticed that there was a sign of boost surging and called this out to Captain Rayment above the noise of the engines. The surging was controlled and the throttle pushed back until it was fully open:

'I glanced at the air speed indicator and saw it registered 105 knots and was flickering. When it reached 117 knots I called out "V1" [Velocity 1, the point on the runway after which there was insufficient runway to stop] and waited for a positive indication of more speed so that I could call "V2" [the speed at which the aircraft should be 'flown off', in this case 119 knots]. Captain Rayment was adjusting the trim of the aircraft. But suddenly the needle dropped to about 112 knots. I was conscious of a lack of acceleration, the needle dropped further to about 105 knots and hovered at this reading. Captain Rayment called out, "Christ, we won't make it!" and I looked up from the instruments to see a lot of snow and a house and a tree right in the path of the aircraft.'

The crash happened because 609 Zulu Uniform failed to 'unstick'. This colloquial-sounding word is the correct aeronautical one for 'take-off' (which, in fact, in the manuals is referred to as 'flying off').

'During the take-off I noticed that the pilot was making every effort to un-stick,' an eyewitness at Riem airport told one of the investigating tribunals. 'The main wheel was raised very high off the ground; the angle of incidence was very large. The tail appeared to be touching the ground.'

Establishing the reason why 609 Zulu Uniform failed to unstick would occupy many expert witnesses, in both England and Germany, over many years. Did a layer of ice on the skin of the wings increase the required un-stick speed? Or was slush on the runway the main cause of the crash? If it was ice, then the English pilot in charge of the Elizabethan, Captain Thain, was responsible: he should have had the wings checked for ice hazard and de-iced before take-off. If it was slush – a 'contaminated' runway, in the argot of official inquiries – then the blame fell squarely on the German authorities at Munich, who should have had the 'jellified, watery mass' of slush swept clear: an aircraft preparing to un-stick in slush could be subject to drag forces so great that they might cause it to slow down enough to prevent it from being able to take off.

Captain Thain said that the descent through thick cloud into Munich had necessitated the switching on of the airframe anti-icing, which permitted air heated to 60°C by fuel burners in the wings to be vented under pressure via ducting at the leading edges of the wings, tailplane and fin. Because of this, any flakes settling on the upper wing surfaces during refuelling simply melted and ran from the trailing edge. The German refueller had had little problem maintaining his footing as he walked over the wing, and in fact had made himself an easy target for the Manchester party's snowballs as they disembarked for refreshments in the terminal building.

Chief Inspector of Accidents Captain Hans-J. Reichel, however, head of the Luftfahrt Bundesamt accident investigation team, insisted that there had been a rough, coarse-grained layer of ice on the wings of the crashed plane and also on some parts of the airscrews. The report of the German Commission of Inquiry, published in March 1959, concluded that ice on the wings had been found to be the 'decisive cause' of the accident.

Back in Britain, aeronautical performance experts, meteorologists, chemists and professors of stream mechanics were consulted and graphs prepared to indicate acceleration characteristics on both dry and contaminated runways; slush drag coefficients were introduced in an attempt to explain the deceleration phenomenon; fresh slush trials were conducted in the United States using ice-making machines to reproduce conditions similar to those at the time of the crash and new evidence was amassed. The British Ministry of Aviation invited the Germans to reopen the inquiry, which they eventually did in November 1965.

At the second inquiry, the English and Germans again pitted experts against each other. Iced-up wings or slush drag? Slush or ice? Ice or Slush? The argument was kicked around between the two sides like, you could say, a football. Stout-hearted England against the oily wiles of johnny foreigner. Exactly the reason the nabobs of the Football League and Football Association had resisted getting drawn into competition with the continental blaggards in the first place. England had treated the World Cup as a sideshow event for the first twenty years of its existence, between 1930 and 1950, and declined to enter. The League had high-handedly told Chelsea, the club champions when the European Cup was begun in 1955, that they were to refuse the invitation to take part. The following season Matt Busby coolly ignored the Football League's instruction not to enter his championship-winning side into the tournament and, in his second run at the title, fate had dealt him the hammer blow of Munich.

'Football is never just football,' Simon Kuper writes in his book *Football Against the Enemy*. 'It helps make wars and revolutions, and it fascinates mafias and dictators.' He quotes a former Dutch Resistance fighter, interviewed on television after Holland's victory over Germany during the 1988 European Championships: 'I feel as though we've won the War at last!' Kuper adds: 'Never before had Dutch journalists been seen hugging players and sobbing, "Thank you."'

By the end of the reopened inquiry into the cause of the Munich disaster, the German authorities had budged only slightly: 'Icing is still to be regarded as an essential cause of the accident . . . slush, however, must be regarded as a further cause.' But, in April 1966 – four weeks before Manchester United's historic European Cup quarter-final victory over Benfica, and just two months before the World Cup tournament was due to begin in England – the Ministry of Aviation issued its own deduction: 'We conclude that there is a strong likelihood that there was no significant icing during take-off . . . we conclude that the principal cause of the accident was the effect of slush on the runway.'

A new British hearing was finally ordered and opened in London in July 1968, more than ten years after the crash. The report of the proceedings, largely exonerating the aeroplane's pilot, Captain Thain, was made public nearly a year later, in June 1969: 'Our considered view . . . is that the cause of the accident was slush on the runway. Whether wing icing was also a cause, we cannot say.'

Man was about to land on the moon by June 1969. The Beatles had formed, transformed the world, and disbanded.

Manchester United were at last European champions. England were still reigning world champions. Best was about to move into the cool geometry of 'Che Sera' in the Cheshire suburbs. The stained-glass windows dedicated to the memory of Duncan Edwards had been in place in St Francis's Church in Dudley for eight years. But were supporters at grounds in south and east London, and City fans across Manchester at Maine Road, already turning to taunt the United faithful with their arms raised at shoulder height, pretending to be limping fifties monoplanes and singing, 'Who's that dying on the runway?' It is an indication of how profoundly Munich has penetrated popular memory that such scenes are familiar occurrences almost half a century later.

Because of the way they are believed to milk the sympathy of most neutrals, Manchester City fans who weren't born at the time – whose mothers and fathers weren't even around in 1958 – refer disparagingly to United supporters as 'Munichs', fifty years after the event. So a referee thought to be favouring United in a derby match might be subject to the chant: 'Who's the Munich in the black?'

People objectified as cities and disaster sites; other people objectifying themselves as pieces of machinery. Fathers introducing their sons to the idea that the harmless word 'Babe' can have dark, undesirable connotations. Parents introducing their children early to the notion that community is based on shared memories, and that the memory of Munich is part of their birthright. Log on to www.red11.org/mufc/edwards.htm and, to a crematorial mellotron backing of 'Yesterday', you will find many messages from men in their forties called Duncan and many teenage Duncan-son-of-Duncans, celebrating the fact that they were named after the most mythic and folkloric of the Babes.

In 1966, twenty years after George was born, Ann and Dickie Best had their sixth child and their second son. They called him 'Ian' and gave him the middle name 'Busby'. Ian Busby Best, a talented footballer with two legendary footballing names who, having seen his brother's career crash and burn and his mother drink herself to death by the time he was eleven, wanted to know nothing about football.

The legend of the holy drinker #5

Phyllis's

> Clearly there was a moment in his career when the private spirit (a unique and highly sensitized one) gave way to the public image, a redundant and coarsened one ... [He] was gored by success. He lingered on the bloody horn of it. He loved it. He loved to suffer it. And so the books diminished. Never again would the body of work after WW2 compare with the work before it.
>
> Bud Schulberg on Ernest Hemingway, *The Four Seasons of Success*

Matt Busby always said that the great years of a player's career were those between the ages of twenty-six and thirty-two. But even before Best crossed the lower threshold, Busby had formed the view that he was hell-bent on self-destruction: he told his friends he believed that one day George would top himself. And all his life from around 1969 on, George was the first to agree, became in a way a suicide note.

Not much got past the Boss. Paddy McGrath, his biggest pal, wasn't known as the Godfather of Manchester for no reason. But Busby and McGrath and their cronies at the Cromford, who had lived through the Depression and fought in the war, were hoeing a different row to the younger generations who flocked to beat venues like the Oasis and the Twisted Wheel and round-the-clock weekend raves.

Bestie and his sidekick Mike Summerbee were never attracted to the rave scene with its ironing-board-chested, boyish birds and bennies and purple hearts: they never went near drugs. They preferred more sophisticated places like Blinkers, with a slightly older clientele, although, as Summerbee once admitted, they grew less choosy where they went as they became increasingly pleasantly jingled and the night wore on: 'We used to start off in the posh clubs and end up in the doss houses [in] Moss Side and Whalley Range . . . There was the Nile Club, which became infamous later because there were a few shootings there, but in our day it was nice. You'd get West Indian cricketers like Clive Lloyd, Keith Barker and Charlie Moore in there, passing round the Cockspur rum, and we were all welcome in the shebeens.'

Best had been dropped by Busby from the first team in an attempt to curb his nocturnal habits as early as 1965. But to out-siders at least, it started to appear that, the more central Best became to the team's success, the more the manager was pre-pared to turn a blind eye. 'Often I get telephone calls and letters about George has been here at this time of night and there at that time of night,' Busby said in 1969. 'And of course I'm after him if I think it's not to his good. But many times I've checked these stories and found them untrue. I've always thought, look-ing at him on the field of play, playing as he does, running as he does, the knocks he gets, he's up and back at it again. And this was always the evidence, to me at any rate, that he knew his life was football to start with and he kept himself, in the true profes-sional way, able and capable of playing the game.'

For players up to and including Denis Law and Bobby Charlton's generation, 'the true professional way' meant get-ting a skinful on a Saturday night and running it off on a Sunday lunchtime. Football culture was a drinking culture in the dressing room as well as on the terraces. It started off as an industrial sport and the players brought to it industrial habits. Before Newcastle played Blackpool in the 1951 Cup Final, Jackie Milburn remembered being so worked up that he went into the 'south' dressing-room toilets at Wembley for a crafty drag, only to find that he could hardly get in there for other players doing the same. (Milburn scored twice; Newcastle won.)

Manchester United's wasn't the only dressing room where

there was a bottle of Jameson's handy for any player who felt he needed a nip before he ran out, and beer was laid on after matches to kick off the long Saturday night. The Boss's son, Sandy Busby, used to go out drinking with the players of around his own age, such as David Pegg and Eddie Colman pre-Munich, and Wilf McGuinness and Shay Brennan afterwards, and he has vivid recall of his drinking partners – bleary-eyed, hung-over, unshaven – pushing themselves through the Sunday morning detoxing ritual: 'You could set your watch by Tommy [Taylor] and Jackie [Blanchflower] every Sunday. They'd pound out 22 laps flat to the boards, no half-pace stuff. That got rid of the ale. It was completely voluntary.'

Atonement for Saturday's excesses also occasionally included Sunday tea at the coach Bert Whalley's house, followed by a service at the Methodist church where Whalley, who was among those killed at Munich, was a lay preacher. Players were occasionally invited to read the lesson at his Sportsman's services, before heading off to a Sunday night dance at Chorlton or the Levenshulme Palais.

As we know, by the mid-1960s 'Sunday tea' had come to mean dolly birds and vodka and a quick bunk-up if you got lucky in one of the luxury bedrooms at Selwyn Demmy's pad at Riverside Court in Didsbury, and then, feeling no pain, on to Le Phonographe in the evening. So began another week.

For a long while, nobody watching Best play could imagine the way he was punishing his body. His performances rang true and clean and he could audibly thrill or quieten crowds of 60,000 people. Quite early in his career, Danny Blanchflower, Jackie's elder brother, captain of the great Spurs League and Cup double-winning side of 1961, and one of George's boyhood heroes, weighed the comparative merits of Best against the claims of Stanley Matthews and Tom Finney, as many were prone to do in those days, and reached the astute conclusion that 'Best makes a greater appeal to the senses than the other two. His movements are quicker, lighter, more balletic. He offers the greater surprise to the mind and the eye.

'Though you could do nothing about it, you usually knew how Matthews would beat you. In those terms, he was more predictable to the audience. Best, I feel, has the more refined, unexpected range. And with it all, there is his utter disregard of physical danger. Think of his ability to beat giants of well over six foot, in the air. He has ice in his veins, warmth in his heart, and timing and balance in his feet.'

'It seems impossible to hurt him,' Matt Busby's old friend, the Manchester City manager Joe Mercer, agreed, speaking at a time when it still seemed easy for Best to turn it on most Saturdays without fail. 'All manner of men have tried to mark him out of the game, to intimidate him and treat him roughly. Best merely glides along, riding tackles and brushing giants aside like leaves . . . I don't think of him as a small man. I only see those beautiful, tapering muscles and that magnificent style.'

'To be an outstanding finisher, you must be able to hit the ball at any angle from any position, even if you are falling over,' Jimmy Greaves once said. 'Right now I can visualize Georgie doing that, just pinging one away as he tumbled. Second-rate finishers want to line everything up like a golf-shot.'

In a contact sport, Best, thanks to his verve and athleticism, was a non-contact player. Like the exponent of the Brazilian capoeira, he had resolved to be completely free. Capoeira is a cross between a dance and a martial art. The dancer wears knives on his heels and dances around his opponent trying to cut him. 'Capoeira is a way of tricking your opponent – not like boxing where if you are stronger you win. It is a body philosophy,' an academic in Rio explained to Simon Kuper. 'The greatest football idols were the great dribblers, people like Garrincha and Pelé, who used to invent movements – the Dry Leaf, the Bicycle – just as the great capoeirista did . . . Brazilian football is not only a sport,' the professor added. 'It's a kind of stage play, a theatrical movement.'

Because he was a player of such natural artistry, it seems inevitable, when trying to find words that describe what Best did, to look for comparisons from outside sport, such as this description of the early, swashbuckling movie star Douglas Fairbanks Sr. 'There was, of course, an element of the show-off in what he did, but it was (and still remains) deliciously palatable because he managed to communicate a feeling that he was as amazed and delighted as his audience by what that miraculous machine, his body, could accomplish when he launched it into the trajectory necessary to achieve those staggeringly long, marvellously melodic lines of movement through which he flung himself with such heedless grace . . . No one has quite recaptured the freshness, the sense of perpetually innocent, perpetually adolescent narcissism.'

'The human heart in conflict with itself' is a phrase of William Faulkner's. By it he meant the complexity of human behaviour and its effect on performance. This is a subject which greatly interested the eminent Harvard scientist Stephen Jay Gould who, when he wasn't writing about biology, was writing about baseball (and when writing about one was often writing about both). Gould was a confirmed believer in what he called 'the universality of excellence'. His experience had taught him that there is no qualitative difference between the highest achievements of the mind and of the body. There certainly isn't the hierarchical relationship that many assume between the two. 'I don't deny the differences in style and substance between athletic and conventional scholarly performance,' Gould wrote, 'but we surely err in regarding sports as a domain of brutish intuition (dignified, at best, with some politically correct euphemism like "bodily intelligence") and literature as the rarefied realm of our highest mental acuity. The greatest athletes cannot succeed by bodily gifts alone. They must also perform with their heads, and they study, obsess, rage against their limitations, and practice and perfect with the same dedication and commitment that all good scholars apply to their Shakespeare.

'One of the most intriguing, and undeniable, properties of great athletic performance lies in the impossibility of regulating certain central skills by overt mental deliberation: the required action simply doesn't grant sufficient time for the sequential processing of conscious decisions . . . [Sportsmen's] mental skill may be harder to verbalize, but not because athletes are stupid or intrinsically less articulate than writers. Rather, this style of unconscious mentality gropes for verbal description in all domains of its operation . . . Indeed, such mental operations cannot proceed consciously and sequentially. But these skills do not therefore become a lesser form of intellect confined to the bodily achievement of athletes. Many of the most abstract and apparently mathematical feats of mind fall into the same puzzling category . . . If I have learned anything from studying the lives of great ballplayers [it is that] I have come to understand the common denominator of human excellence.'

Gould's hero was the 'Yankee Clipper', Joltin' Joe DiMaggio, who had gained his lifelong devotion when he autographed a baseball for him when he was a boy. DiMaggio, like all sporting heroes, was flawed: mean, snappish, vain, a compulsive womanizer, somebody who, according to his biographer, kept the Paul Simon song that contains a line about him – 'Where have you gone, Joe DiMaggio? A nation turns its lonely eyes to you' – on permanent repeat in his car, along with Hemingway's novel *The Old Man and the Sea*, with the pages that mentioned the Great DiMaggio dog-eared at the corners. But 'to hell with what might have been', Gould once wrote. 'No-one can reach personal perfection in a complex world filled with distraction . . . What happened is all we have . . . He played every aspect of baseball with a fluid beauty in minimal motion, a spare elegance that made even his rare swinging strikeouts look beautiful . . . [He had] a fierce pride that led him to retire the moment his skills began to erode.'

'That thing about being an icon, the Fifth Beatle, I just found it so freaky,' George Best once said. 'I even found it difficult to watch myself playing on TV because I couldn't identify with the person on the screen. I couldn't get to grips with it. It was as if it was all happening to someone else.'

'Nobody knows me.' This was the note he once left propped up against the bedroom mirror of a woman he had just slept with, as he vamoosed silently away.

'I don't find it easy to get really close to people or maybe I should say I don't find it easy to let them get really close to me,' he admitted at the height of his fame. 'I can count my friends on one hand. The thing is that I don't really need other people all that much, at least I don't have to lean on them emotionally. In fact, when I feel I'm getting involved it makes me uneasy.'

His naturally taciturn nature and the firewall of emotional distance he threw up around himself persuaded those who came into his company that something was on top of him that had called a halt to him. 'This is the jar you cannot open. This guy cannot be cracked by thinking,' to quote Philip Roth on one of his later fictional sporting heroes, Seymour 'The Swede' Levov. 'That's the mystery of his mystery. It's like trying to get something out of Michelangelo's *David* . . . There's nothing here but what you're looking at. He's all about being looked at. He always was.'

'Best says that no-one knows him,' his preferred articulator, Hugh McIlvanney, wrote in 1969. 'But is he enigmatic because he's simple and insensitive, or because of a quality of containment and self-sufficiency that keeps him a private man in a crowd? Maybe the answer is he knows he has a beautiful talent and is content to let the world take him or leave him on the strength of it.'

The body is one of the ways we express ourselves when we run out of words.

> *Went up to the bar and ordered*
> *these drinks, lost those*
> *somewhere ordered a couple more,*
> *found that we had forgotten*
> *the others so we had another*
> *round, found some and tended*
> *to lose track a shade.*

Golf; golf, folk music; golf; cricket, reading, gardening; golf, cricket; golf; golf, cricket; golf; pop music, watching football; tennis, fishing; tennis, clothes, pop music; golf, tennis; cricket, table tennis; tennis; golf; swimming, tennis, pop music.

During the season he spent with Tottenham Hotspur at the beginning of the seventies doing the research for his book *The Glory Game*, Hunter Davies got the players to complete questionnaires asking about things like their outside interests. He asked the senior players, such as Alan Mullery, Martin Chivers and Joe Kinnear, to list what business interests they had, and got the following answers: sports shop; garage rep; sports shop; timber firm; Martin Peters Promotions; fish-and-chip shop; property company, furniture-shop director; builders merchants; garage director.

In a documentary film the BBC made about George Best around the same time, they showed him sitting in Mrs Fullaway's front room sticking sparkly stuff from a hobbies kit on to a framed piece of hessian, composing a pretty picture; placing a disc on to the old-fashioned mahogany radiogram; watching the telly with his feet up on the sofa with the family pet, Kim, next to him, and enjoying a chin-wag over a cup of tea with Mrs F. At one point he nips into a favourite rendezvous, Blinkers, shakes hands with the owner and some businessmen customers, eyes the go-go dancers frugging in their wooden cages while enjoying a bowl of spag bol at the bar and heads off for an early night before resuming training in the morning. Item one not screened in this documentary: girls climbing up a ladder to his first-floor bedroom window. Item two not screened: Mrs Fullaway making girls leave by the same way they had entered, the following morning, to the amusement of her Aycliffe Avenue neighbours.

Neither Wilf McGuinness nor Frank O'Farrell were golfers, but it seems their brief stints in the manager's job at Manchester United could have been less brief if they had taken the game up. Matt Busby – Sir Matt, as he had become after the European Cup victory in 1968 – was a keen golfer and, after he retired upstairs to become the club's general manager in 1969, it was those who accompanied him on the fairway who got his ear. Inconceivably (inconceivable to Denis Law and Bobby Charlton, at least, who remained too in awe of the man they still thought of as 'the Boss' to think of socializing with him as equals), Busby's regular golfing companions were two players from the first-team squad.

'Sir' Willie and Matt. That was the joke that had started doing the rounds in the dressing room. George Best-pretender Willie Morgan had arrived at Old Trafford from Burnley in August 1968 and had gone about establishing himself in a less than shy way. Within a few months, with the goalkeeper Alex Stepney and their wives, he was joining Sir Matt and Lady Jean for dinner at the Cromford Club on Saturday nights and part-nering Busby at Davyhulme golf course on Sundays, Mondays and sometimes other days during the week.

It was thanks to Best, whose face by then was on everything from tea mugs to bottles of aftershave, that footballers had started to look beyond fish-and-chip shops and builders merchants for ways to secure their futures. In London, Rodney Marsh, Alan Hudson, Terry Venables and a handful of other Jack-the-lad players had actively begun trying to market them-selves as 'The Clan' – a Plaistow version of Sinatra, Dean Martin and their gang of tail-chasing Vegas 'swingers'. 'We've already had a free suit each,' founder Clan member Phil Beal of Spurs had announced. 'We might sell ourselves to a big com-pany, the way Georgie Best has done. We're just starting. Whatever happens, we can't lose.'

Sir Matt had put his foot down and blocked an offer, reput-edly worth £7,000, for Best to make a record. He didn't under-stand. He *couldn't* understand. He still thought they were in the football business.

Despite being the biggest draw in world football, in 1970 United were still paying Best less than they were paying the ageing Charlton and Law but, although it niggled, Best didn't really care: the £170 a week he was collecting from the club was only a fraction of the earnings that were pouring in from other sources, such as endorsements and modelling and a ghosted column in the *News of the World*, in addition to the Manchester boutiques.

Willie Morgan, proprietor of the shop selling Burnley's hottest groovy gear, was clearly mystified as to why the marketing men weren't beating a path to his door. 'He thought he was the James Bond of football,' Morgan complained of Best. 'He had everything he wanted, and he pleased himself. He had money, girls, and tremendous publicity. He lived from day to day. Until right at the end, he always got away with it when he missed training or ran away. So he didn't care. People always made excuses for him. He didn't even have to bother to make them himself.'

Mrs Morgan, Willie's mother, had grabbed hold of Best and told him as much one day, as he was leaving the field after a United game against Burnley at Turf Moor. 'She grabbed my arm and literally dragged me into the little tearoom they had there,' he said. 'In front of other people, she proceeded to tell me in no uncertain manner how her son was a better player than me, how he'd grown his hair long before I did, and that he was worth more money than I was. "Good luck to him," I said. "I'm not going to argue with you."'

He could afford to be casual. Morgan was no threat. As far as Best was concerned, he was one of the mediocrities who, from 1969 onwards, made up the Manchester United team. It was an opinion shared, as it happened, by both of Matt Busby's immediate successors. But it didn't matter. Morgan, Crerand and Stepney had joined the Busby inner circle. Busby's placeman, the millionaire Manchester butcher Louis Edwards, was now chairman of the directors and the major shareholder in the club. The seat of power, though, was the office at the end of the long corridor with the plaque saying 'Sir Matt Busby – General Manager' on the door. In April 1969, just as he was about to turn sixty, Busby had handed on the succession after twenty-four years in charge.

Wilf McGuinness was that most important thing at Manchester United: he was family. An injury had kept him out of the squad for Munich. A badly broken leg less than a year later had ended his career. But, being family, a place was found for him among the pipe-smoking, white-store-coated good old lads on the backroom staff. He had only won the FA Youth Cup once in the time he had been in charge of what would now be called United's 'academy'. But the players he had brought through – they included David Saddler, Bobby Noble, Brian Kidd and John Aston, as well as Best – suggested that he was able to work in the tradition started by Busby and Jimmy Murphy, which involved turning raw schoolboys into integrated, mature first-team players without sacrificing the individual qualities which had made them stand out in the first place.

McGuinness was thirty-one in 1969, roughly the same age as Law, Crerand, Charlton, Stiles and other variously dimming talents of the championship-winning sides of 1965 and '67 and the European Cup winners of 1968 who he was now expected to, if not pick, then at least placate. Naturally, they weren't happy. Who was he? He was only Wilf, who had been dogs-bodying around the place for years while they were star turns, bringing home the bacon. Best was twenty-three, reigning European Player of the Year, and looking for a clear-out. He believed that United were already on the way down when they became European champions, a shadow of the team they had been in 1965 and '66.

His position was simple: give him some talent to work with. That's all he needed. He was drinking – going on benders, sometimes getting blackouts at the end of particularly alco-holic weekends (he had been banned from driving in 1968 after crashing his car) – but he was also training hard, staying behind to do shooting practice with the apprentices when the rest of the first team had gone home. He had missed only two League games in the previous three seasons. He was filling Old Trafford every Saturday, so where was all the money going? They had only signed two new players – Morgan and Stepney

– in four years. At the time McGuinness took over, United had just finished eleventh, their lowest position since Best joined the club.

'You hate to be cruel,' Best said, 'but we had players like Steve James, who went on to play for Kidderminster Harriers and Tipton Town, and Carlo Sartori. He's now making a successful living as a knife-sharpener in Manchester and I'd say as a footballer, he was a pretty good knife-sharpener . . . Losing isn't in my vocabulary. After playing with Denis and Bobby and Billy [Foulkes] at their peak, the declining standards were hard to take. But I was left struggling among players who shouldn't have been allowed through the door at Old Trafford.'

It was like playing for Northern Ireland, without the team spirit and the behind-the-scenes madness and the late-night laughs. The Northern Ireland selectors always had to make up the numbers with cloggers from the Second or Third Divisions, sometimes even the Irish League – the equivalent of an actor such as John Gielgud being denied the National Theatre stage and being forced to appear on the fringe with a small workshop company, as Best's Northern Ireland teammate Derek Dougan once pointed out. Best himself didn't disagree.

'You could play a lovely pass, one of the makeweights wouldn't run on to it and you'd get booed for what the punters thought was a bad ball. I suffered the same thing when I played in America . . . With Ireland we were always struggling. We did win a few games, but we were always up against it, and the results, and lack of expectation, made it difficult to take the whole thing seriously.'

By Christmas of Wilf McGuinness's first season as chief coach (he wouldn't see out a second one), Best would be saying the same thing about playing for the hobbled, faction-riven, underperforming Manchester United. 'Team spirit was falling apart. Cliques were forming, which we'd never had before, and there was a fair bit of back-stabbing going on. People started bickering, slagging each other off, then there were fights, fists-up jobs. I hated what was happening.'

In the same way that he welcomed the challenge of having to raise his game against top-notch opposition on the park, Best liked to feel he had been presented with worthy adversaries off it. Sir Matt had been around the block enough times to make it hard to sell him a dummy; he might have been the product of a different era, but he was a tough old bird. (The rumour that, in place of the directorship he had been wanting, Busby had been rewarded with the right to sell 'bunce' – club scarves, replica shirts – from a caravan outside Old Trafford was slightly undermining, but not fatally.)

McGuinness was a Collyhurst Catholic like Paddy McGrath and Nobby, and he thought he shared their sharp Manc knowingness and nose for a scam, but George believed he knew different. Wilf developed a particular obsession with Best's irrepressible cock-happiness, especially on those occasions when he was away from home with the team and, according to the wisdom of the ages, should be conserving his energies for the game. ('He had this weakness,' McGuinness pronounced wisely. 'He followed his dick.') McGuinness became as driven in his quest to keep him out of strange beds as the Ferret had been keen to watch him in action in them. Both, of course, as far as Best was concerned, only gave his adventures extra relish.

The best-thumbed story from around this time, but one which illustrates how his focus was moving increasingly away from football, unfolds on the occasion towards the end of the 1969–70 season when United faced their old rivals Leeds in the semi-final of the FA Cup. After the first game ended 0–0, the replay was to take place at Aston Villa's ground in Birmingham, and the United party were booked into a hotel in Worcester where, having clocked a middle-aged woman in the bar giving off the right signals, Best resolved to make good on a promise he had long ago made himself: 'I always fancied having a quick fuck before a game. I mean minutes before, not the night before. I fancied the dressing room at Wembley just before a cup final.'

It was a business hotel in the Midlands before a semi, and

despite the manager's best efforts – McGuinness had personally evicted him from the woman's room ninety minutes before
the match was due to kick off, having monitored proceedings
from the room occupied by Stiles and Charlton next door –
Best still managed to keep the team coach waiting while he
completed his business upstairs. He played like a donkey,
falling face-down in the mud at one point as he was about to
shoot, to hoots of derision from the Leeds supporters. After a
second replay, United went out of the Cup and, pretty soon
afterwards, McGuinness, 'family' or not, found himself out of
a job.

Best had started that season well. But after Christmas he
found himself in a series of stupid disputes with referees. He
was fined £100 and suspended for a month for knocking the
ball out of a referee's hands. Three months later, playing for
Ireland against Scotland in Belfast, he was sent off for spitting
and throwing mud at the referee. His next game was against
England at Wembley, where he was booed every time he
touched the ball. The root of it all, he claimed, was the stress
he was under, trying to carry a poor Manchester United side by
himself. But the truth was that the lifestyle feedback he had
generously allowed himself as the reward for success – the
birds, mostly the booze – had turned into a lifestyle standing
increasingly independent of any achievement that might once
have lent it respectability. Drinking to celebrate success; drinking to drown failure. Same difference. It was all drink.

Shortly before McGuinness was given the elbow, Best
received another visit from the pretty young *Daily Sketch*
reporter who broke the news that his Danish 'dream girl' had
been ditched. She hopped out of bed with another exclusive.
'I've been playing badly for a couple of months now – due
mostly to late nights and drink,' she quoted him saying. 'I didn't
think about it at the beginning. I just knew I was fed up with
everything and everyone around me. So I went on going out
every night and drinking when I should have been training.'

Mr Ernest Garnett, the chairman of Bellair, who were paying Best £12,000 to publicize their aftershave, was livid. 'We are trying to promote a clean-cut image and Mr Best is not helping,' he declared. 'He will have to keep his nose clean in future, a lot of our dealers have a puritanical outlook on life.'

'I'll straighten him out if it's the last thing I do,' Sir Matt Busby promised, and he was soon in a position to make a hands-on attempt. Having shown McGuinness the door, Busby had to resume control himself at Old Trafford until another manager could be found. And so, immaculate as ever in Crombie overcoat and trilby, he found himself on Piccadilly station in Manchester on a January morning in 1971, waiting for George. George was due to appear before an FA disciplinary committee after picking up three cautions for misconduct on the field over a period of a year. But George was still in bed. George was hung-over. He missed the train. Busby made the journey to London on his own, and Best arrived only three hours late to hear that he had incurred a (laughably lenient) £250 fine and a six-week suspended sentence.

Four days later, the scene on Piccadilly station was repeated, only with the whole team awaiting Best's arrival this time, and the whole team travelling to London for their match against Chelsea without him. He was consistent. He caught a later train but, on arrival at Euston, taxied away from Stamford Bridge in the direction of Islington, where he had arranged to spend the weekend with the actress Sinead Cusack, whom he had met when they appeared on a chat show together in Ireland.

Cue media shitstorm. Cusack's flat was besieged by television and the papers. Outside-broadcast aerials were erected; transmitter vans blocked the street. Gangs of kids stood outside and eventually gained access to the building, chanting, 'We want Georgie' or 'Come out, Georgie,' and, after they'd seen the following morning's papers, 'Georgie Best is on the nest.'

The siege of Noel Street went on for three days, with bulletins being given at hourly intervals on radio and television. 'Sinead and I just sat there and watched the story on the television news,' Best later said. 'It was unreal watching pictures on the telly of the flat you were sitting in. It was like acting in a play in a packed theatre without the curtain going up.'

Eventually, on the Monday morning Best's friend Malcolm Mooney made a mercy dash from Manchester and smuggled him out of a rear door of the block of flats and back up the M6 in his car. A breakdown on the motorway meant they were six hours late for the carpeting in front of Busby at which Best was suspended for two weeks without pay. Reviewing the incident in his autobiography, Sir Matt said: 'I don't think any other single thing that happened to the boy brought home to me his problem. All right, he had been silly and irresponsible. But for three days and nights he was front page and back page news. Cameras watched all night for him. He was on television news. I sat there and wondered how he was to survive it all.'

'I had been conditioned from boyhood to win, to go out and dominate the opposition,' Best tried to explain many years later. 'In our good years, as soon as I finished training I was looking forward to coming in the next day, or playing the next match. From 1970 onwards, it was very different. Instead of revolving around me, the team depended on me, and I couldn't handle the pressure. I was doing it on my own and I was just a kid. I had always played for fun. Now that there was responsibility, it was just a job.

'I'd lost all my enthusiasm for football. I wasn't looking forward to the games any more because I didn't want to go out and get stuffed 4–0 by teams who wouldn't have held a candle to Manchester United two or three years earlier.

'Whenever things got too tough, whenever I got depressed because the team was playing bad and I couldn't take all the limelight and wanted to get away I used to find myself a bird. That's what happened with Sinead. Girls like Sinead were the cure for all that. She is one of the few I really liked.'

Even before he was knighted and made a Freeman of the

City of Manchester, words like 'paternal' and 'patriarchal' attached themselves automatically to Busby: 'In his control of the club there is a lot of the character of a stern, devoted grandfather, making all the big decisions, ordering and disciplining in some huge, unpredictably gifted household,' Hopcraft wrote. Such descriptions were not only typical, they were true. But there was a harder, unforgiving side to him – a fine ruthless streak – which had showed itself sporadically over the years. The decision, for example, to jettison Wilf McGuinness, who had joined the club as a fifteen-year-old, when he became surplus to requirements. The blanking of his great old friend and comrade-in-arms Jimmy Murphy in later years when it became apparent that his face no longer fitted around Old Trafford.

It went without saying that any player who questioned his authority as manager could expect to be roughly chopped off at the knees. Johnny Morris of Busby's fabled 1948 team was one who tried it, to his cost. Morris discovered he was expendable, despite being the most valuable player in the club. Most notoriously in the post-war years, John Giles was given his marching orders when he had a falling-out with the Boss over which position he should play. Giles went on to become a linchpin of the Leeds side who were to become United's great bugbear of the sixties, but Busby, while acknowledging it was his 'greatest mistake', never betrayed any regret about helping Giles on his way.

'His standards are very high. He is a man of great principle,' Busby's friend, the Manchester painter Harold Riley, once said. 'If people disappoint him, don't conform to those standards, he will just step away.'

Except, in Best's case, as everybody kept noticing, he didn't. He didn't step away. And then he didn't step away again. What would have seemed unimaginable outrages to Busby when he took over at the club, when the football business was still about football – crashing cars, missing training, turning up for training stinking of drink, three-in-a-bed sessions with prostitutes in the team hotel – were minimalized, accommodated, forgiven over and over again. The great Celtic manager Jock Stein once said that his most satisfying feat in football was not winning the European Cup in 1967 but extending the way-ward Jimmy Johnstone's career. For many people, history is proof that Matt Busby's biggest mistake was not to recognize sooner the weakness that grievously afflicted George Best's life.

'What were we supposed to do,' Busby later said, 'shoot him? I always looked for a cure with George. It would have been easy to have transferred him, but that wasn't the answer. Special rules for George? I suppose so, but only in the sense that he was a special player. I mean, you make it different once you say someone is a good player and the man next to him is a genius. George is a genius.'

Commerce, of course, came into the equation: Best was the biggest box-office attraction in world football. He was money in the bank. But Arthur Hopcraft had a characteristically pen-etrating comment to make about Busby's indulgence of Best which linked it to the cataclysm of Munich: 'It has been com-plained against Busby that for so important a figure in the sport he permitted too much petulance by some of his players, too much flaunting of personality both on the field and off it. Perhaps the team he created in the fifties, linked so closely to his own character, would have been less offensive in this way; perhaps a man who has seen so much exuberance crushed in a single, frightful moment could not be expected to be harsh, when it appeared, even if more showily, in a later generation.'

As ever, Bobby Charlton – the chastening reminder of Munich, dolorous, unexuberant – remained unimpressed. As captain, it was Charlton's responsibility to report any signs of restiveness in the dressing room to the manager. And within a few months of the quiet, serious-minded Irishman Frank O'Farrell being appointed as Wilf McGuinness's successor in the early part of 1971, the players were on the point of revolt over what they regarded as the club's unwarrantably lenient attitude towards 'genius George' Best.

Just as with McGuinness, Best had started off playing well for the new man. He scored fourteen goals, including two hat-tricks, in the first half of the 1971–72 season, and Manchester United were at the top of the First Division. 'When I looked at the team I realized their reputations were better than their performances,' O'Farrell said. 'The results were due to one man: George Best. He was fantastic. After some games we won when we shouldn't have I used to say, Thank God for George.' O'Farrell rewarded Best with a pay rise which pushed his wages up to £225 a week and put him on a par with Law and Charlton.

The first time he went missing under O'Farrell was before a Cup tie at Southampton. O'Farrell fined him but didn't drop him. United got a draw. 'In the return at Old Trafford we were struggling,' O'Farrell remembered. 'All of a sudden George scores two great goals and we've won.' This was his dilemma.

One day, Best came in after a spell on the run and gave as his excuse the fact that his parents had been threatened by para-militaries in Northern Ireland and he had been over to comfort them. This wasn't true. But Best himself had become the target of IRA threats when he was told he would be shot while playing for Manchester United at Newcastle. This was in retaliation, it was claimed, for the sum of £3,000 he was rumoured to have given the Protestant leader, the Revd Ian Paisley. The rumour was false but, as Best remarked, 'It's the kind of lie that can get you killed.'

He was assigned an armed guard at his hotel in Newcastle and armed police mingled with the crowd at St James's Park during the game. Afterwards the police gave the team coach an escort of two cars for the drive back to Manchester. Best's house in Bramhall was placed under surveillance. A letter signed by 'The Striker' threatened a knife in the back and said, 'Next time you will miss your own biggest headline.' The Brown Bull beckoned.

He was going out and staying drunk two or three nights in a row. He was always the last one standing. Increasingly often he was missing training. After failing to turn up at the Cliff every day for a week just after New Year in 1972, he was traced to the London flat of his latest girlfriend, the reigning Miss Great Britain. O'Farrell, to whom this kind of behaviour was as exotically otherworldly as it was to Matt Busby, fined him two weeks' wages and ordered him to train mornings and afternoons until further notice, with no day off for five weeks.

United collapsed in the second half of the season to finish eighth in the First Division. Best did what he had been doing every summer since 1965 and got a group of mates together and took off for Spain for three months of sun, sex and sangria (and vodka, wine, Dom Perignon champagne, schnapps, sambuca and Courvoisier brandy – 'lakes of drink, wall-to-wall fanny') in a rented villa in Marbella. A friend drove the Rolls or the E-Type down as an extra chick magnet.

It was in Marbella that, two days before his twenty-sixth birthday in May 1972, Best announced his retirement in a *Sunday Mirror* exclusive. The paper paid him £5,000 for the story, which was enough to keep everybody in brandy-and-cokes for a long time and the executive staff at Old Trafford apoplectic. In London, a public-relations man announced that 'Best's brand awareness has never been so high,' and O'Farrell issued a confession of his perplexity, admitting that 'He is, like all other geniuses, difficult to understand.'

By August, the *Mirror* cheque safely banked, Best, apparently bored with the licence that 'retirement' had given him to act like an ex-professional footballer, was back and reassuringly missing from training once more. The situation was as he had left it: factions, feuds, a collection of dinosaur greats.

In September, he marked the occasion of Bobby Charlton's testimonial, in which he should have been playing, by staying in the Brown Bull getting plastered and chucking eggs that Billy Barr had let him have from the kitchen at the painting of Charlton that was hanging in the bar.

'The club was a mess,' Best said. 'It was burning me up inside but I suppose I didn't have the guts to tell the great man to his face. When we lost badly, I went out to get absolutely slaughtered. I went straight out and got pissed.'

December 1972 saw United anchored at the bottom of the First Division. Relegation was staring them in the face.

*There's not an awful
lot to be said for the
case of getting home
in time sometimes.*

The slide from committed drinking to full-blown alcoholism probably started in 1968. Two celebrations which were mopped up into the bigger, ongoing Manchester Euro celebration were the weddings of Best's two closest 'social companions'. Mike Summerbee and David Sadler both got married in 1968. Summerbee abdicated his long-held post as chaperone and small-hours hellraiser to marry his girlfriend Tina (George was best man), and Sadler, the one person George could talk to in his cups, when the demons were dancing and he was hallucinating dioramas of razor-clawed dust mites and gnarling faces, moved out of Mrs Fullaway's to live in a club house with his new wife.

Head of the Manchester United Former Players' Association in later life, Sadler, while remaining close to Best, owned up to some feelings of resentment. 'I thought he was wasting that great talent', he said, 'and sticking two fingers up at the rest of us who were less gifted but more diligent in our approach to training and preparation for games. We had words. He reacted, more or less saying sod off, I'll live my life the way I want to. And to be fair to George he was putting bonuses in our pockets and he was probably the only one doing it. That goes back to Wilf [McGuinness]'s time.'

Manchester City won the League in 1968, and it was clean-up time for Summerbee: he sold his half of the Sale boutique to George and turned in the keys to the flat that they had been sharing in Crumpsall. He claimed that he had never had

George's staying power and never drank more than he could run off easily at training the following morning. Even so, after he got married Summerbee slowed down considerably. For example, he was never an habitué, but after his marriage he stopped going to Phyllis's completely, because Phyllis's never properly got going – never turned into the Phyllis's that everybody thought of when they said the name – until at least three in the morning. After he'd been left the last one propping up the bar in the Brown Bull, and even the residents had crawled off to bed, Phyllis's in Whalley Range is where George would invariably aim himself – somewhere where scurrilousness and wit were the norm, and the only disqualification from entry was being boring. He was safe from bumping into any footballers there, and his respectable friends were always trying to talk him out of going, which made it even more irresistible. Malcolm Wagner was one of them.

'I think the Phyllis's run was very, very bad for George,' he said. 'You'd had your fill by the time you'd done the nightclubs, and then to go on to Phyllis's and come home with the birds singing wasn't good for anyone. All you would do in Phyllis's is drink, there was nothing else happening. I'd had enough to drink by two in the morning. But it became a habit for George, when the clubs had shut.

'That's when all the talk started about hangers-on who were a bad influence on him, but his mates – his real mates – never went to Phyllis's as a regular thing. We all made a pact that we wouldn't go, and that we would try and discourage him from going, but it was a waste of time. George has always done what he wants to do. Persuasion has no effect.'

'My mates,' Best said, 'the ones people rubbish who are supposed to lead me astray, used to pray with me to stop drinking. They used to come round the house and offer to sit with me, to stay with me like a fucking babysitter, to stop me going out. But I wouldn't listen. I had a fight with a couple of them. I was literally crazy with drink. The funny thing was, or is, I can stop when I want. In those days I didn't want.'

It was dark in Phyllis's – a permanent twilight time. And snug. And permanently out of time. There were no clocks. There were heavy velvet curtains, always drawn, to keep the world at bay. And Dennis, Phyllis's other half, posted at an upstairs window to give the warning if the police showed up. Cut-moquette armchairs and sofas and antimacassars to give a respectable, almost vicarage tea party, Miss Marple-ish air. Boudoir carpets. Nice pieces of bric-a-brac. Peach mirrors, tasselled lamps. And Phyllis herself, permanently perched on her high stool at the end of the bar, as comforting as Christmas – lit up like Christmas when one of her regulars came in – brash and maternal at the same time, always nice.

Phyllis had a son called Phil, who would go on to form the band Thin Lizzy and record a song that could have been based on George Best: 'Oh the boy he could boogie / Oh the boy could kick a ball / But the boy he got hung up / Making love against the wall.' Phil Lynott would die a junkie, but at the time Best knew him he was still a schoolboy going to Princess Road junior school at the Moss Side end of Whalley Range, a few streets away from the Victorian corner-terrace house that contained his mum's drinker. Phyllis's was situated between the pincers of Wilbraham Road and King's Road, the two streets where Sir Matt and his family lived all their lives, but it's unlikely any of them ever realized it was there.

Irish stew. That's the smell George would always associate with Phyllis's place. She often had a pan on which had been bubbling for three days. Irish stew and vodka. His idea of a perfect breakfast after another night on the sauce. The regulars were members of the Manchester night-time economy – croupiers, bar workers, entertainers, bookies, bouncers, car dealers and the Quality Street gang (Waggy the hairdresser, Big Frank the builder, Danny the United nutcase) who – excepting the summer months, when they were in Marbella with Bestie – kept a fond, respectful eye on Phyllis's welfare. Phyllis's was a drinking den 'providing a night-life for workers from the night-life'. Day or night, it was always open and she was always there. She never seemed to sleep. There was no trouble at Phyllis's.

Entry came via a ground-floor spyhole, although Best always went up the outside fire escape direct to the first floor. (It was a route he had got used to using in hotels in order to avoid awkward encounters in lifts in the middle of the night.) In the early seventies, Michael Parkinson enjoyed a night on the town with Best – 'a few drinks and then a good gamble, then a tour of the discos looking for crumpet' – which inevitably ended with them taking the fire escape up to Phyllis's side door. It was during his dog days at United. George had a paper bag under his arm containing his winnings from the casino, about £600 in notes.

Parkinson described the drinking part of the evening as follows: 'He stood at the bar all night, never moving, just steadily drinking. One day one of his mates had said, "Have you seen my imitation of George Best?" and he just stood in a corner with a drink in his hand saying nothing.' At the casino, the croupier greets him with the words, "Go home. I was having a good time till you came in." Around him', Parkinson wrote, 'the faces of the other gamblers were elated with concern or excitement or studied nonchalance. He just looked bored.'

After the discos, they washed up at Whalley Range: 'George liked Phyllis and whenever he was troubled he went to talk to her . . . "Fed up again?" she asked. "Choked," he said. "It's a small town," she said. "A bloody village. Just like *Peyton Place*," he said. "Same anywhere, George love," she said . . .

'He got bored during the day, so he drank, he was bored in the evening so he drank some more. Then he didn't want to go home because he couldn't sleep properly so he got drunk again. Just like tonight . . . He said goodnight to Phyllis and went outside. It was daylight. Children were on their way to school. He went to his car and two kids stopped and watched him driving away.'

One quiet midweek night he was in a club called Reubens,

186

sitting at the bar with a friend who was the owner of another Manchester club. A girl from a group of girls who wasn't unknown to him came up and asked him to dance. He said he didn't dance in clubs. He was from Belfast. Remember? She was pretty drunk. Brandies with Babycham. She called him a big-headed bastard and swung one at him. Threw her drink in his face. He didn't think he hit her hard – it was a slap like a father would give his daughter. Unfortunately, it was enough to cut the inside of her mouth and give her a hairline fracture of the nose.

He had been dropped from the team earlier that morning – 29 November 1972 – after missing training again the previous day. By the time he was found guilty of causing actual bodily harm five weeks later and given a suspended sentence of twelve months, Tussauds in Blackpool had melted down his wax figure to make one of Rodney Marsh, who Malcolm Allison at Manchester City had signed as a rival attraction to Best, and his career had hit a brick wall.

The night of the trial found him in his friend Dougie Welsby's Queen's club, chatting to a girl. It was Welsby who had been with him the night of the Reubens incident. The girl was a friend of a friend, and when the club closed she moved on with a few of them to Phyllis's. Around five or six in the morning she suggested he might take her home. When he said he couldn't – he was due to be poured on to a flight to Toronto in a matter of hours – she cut up rough; she threatened to call the police to tell them they were drinking illegally and lurched out into the hall in the direction of the phone. He was on twelve months' suspended, picked up only fifteen hours earlier. He grabbed the phone from her as she was dialling, and as he did so she turned away from him and caught her head on the coin box, suffering a hairline fracture of the skull.

He sent flowers – got somebody to send flowers for him – to the hospital and skipped the flight to Canada. The same time the next day he was back among the night people in the safe embrace of Phyllis's, the previous night's sordid episode already diffused by repetition among the punters, seeping invisibly like a stain into the fabric, a metastasized atom of a malign fragment of the legend of the holy drinker.

Those early floodlit matches at Wolves he used to listen to on the wireless. Floodlighting didn't arrive at Old Trafford until 1957. It was the old story: short arms, long pockets; directors who thought it was a gimmick. The Wolverhampton Wanderers directors and Stan Cullis, the manager, were more progressive. To a whole generation of football fans in the 1950s, Molineux was a place of magic, as the new night-time lights blazed down on exotic foreign competition like Moscow Dynamo and Racing Club of Buenos Aires, flipping them from drab post-war sepia into supersaturated technicolour.

Like Duncan Edwards, as a boy Best was a hard-core Wolves supporter, and part of the reason was the glamour that attached to the lights – the great batteries of lights slicing through the dark like a crazy extravagance in such pinched times, illuminating the possibilities of that mean industrial place.

Foreign teams playing in Britain, and the lights themselves, were such a novelty that Wolves's international matches were televised live. The Bests didn't have a television themselves, but a neighbour called Mr Harrison did and Geordie used to watch the Wolves games with him. Every time he knew there was a game on he'd stand outside kicking a ball against the wall until Mr Harrison invited him in. It was only a small black and white television and the famous old-gold shirts of the Wolves could have been pale blue or light green or even boring old white. But George was spellbound. 'I was mesmerized by those games,' he'd recall many years later. 'The football was fantastic and there were 55,000 fans locked inside Molineux for every one of them. But it was the floodlights which made them magical for me. I had already begun a scrapbook on Glentoran, in which I pasted all the match reports from the *Belfast Telegraph*. Now, I turned the book upside down and in the back I began pasting in reports of Wolves.'

Like his Belfast contemporary, the snooker player Alex Higgins, who rarely performed well in daytime sessions, Best came to love the big European nights, which were always under lights and took him back to Mr Harrison's front room, kept darkened to get a better picture, the light from the television flooding the room the way gantry lights created a tall, clear-walled yellow tank of light at the football ground.

He played his last game for United on New Year's Day 1974. When he turned up for the next match – 'He was standing there pissed out of his mind, and with a young lady,' the latest new manager Tommy Docherty said (Best always denied this) – he was told he wasn't wanted. He sat out the match in the players' lounge, watching racing on the television, nursing a cup of tea. An hour after the final whistle, when the crowd had cleared, he went on his own up into the stands.

It was mid-winter. It had been a floodlit game. Now the lights were out and the pitch was in darkness. Lights glowed in the press box and in the various hospitality places and offices. There were tears, of course. Of course there were. But also some sense of solace in being relegated to the shadows rather than performing in the glare, the focus of so many indiscriminate fantasies, hopes and yearnings. 'I could make one mistake, one slight mistake only, and the whole tragedy of living, of being alive, would come into the crowd's throat and roar its pain like a maimed animal,' the big prop forward Arthur Machin in David Storey's *This Sporting Life* says. A relief to be spared that at least.

'What is your nationality?'

'I'm a drunkard.'

Bogart in *Casablanca*. It was Best's favourite film, with a script he knew word for word. 'Last night? That's so long ago I can't remember it. Tonight? That's too far ahead for me to plan.' All of it.

Somebody who spent every waking hour in a bar. In Rick's Bar, as in the small, tarnished, smoke-filled room that was

Phyllis's, visitors could be sure of finding someone they either knew or wanted to talk to. Adrift in the timeless twilight that took you back to Mr Harrison's on the Cregagh, with the TV screen light making a ghostly glow and the light-flooded spectacle happening on the other side of it.

'Sometimes what is happening on the field seems to speak to something deeper within us,' America's baseball laureate Roger Angell once wrote. 'We stop cheering and look on in uneasy silence, for the man out there is no longer just another great athlete, an idealized hero, but only a man – only ourself. We are no longer at a game.'

The sound of a crowd could give him the horn. A crowd comprised of the owners of the crushed beer tins and swirling newspapers and waxy wrappers, now dispersed. Printed ephemera. Days on the brush when they were apprentices, dragging their sacks along the terraces, they would find plenty of dropped pennies and halfpennies and Corona pop bottles, which they took back to the shop opposite the Stretford End to collect the penny return.

In the vocabulary of their little world, they were gutties. Proper football boots were far too expensive. 'Mitching', which meant playing truant, wagging off, going on the missing list, getting the fuck away.

'He went like that,' as Bogey says in another of George's favourites, The Maltese Falcon, 'like a fist when you open your hand.'

Eight

In the foyer at Dudley Leisure Centre, a receptionist was struggling to explain to the husband of a Muslim woman dressed in the traditional *hijab* that she would not be allowed to accompany their children into the pool unless she wore a swimming costume. The husband insisted that it was against the rules of their religion for his wife to expose her body in public in this way, and the receptionist was just as insistent that she would not be allowed into the pool wearing the concealing *burqa*-style garments she wanted to wear. 'She can wear leisurewear . . . er, lycra. That would be permitted. Also, under the health and safety, one adult can only take in two children under eight . . .'

All around them hung evidence of what, in different circumstances, could be seen as an aggressive nationalism: the three-lions England jerseys and shields and patriotic trophies of Dudley's favourite son, Duncan Edwards. The display cases occupied every inch of a large wall and rattled occasionally in response to high-spirited noises from the pool.

It was July 2005. Three weeks earlier Islamist extremists had bombed the London tube, killing and maiming many people. Just the day before, four people had been arrested in dawn raids on houses in Birmingham in connection with the failed 21 July suicide bombings. Hay Mills and Washwood Heath were near enough to feel like suburbs of Dudley. Feelings were running high. The sturdy metal gates had been locked and the windows boarded at Dudley Central Mosque on Castle Hill. (Although this was also true at the former art-deco cinema – Priestley's 'ridiculous terra-cotta music hall' – which was now the Assembly Hall of the Jehovah's Witnesses. Both buildings stood on Castle Hill, under the shadow of Dudley Zoo, separated by a casino.)

In the high street, on the edge of the market, a group of

women had become exercised by a sign in the window of Chicken Hut advertising an Islamic youth camp and giving the website address www.pathofknowledge.co.uk. 'Al Fatiha Youth Camp,' one of the women read out. 'After all that's gone on,' her friend said, rummaging in her bag for her glasses to take a look. They were soon joined by a heavily tanned elderly man wearing a white T-shirt and fat-linked gold chain necklace; he had more gold round his wrists and on his muscular-looking fingers.

'They're takin' the piss, aren't they?' he said, when he saw what the women were looking at. 'It's a fookin' Trojan horse 'ere, an' no joke.' The women murmured agreement. 'Like that Guantanamo mob,' he said. 'They're all fookin' guilty. They've handed the coontry owver. When you read about the millions for this new mosque. I've been over and baptized the fooker.' He held his hand in front of his trousers and mimed pissing in the Chicken Hut doorway. The women laughed.

In the market, stalls selling Asian goods – sari fabrics, silk slippers, turmeric and okra – co-existed alongside stalls selling Black Country staples like home brew and takeaway home-made faggots and peas; terrazzo-marbled slabs of brawn. A particularly busy lunchtime crowd had gathered round the Castlemoor Farm's hog roast, where a whole pig on a spit was being carved and served in floury baps with stuffing, crackling and apple sauce. Some of the older lunchers with time on their hands rested on benches and, between mouthfuls and appreciative mumbles, called out encouragement to Malcolm Sier, who was on his knees behind a high metal-mesh barrier using a chisel to carve the details of Duncan Edwards's short life and career on to the pedestal of his statue.

'Quality work!' one man shouted. 'Great to see it!' agreed another. 'A handsome character 'e was, was Duncan,' added a third old boy of around seventy, which is the age Duncan would have been if he had still been alive. Six years after the statue's official unveiling, Dudley Metropolitan Borough Council was finally beefing up the basic information of

Edwards's name and dates which they had had carved on to the plinth in 1999.

It was as if all of it – the sweet pork, the homely British crackling, the artisan craftsman, the dirt of his labour (the lettercutter was down on his knees in the dust, wearing knee-pads and goggles), the clarity and finality of the unfolding inscription, the virile figure of the heroic young sportsman, rendered tangible, explicable and solid in bronze – it was as if it all coincided in a moment that was immensely reassuring to a generation for whom the world had become – was, even as they digested their pork 'belly-busters' and watched Malcolm Sier tapping mallet on chisel, still becoming – daily more unpredictable, alien to their experience, and threatening.

The month or so that it took Sier to complete the commission brought him a regular audience; his work seemed to appeal to that instinct for nostalgia and regression so deep in the English character. Edwards was Kid Dynamite, the Baby Giant, the Gentle Giant, the Boy with the Heart of a Man after he'd died, although nobody ever seems to have called him those things while he was alive. 'He was somebody who had the gift of greeting life with a glad heart,' an elderly woman came and confided when she knew I was there to write about Duncan Edwards.

It was as if Edwards himself, placed before them in the solemnity of bronze, an honour exclusively reserved in the past for civic dignitaries and old soldiers, had become not only a reminder but a symbol of a way of life that was on the ebb. Malcolm Sier, in the act of inscribing Edwards's achievements, was plugging a gap in the British way which had been opened up and was getting wider. At the cemetery somebody had recently gone and planted a flag of St George at the base of Edwards's grave. Everybody knew Duncan, watched him, said hello to him, loved him, in a way.

Sier is a local man, from Wolverhampton, with a studio in a place just outside Dudley on the green edge of the Black Country called Himley Hall. He is used to working out of sight and in unusual isolation: he has no website to showcase his work, no email address, no mobile phone. Although a generation younger than them, he had this in common with the pensioners who came to the market to sit and watch him concentratedly, methodically go about his business. A local community brought together in a display of order and consensus.

The original brief pedestal inscription giving only Edwards's name and dates had been completed in the studio. The new work had to be done on site, and Sier admitted that he had been apprehensive before he started. But he had drawn reassurance from the fact that he was sure Duncan Edwards himself had known what it was to be nervous – 'Nobody is confident all the time' – and had had to overcome that. He had decided to cage himself in because he realized he was a vulnerable figure, working on his knees with both hands occupied and his back to the world. And there had been the inevitable local drunks and druggies bending his ear, lurching about. But on the whole, he said, he had been amazed by the interest shown and the constant expressions of appreciation. They had confirmed his belief that 'anything commemorative is not for the dead, it's for the living – it's uplifting, it speaks for itself, it's an absolute expression of a human being . . . Your impression fades in one sense over time,' Sier added. 'Someone once existed who is no longer there. But you're left with an essence. And it's this essence I'm trying to bring into the real world, into our world.'

And all this from lines chiselled in stone. (The bronze figure of Edwards looming over Sier as he worked had been the work of other hands.) The physical attitude that Sier's job obliged him to assume – on the ground, in the dirt, literally labouring at the great man's feet – could have been what encouraged others to step forward and reveal themselves. But Sier himself puts it down to another reason: heartfelt affection for Duncan Edwards. 'I've known of Duncan for most of my life, very much so, coming from this area,' he said. 'But that was Duncan the legend. I already knew what he was standing for, in that sense. But there was this absolutely pervading feeling that, in his short lifespan, he was . . . It's not just somebody who was a footballer. He was somebody else.

'It was the people all the time. All the people. So many people wanting to share their memories of the Duncan they used to kick a can around with, or go hop-picking with in the summer, or mending bikes . . . Endless, endless stories of when people came into contact with Duncan which gave you an overview of how their lives had evolved. One dear old lady, she was very passionate about Duncan. Very, very passionate. She was a big fan of . . . what was it again now . . . Oh yes – his legs!

'So it's their energy that surrounds that object. It was quite overwhelming at times, but it's that that gave it a real sense of celebrating Duncan. It's for and about them.'

'Sculptor, lettercutter and memorial artist' is how Sier describes himself, and his is a job that brings him in constant contact with death. I wondered how he would react to being asked to work on a memorial to George Best? He referred several times in conversation to the 'gentlemanly way' in which footballers of the Edwards era conducted themselves, and I had read into this a disapproval of players from the Best tearaway tendency. Surprisingly, though, he quoted something Best had been reported as saying before he died: 'It wasn't all sour. Life is not all regrets. When you really think about it, it doesn't even seem worthwhile regretting the bad times because they're all part of the same life.'

'To me,' Sier said, 'that was getting pretty close to the man as he was. We saw what his final days and years were like, and how he physically suffered. He was somebody who came wise after the event. So I wouldn't have a problem with George Best.'

Sier uses a V-cut chisel to make valley-shaped numerals and letters to fonts of his own design. The pedestal of the Edwards statue is faced with what Malcolm Sier regards as 'one of the Rolls-Royces of stone' – pale Hoptonwood limestone from a

Derbyshire quarry that is now worked-out. 'It's very tight, a very clean stone to use,' he says. 'A very consistent stone, because it's a dense, fine material. You get nice clean edges.'

BORN IN DUDLEY
'The most complete footballer
I have ever seen'
Assistant Manager
DUNCAN EDWARDS
1936–1958
ENGLAND INTERNATIONAL HONOURS
18 appeara

The inscription was a work-in-progress the first time I happened across it. Jimmy Murphy's name was pencilled in before 'Assistant Manager' but hadn't been carved. The metal-mesh barrier was still in place around the statue and there was a sign with Malcolm Sier's name and areas of expertise listed on it. But it was still strangely unnerving. Half the inscription had been written in stone, committed to the ages, and the other half – the part listing Edwards's England appearances as 18, with 5 goals; his Manchester United career as 175 appearances with 21 goals and 2 League Championship medals – had been lightly pencilled in as if it was still provisional – as if it could still be subject to change and possibly hadn't even happened yet.

It reminded me of how, on gallery walls, the birth date of artists is always given and space left inside the brackets for the second date of a life – the death date – which has yet to be recorded. You sometimes see the same thing on headstones when space has been made for a husband or wife or son or daughter in a plot: 'Also her dearly beloved husband Marcus, 1963–   .'

It was as if Edwards's life was unfolding all over again at the hands of a monumental mason, and the result could only be verifiable – the life wouldn't really be over – when he had carved the last letter on the last word and excised the horizontal pencil guidelines from the surface of the tablets of Derbyshire stone.

'Haven't you got a machine that can do that?' Sier was forever being asked in Dudley market. And he'd tell them he hadn't: 'No, this is me.'

'Seeyaz, mooker!' the old Black Countrymen would call out to him, having seen off their pork with the trimmings and unburdened their stories of Duncan, as they meandered on their way.

Nine

And when the sun comes up over the Quarter
next morning and that pretty woman
you've had and had all night
now wants to go home with you,
be tender with her, don't do anything
you'll be sorry for later. Bring her home
with you in the Citroen, let her sleep
in a proper bed. Let her
fall in love with you and you
with her and then ... something: alcohol,
a problem with alcohol, always alcohol –
what you've really done
and to someone else, the one
you meant to love from the start.

   Raymond Carver, 'Alcohol'

*The demands placed upon surgeons by society are increasing
... The challenge for the liver surgeon is not only to ensure surgery is safe, but also that complications, such as bleeding and
the need for transfusion are low ... There have been important
advances in topical haemostats and surgical sealants with many
different products now becoming available ... Knowledge of
these products and an appreciation of their potential use and
application are invaluable for surgeons involved in performing
advanced hepatobiliary and liver transplant surgery ...
Surgeons are continuing to improve the results of liver surgery
and are performing liver surgery in higher risk patients. It is
increasingly likely that they will need to incorporate the use of
haemostats and surgical sealants into their clinical practice and
the best use of these products comes with experience, when the*

differing properties of sealants and haemostats become readily apparent . . . Haemorrhage is a major cause of morbidity in liver surgery . . . Different methods may be used for generalized bleeding from a cut or raw surface compared to a difficult bleeding point from within the liver . . .

There was consensus that Quixil® is more adherent and flexible than traditional fibrin sealants. It is less likely to crack or peel away . . . Discussion around the advantages this conveys pointed to the speed of clotting with Quixil®, which means there is less opportunity for bleeding to pool and rupture the sealant. It is more effective at lower temperatures and during reperfusion, as the liver expands, Quixil®'s flexibility means it is less likely to shear off. This is particularly important in the use of segmental grafts such as after split liver transplantation.

Quixil® also has a clear clot, making it easier to observe and manage bleeding points . . .

FloSeal® was identified as useful in a localised setting where a hole needs to be 'plugged' and where sutures might narrow the vessel, for example in hepatic venous bleeding, or where a suture is difficult to place. It expands within a hole and then coagulates. It was also suggested that FloSeal® is useful in small areas of profuse bleeding.

Bioglue was also discussed. This is extremely rigid, making its indications limited . . .

SURGICEL*NU-KNIT™ are useful for applying pressure to a cut surface while the patient's coagulopathy is stabilised. They may be left in, and are absorbed, although NU-KNIT™ may cause staining of the drain that can be confused with a bile leak.

Extracted from 'Advances and Methods in Liver Surgery', *European Journal of Gastroenterology & Hepatology* (2005), by Nigel Heaton, consultant surgeon, King's College Hospital, London, who performed George Best's liver transplant in July 2002.

'Hello?! . . . Canyi heariz?! . . . Hello, man! . . . Mam!' The GNER 10 a.m. London–Newcastle service has just pulled out of King's Cross. We're in coach 'G', the 'Quiet Zone', the part of the train designated for the use of passengers – customers – who want to get away from other customers who are nuisance-users of personal stereos and mobile phones. But does Gazza care? Gazza, because he's Gazza, 'the mouth of the Tyne', doesn't give a monkey's. He'll ride his mobie – 'Hang on, we're just gannin' in a tunnel! . . . We're oot! Canyiz heariz noo?!' – until the train edges into Newcastle Central station a touch under three hours later. By then we will all know that he's two days away from making a return visit to the no-frills, tough-love Cottonwood addiction treatment centre in Arizona where he'd first gone to be dried out and deal with his demons a year earlier, that he wants his mam to throw some of his shorts and T-shirts in the washing machine and nip down the town and buy him some flip-flops – 'Ah, man – flip-flops! Canna believe this. Forya feet! For the clinic! The clinic in Arizona!' – that he's trying to get two hundred grand back in tax from the tax man ('It doesn't come out of my money, does it? . . . How much is that? . . . Is it a good thing or a bad thing?'), that he's going to get his hair done at four and that he'd kill for a tab ('Are they the same as English cigarettes? Yi knaa, the ones you buy in the shop?').

A fat lad for most of his career in top-flight football with Tottenham and England, he's looking scarily thin, even gaunt, and – even for Gazza – weird. His hair has been dyed a sci-fi silver-blond, as have his eyebrows and goatee beard. His skin has been broiled to a fluorescent, burgundy-orange tandoori tan. He seems wired, hyper, something he puts down – as he'll eventually confide to nobody in particular and the carriage in general – to mixing his medication with too much Red Bull.

'We must conclude that within certain individuals a genie resides,' the American novelist Evan S. Connell once wrote, 'directing them to eminence of one sort or another, however commendable or bizarre. [W]e wish to descry this genie, to find where he or it lives, and fathom its nature; knowing that if we too possessed the demon we would not go unrecorded. The Earth's bright doors should spring open for us as well.

'So we look after the celebrities of the world, whether they are statesmen, actors, athletes or murderers, wondering at their essence . . . We seek to make friends with them in order that we may divine their secret and appropriate this to our own purpose. But the secret is hidden, ordinarily. We look and wait and listen, but divine nothing. The genie is not visible, not audible . . . The spirit is bottled, the radiance concealed, the mask set, a curtain drawn, so that you spend hours, days or weeks in the presence of some exceptional person without detecting much.'

Well, maybe. Gary Lineker, yes. Michael Owen, yes. Alan Shearer, perhaps. (Shearer had been in the same carriage on the same Newcastle-bound train two weeks earlier, travelling on a Sunday morning with his wife, and the 'keep out' signs had instantly gone up, creating an unbreachable cordon sanitaire; Shearer's wall-eyed, 'what-you-looking-at?', intimidating hard-man glare was as effective off the pitch as on. He had perfected the difficult trick of being unmissable and invisible at the same time.)

But Paul Gascoigne has never known what it means to keep the spirit bottled. There's no mask; he's always been as open as a book (and 'daft as a brush', as the former England manager Bobby Robson once said). Drunk or sober, George Best built walls around himself; he remained quiet and withdrawn. If he had a problem, his solution was never to talk about it but to go off and drown it in drink. He once said that he drank in order to withdraw even further into himself: 'It's always been that way, and when I'm on my own I think too much, it makes it worse. I don't talk to anyone, I don't stay, I just skip from place to place until I come to my senses.'

'Lonely. He was always lonely,' his first wife Angela said. 'But he brought his loneliness on himself because he didn't know how to relate to people. He never really became close to anyone. It was difficult for George or anyone else to break down those barriers he put up. He'd been pulled in all sorts of different directions throughout his life and career, so the withdrawal was very much in self-defence. It was very hard for him to give himself to any one person at any given time.'

He resisted revealing himself to psychiatrists or opening up at the few meetings of Alcoholics Anonymous that friends got him to attend. (Odd for somebody who, in the course of his lifetime, put his name to upwards of a dozen apparently 'self-confessional' books of autobiography. But the books had more to do with his personal finances than any genuine attempt to explain himself to himself. That was for wimps and wusses.)

'He sat there with his bloody glasses on the end of his nose and started asking me the same bloody silly twenty questions the press had been asking me for the past five years,' Best recalled of the psychiatric consultation Manchester United made him have in his final drunken days at the club. 'At some point I thought, this is madness, I'm sitting here being interviewed at great cost by some prick who's going to tell the club what they already know, that I'm daft as a brush. And I started laughing. Just burst out laughing in the middle of the interview. He looked at me in a funny way and then jotted something down.'

He twice went through the motions of checking himself into an in-patient rehab centre in northern California in the early eighties when he was playing for Milan Mandaric's San Jose Earthquakes, but later said he got himself released early from 'the prison' by spilling his guts in the way he knew they wanted and giving the counsellors (who in fact labelled him 'dishonest and superficial') the answers it was obvious they wanted to hear. 'If I was going to have to go dry for a while, then I wanted to suffer the horrors of withdrawal in the privacy of my own home, rather than in a hospital bed gawped at by all sorts of people,' Best later said. 'That form of therapy has proved useful to a lot of people and I don't have anything against it. I'm just not the sort of person who likes to talk about my inner feelings and found it near impossible to do so in front of a bunch of strangers.'

'I'm an alcoholic.' Gazza has been desperate for a bit of company. An unsuspecting young woman boarding the train at Peterborough and taking the seat opposite him has given him the opportunity to launch into the story of his life. He has established pretty quickly that his new travelling companion has never heard of him. 'You divven knaa who I am? You divven recognize iz? Okay,' he says. 'Right. Well. I was pretty well-known in me day, like. I did *Wogan* an' all of them. Ah've just telt me story to a book-writer to come oot in a few months. D'you knaa him? Hunter Davies. He wrote a book aboot the Beatles. He's pretty well known. He writes for the big papers – yi knaa, not the ones like the *Sun* . . . Ah've been in London just to see me counsellor. I need to change the medication . . . A lot of people have given iz a pat on the back for tellin' the truth an' that . . .'

His flow has been interrupted, as it will be repeatedly, by his mobile going. 'We desperately need that five grand,' Gazza says. 'Ah've got to give some to me dad for the car . . . There's a grand in it for you. Wedge . . . Cheers, pal.'

'Sorry,' he says to the girl sitting across from him. 'What was ah sayin'? Oh aye, 'boot bein' an alcoholic. I've been off it more than a year now. I'm going back to the clinic in Arizona in the middle of the fu . . . . Er, it's in the middle of the desert, miles from anywhere, on Wednesday. They're pretty hard. But it's worth it, like. Feels pretty good to wake up in the morning not feelin' like shit and bein' able to remember where you've been. But what's started to worry iz is, if I stay sober, will I turn into a boring person? Ah've always been well known for bein' a laugh. What if the price for being sober is turnin' into a sensible, boring tw . . . . It might soond daft to you, but I worry aboot that.'

'There is another Pelé called Maradona and there is another George Best called Paul Gascoigne,' Brian Glanville once wrote. Stan Seymour, the chairman of Newcastle United,

Gazza's first club, called him 'George Best without brains'. Gazza in turn had said that Best was 'scum', to which Best replied that at least he was by far the better player of the two: 'He wears a number 10 jersey. I thought it was his position, but it turns out to be his IQ.'

Gazza was twenty years younger than George Best – young enough for the trajectory of Best's career to be there as a blueprint for what not to do. Instead it turned into a gazeteer. Gascoigne went from Newcastle to Spurs to Lazio in Rome to Glasgow Rangers to Middlesbrough to Everton to Burnley to Gansu Tianma in the Chinese B league to Wolverhampton Wanderers reserves, in a professional career which lasted eighteen years.

In the six years after he left Manchester United, Best's travels took him to Dunstable Town, Stockport County, Cork Celtic, Fulham, Hibernian at the bottom of the Scottish First Division, and then Los Angeles Aztecs, Fort Lauderdale Strikers and San Jose Earthquakes in the Mickey-Mouse North American Soccer League. But right to the end he maintained that the common perception of wasted talent – that he was somebody who once held mountains in the palm of his hand and threw it all away – was wrong. The story of Best in bed with a bottle of champagne and a Miss World which ends with the words 'Oh, George, where did it all go wrong?' has been told so often that it won't bear repeating. An alternative version has an old newspaper seller standing in a raw Edinburgh wind turning to Best in his warm Turbo Saab listening to Fleetwood Mac and asking him why he threw it all away.

'He'd read the stories, he'd categorized the failures. He didn't want to know I'd had some fun along the way,' Best said through one of his ghosts. 'I may not have won as many medals as other players or appeared in the F.A. Cup final. I've never played in the World Cup finals. On the other hand I've done things most people only dream of: seen places, met all kinds of people, enjoyed the luxury of the best hotels in the world.'

'There are people who think I threw it all away,' Paul Gascoigne tells *his* ghost, Hunter Davies. 'They believe I could have done so much more with my talents if I hadn't been so self-indulgent and daft and drunk and stupid. I think the opposite. I think I have achieved far, far more than I ever expected to achieve, considering I'm me, stuck in this body and this head with all this going on . . . I've met so many people, earned so much, achieved so much, seen so much . . . I would have done much less in life if it hadn't been for football.'

As the train slows on its approach to Newcastle, Gazza is suddenly struck by a thought. 'You're not a journalist, are you?' he asks the woman whom he has been gabbing away happily to for two hours. 'Ah . . . I just thought you could be a journalist.' He hoists his Louis Vuitton carry-all on to his shoulder, grabs the matching weekend bag and pockets his phone, which rings straight away. He looks at it and shakes his head sadly. 'I wish they'd never invented mobiles,' he says.

In October 2005, Gascoigne was appointed manager of non-league Kettering Town. He was sacked thirty-nine days later, on what happened to be the weekend of George Best's funeral. The Kettering owner Imraan Ladak claimed the reason for the dismissal was that Gascoigne was 'under the influence of alcohol before, during and after several first-team games and training sessions' and urged him to seek 'professional medical assistance'.

'I'm No George Best' the headline in the *Sun* roared. But Gascoigne admitted he did have 'a double brandy before the match on the day after my friend George Best passed away'.

'The very nature of professional sport is in a way addictive – adrenaline can be very addictive – and that's why it's hard for players when they stop playing,' Gordon Taylor, the Professional Footballers' Association chief executive, said. 'We witnessed the problems with George Best and it looks to be repeating itself [with Gascoigne].'

'At the moment I think it is extremely unlikely he will live to the age that Best did,' Peter Kay of Sporting Chance, the charity set up to help sportsmen with addictions, added.

'I can never have a drink again,' Gazza had told the girl on the train that day. 'It's too nice.'

The legend of the holy drinker #13

Bestie's

'The rain falls hard on a humdrum town, this town has dragged you down.'

Manchester weather is a popular joke; it was a staple of broad, beery-faced music-hall turns for generations. The lumpen figures in the most sought-after L. S. Lowry paintings lean into a keening wind, weighed down by flapping tweeds and lumpy jumpers that are perpetually sodden from the smutty, ever-falling rain.

If folklore, and the filmmaker Mike Leigh, are to be believed, the weather is one of the main things Mancunians miss when they are away from what, before it developed a reputation for being a twenty-four-hour party place and the club capital of Europe, used to be known everywhere as 'raincoat city'. Towards the end of Leigh's film *Naked*, the Salford sociopath Johnny (part Liam Gallagher, part Shaun Ryder, all Manc chippiness and cutting sarcasm) and his downtrodden girlfriend, also from Manchester and also adrift in London, sing the following song, which Leigh apparently remembered from his childhood:

> Take me back to Manchester when it's raining.
> I want to wet me feet in Albert Square.
> I'm all agog
> For a good thick fog.
> I don't like the sun,
> I like it raining cats and dogs!
>
> I want to smell the odours of the Irwell.
> I want to feel the soot get in me 'air.

> *Oh, I don't want to roam,*
> *I want to get back 'ome*
> *To rainy*
> *Manchester . . .*

'I've got an 'ard-on,' Johnny says to Louise when they've stopped singing, sniggering, close to tears. We understand that he is as excited as much by the perversity of his longing for the direness of the grim north as by the fact of Louise lying next to him on their narrow Crouch End bed.

In 1976, Best flew out of the city of perpetual night into the cauterizing light of California. Taking his nightclub pallor to show it some rays. The problem with changing locations, though – 'doing a geographical' as addicts know it – is that you take you with you. No matter where you go, there you are.

Just before Christmas 1973, in partnership with his friends 'Waggy' Wagner and Colin Burne, co-owner of Reubens, he had opened Slack Alice's in an unpromising location in Bootle Street, one floor above street level when conventional wisdom about clubs always said go for a cellar, with a major Manchester city-centre cop shop on the corner. But *whoosh*! It had been a big whoosh, with Georgie himself proving a major attraction, and a licence to print money. It had brought in, on the one hand, Bruce Forsyth, Dave Allen and Jimmy Tarbuck, and on the other Mick Jagger, Brian Ferry, Eric Clapton, stars of show business old and new, plus the Granada Television regulars. They had persuaded a fantastic guy called Felix, who George knew from the Gomilla Grill in Majorca – always known as the 'Gorilla' Grill to the Quality Street gang and the others – to come over and take care of front-of-house. He was the Spanish waiter from central casting, and fronted up for George with the wisecracks and the corny patter and so on the way he liked.

A year later, in time for Christmas 1974, seeing Slack's doing such fantastic business they had opened Oscar's in what used to be the old Waldorf Hotel and devised a brilliant plan to make it a multi-purpose club to cater for all tastes at all times of the day. The first floor was Oscar's itself, which did real pub grub, bangers and mash, steak and kidney pie; on the top floor they had a private banqueting suite called the Dorian Gray; between that and the pub was a disco, but the real money-spinner was the wine bar on the ground floor, which opened for two hours around eleven. *Whoosh*!

Before long, Best and Colin Burne were helping themselves to £500 each in cash from the safe every night and taking it down to Soames, the upmarket Manchester casino. Malcolm Wagner wasn't a gambler, but his partners in Slack Alice's and Oscar's were soon at it during daylight hours at the races as well as at night, giving it some, doing their money.

It was a second addiction to add to the drinking (a third, if you included the sex). Manchester United had been relegated to the Second Division four months after he played his last match for them, at the end of the 1974 season. He didn't give football a thought for over a year but, by the time Fourth Division Stockport County approached him with an offer to turn out for them on a pay-for-play basis at the end of 1975, he wasn't in a position, what with the multiple addictions, the snowballing gambling debts, to say anything but yes. They cleaned up, as they knew they would, on the gate money, with 8,000 rather than the 3,000 they usually got coming in order that one day they would be able to say they had seen 'genius George'. It wasn't quite the Elephant Man yet, but things were headed that way, and he still hadn't turned thirty.

Only a few years earlier he'd loved getting his fame out and taking it round the block for a spin; he'd found it a turn-on being recognized. 'It was a marvellous feeling to walk down a street knowing everyone was looking at you and wishing they were in your shoes,' he said. 'Later on I would have given anything to go somewhere and be anonymous. I needed to be somewhere I could open a newspaper and not find my name in headlines, talk to a girl without it being in the gossip columns, walk down a street without somebody touching my clothing in the hope of a miracle cure – or a five-pound note.

'It got to be a real problem. Whereas once I'd get silly drunk, I'd just get nasty drunk because I knew that someone would try something bloody stupid. At the time, anywhere would have sounded better than another day in Manchester.'

With no training to do, and no boring commitments to give a shape to his day, he was staying drunk for months on end. 'I'd kill a bottle of vodka a day, easy, and a few more besides. I'd wander from club to club at night just drinking myself silly and then I'd not go home unless I had a bird. Any bird, it didn't matter.'

He once confided to his pal Parky that his number-one rule for success with women was to not be too particular: 'To be successful with ladies you must not make rules – like some people I know won't sleep with their friends' wives. Some won't sleep with married women, others don't like black girls, or Jewesses, or girls with big knockers or bandy legs. You shouldn't make rules about women because if they are willing they are worth while no matter who or what they are.

'That last piece of advice is very important because one or two ladies of my acquaintance would have had a bad time in a beauty contest, but they remain in my mind a long time after I've forgotten some of the lookers.'

In the book she wrote about the tempestuous time they spent together in California in the late seventies, Angie Best explains what George was referring to when he talked about his 'Coyote mornings': 'Coyotes, you see, when caught in a trap, will chew their own leg off rather than remain in the jaws of the trap; "coyote morning" refers to the fact that a man would rather chew a limb off than wake up the girl he'd slept with as he left, because she was so damn ugly.'

Best met Angie Janes in Los Angeles in 1976. He had just signed for the LA Aztecs and was sharing a 'bachelor pad' with the former Port Vale and Stockport County player, and his latest gags-man, Bobby McAlinden at Hermosa Beach. She was working as a personal trainer for Cher and other Hollywood types and living at Cher's house in the gated celebrity community at Malibu. And, given the ongoing melodrama surrounding George's relationship with women and booze, the monotony of his endless round of affairs and binges, this is more or less how they would go on living during the six years they spent shacked up together in (despite her best efforts) varying degrees of squalor in the sun. She grew as used to him ruining carpets and sofas with vomit ('furniture never did last very long in our house') as she did to him disappearing for days, even weeks sometimes, with the latest beach bunny or douche-bag waitress.

There was the inevitable occasional physical violence ('I quickly regained my composure and began to clean up the blood'), as well as the attritional emotional bludgeoning that is the consequence of living with a drunk: 'Whenever he came home like that he would always be aggressive and nasty because he would always be angry with himself for being in such a state. His best defence was usually offence at my expense.' When she wasn't around personally he would vent his frustration on her things: 'Our place on Hermosa Beach had a rubbish chute that fed a big container underneath the building, and on several occasions I had to grab a torch and climb into that damp, dark container to fish out my possessions. In fact, it got to be something of a ritual . . . He'd shoved everything down the chute, dirty and smashed up, just like the mood he was in.'

(It was a pattern that was to be repeated with his second wife Alex. On one occasion she came home to find her teddy-bear collection dumped in a hole that workmen had dug in the road outside their flat. Another time he burned her favourite Chanel suit and threw it in the bin.)

But, as even Best himself admitted, Angie was remarkably understanding about his sleeping around. 'I don't know to this day who that [latest] waitress was,' she writes in her book *George and Me*. 'But it's not about who she was or who any of them were. They were just warm bodies as far as George was concerned, warm bodies that gave him the attention he craved.

He just had a need. It didn't matter about anybody or anything, he just had to feed this need to have a warm body next to him when he was drunk. It really wasn't a personal thing . . . He just wanted someone near him to stop him feeling lonely when he was drunk and he always picked the nearest woman (he never drank at home on his own because we never kept any in the house). It didn't even matter what she looked like, as I found out later on several occasions when I disturbed him.' *Nobody is ugly after 2 a.m.*

In autumn 1976, Best flew back to England to play for Fulham in a team which also included Rodney Marsh (who was in the States playing for Tampa Bay Rowdies in the NASL) and Bobby Moore. The following spring he returned to California to play for the Aztecs, and so the pattern was set for the twilight years of his underperforming, drink-hobbled career.

The strange thing was that, for a while, he was happy. Rod Stewart came in some days and trained with the Aztecs, and Best hung out a bit with Rod; he made it in for training the mornings Rod was coming. And there was a Hugh Hefner-type called Ed Peters, whom he had been given an intro to by Malcolm Wagner back in Manchester and who was legendary for his pool parties awash with naked flesh and dope (although George never touched the dope): it was at an Ed Peters party that he met Angie Janes for the first time.

And there was Bestie's, formerly Hard Times, the beach bar he opened with Bobby 'Macca' a pleasant stroll from their bachelor sock. 'We'd go off there towards the end of the afternoon for a game of pool', he remembered, 'and some more drinks and it seemed like paradise.' Bestie's. His name above the door. Like Rick's Bar in Rick's Café Americaine. 'Of all the gin joints in all the towns in all the world . . .' He knew it all. Phyllis's. He would do tricks. One of them was to drop a penny piece on top of his shoe, then flip it up into the pocket of his shirt. He never failed.

He knew a place called Fat Face Fenners which catered for

those with a mid-morning thirst, so he'd roll up there for a few liveners. Then he'd go to the beach for a burger and chips with tortillas and salsa on the side. After that he'd head down to the Mermaid, a bar on the beach, where he could sit and watch the girls go skateboarding by in their bikinis and have a kip and get a tan for a couple of hours.

Naturally, the standard of football they were playing wasn't high, and the fans hadn't got a clue what they were watching. It was a very long way from Sir Matt's dream: 'this beautiful, unsullied expression of life'. But the sun never went in and the sand stayed warm and some nights he dossed down with the beach bums on the beach. That scene in *Casablanca* where Sam goes, 'Boss, boss! Ain't you going to bed?' and Bogey goes, 'Not right now,' and Sam goes, 'Ain't you planning on going to bed in the near future? . . . You ever going to bed?' and Bogey tells him, 'No! NO!' Bestie always wanted to feel that he was the last man in the world going to bed.

Which he often was. And too drunk or hung-over to go training. And snappy until he had put away the first few steadiers the following morning. Sound familiar? And then the benders and the guilt and the self-loathing and the taking it out on Angela when he got home – if he got home – not remembering where he had been or for how long on account of the blackouts and hallucinations. And so the suspensions. And the recriminations. And the moving on, to another team in another city, being whooped at by another load of lard-arse, know-nothing fans.

Two landmark events – their marriage and the birth of their son Calum – give the tenor of the lives they were leading in California as the seventies turned into the eighties. George asked Angie to marry him in January 1978, but said she had to be quick. She had walked out on him in London after he had wrapped a borrowed Alfa Romeo around a lamp-post outside Harrods while he was drunk. Visiting him in hospital next day she had walked in on a 'little soccer groupie' giving him a blow job on the bed. She was working as a bunny receptionist in the casino at the Playboy Club at the time, and a few days after the accident George had sauntered in. 'He had on the clothes he had been wearing when the accident happened,' she remembered, 'and they were covered in blood. His hair was still slightly matted too, and it looked as if he hadn't shaved for days. Luckily . . . the club were very understanding and let him in. But all he wanted to do of course was drink and gamble. He never once came over to talk to me, but I could see him watching me out of the corner of my eye. When he'd lost all his money, he stumbled out of the door and went home.'

They didn't live together, and barely saw each other, for nearly a year, and then suddenly he was on her doorstep in California begging her to be his wife. Now. Or, at least, pretty quick. They have given conflicting versions of who did the deal: he claimed she sold exclusive picture rights to the *Sun* ('which was romantic'); she says it was Ken Adams, his manager, who made the call ('I didn't know you could do something like that in those days!'). One thing is certain: the 'wedding' at the Candlelight Wedding Chapel in Las Vegas was a fiasco and a tabloid scam. They flew in and flew out, and by early evening he was changing to go and meet the boys down at Bestie's: 'I was dumbfounded. It was our wedding night. As he walked out the door, he said, "Don't wait up."'

By the time Calum was born in 1981 they were living in San Jose and he was experimenting with ways to cheat the Antabuse tablets that were supposed to make him sick if he so much as looked at a drink. He'd promised the people at the Earthquakes and he'd promised Angela, but he was actually holding the pills in his mouth or coughing them into his fist instead of swallowing them. He had had to make the concession to go on medication because in the early part of 1980 the drinking, even by his own standards, had become catastrophic. Instead of playing his first games for Milan Mandaric's team in San Jose, he had been on a seven-day bender at Bestie's – 'he was as drunk as a skunk and he smelt like a rat' – when Angela tracked him down to tell him she was pregnant. 'That's great!'

he told her. And then: 'I can't come home yet, I've got to finish this' – meaning his drinking session. 'As he picked up his glass again, I quietly left the bar.'

He had started using the Lancashire Hot Pot pub in San Jose as his local, and he was playing darts there the night Angela called him to tell him she thought she was going into labour. Calum was born on 6 February 1981, the twenty-third anniversary of Munich. The time of birth was given as 07.02, and George worked out that that meant it was two minutes past three in the afternoon, British time, the exact time of the crash.

'Having Calum proved one thing,' Best later said. 'Alcohol had become the most important thing in my life.' He was bang on it again within days of Calum coming home. Drinking heavier than ever, in fact. Having blackouts, DTs, hot and cold sweats. It was agreed that he would seek help at the Vesper Hospital's rehabilitation unit. The football club's insurance company would cover most of the treatment costs.

The problem was, he didn't think he was a bad man, as active alcoholics often feel, trying to get good. Neither did he think of himself as a sick man trying to get well, as recovering alcoholics are encouraged to do. He was George Best. 'Genius George'. Somebody who was standing up giving them all the 'My name is George and I am an alcoholic' bit, but who was only counting the days until he could be out having his next drink. Bestie's beckoned. Nights on the lash. His name was over the door. AA stands for Alive Again. It also stands for Altered Attitudes. George's were deep-seatedly, apparently unalterably, certainly suicidally the same. It was just over two years before Calum was born that Ann Best had died after refusing to get professional help.

'Hitting bottom'. This is perhaps the single idea of Alcoholics Anonymous with which non-alcoholics are most familiar – the car-crash moment after which nothing can be the same. AA attaches great importance to this phenomenon and regards the alcoholic who has not hit rock bottom as a poor prospect for their help. Conversely, they are inclined to explain their failure by saying that the individual who goes back to his alcoholism has not yet 'hit bottom'. AA says that bottom is different for different men and some may be dead before they reach it.

Angie Best believed that that moment had come for George on the morning she had to swerve to avoid the tramp weaving unsteadily down the centre of the highway and then realized when she looked in her rear-view mirror that the tramp staggering through the rain in the tattered tracksuit was her husband. It was a low point, but it wasn't the lowest. Maybe that was the time he went missing at Christmas for two days, then eight days, then New Year came and went and it looked like she might have to bring in the police. But then he came back and aimed an onyx ashtray at her head, and she stabbed him. He came home after two weeks away, called his latest girlfriend to come and collect him, and she took a carving knife and stabbed him a deep stab in the buttock. 'He looked from the ashtray to me, and back at the ashtray . . . Luckily, it was a drunkard's throw and I managed to duck out of the way. It hit a cupboard and broke it . . . I had never seen so much blood before.'

By this stage he was resorting to stealing money to get his next drink – taking money from Angela's handbag and from the bottle in the kitchen where they put their loose change. She had taken to hiding the car keys, and so he would have to walk a long way – seven or eight miles – until he found a bar. Once there, he would install himself at the counter and hope one of the regulars would take pity on him when his dimes and quarters had run out. One day, finding himself with only a few cents left, he had dipped a woman's handbag for a ten-dollar note. 'I looked up and saw that the barman was talking to the guy at the other end of the bar', he later remembered, 'and, in an instant, stuck my hand into her bag. I fished around and pulled out a bill, which I stuck straight into my pocket. My heart was thumping at what I'd done and I couldn't face seeing the girl when she came back. So I drained the last of my beer, shouted goodbye to the barman and walked out . . . I wasn't going to give it back. I needed it for more drink and I walked to another bar a couple of blocks away to get it.'

He hated San Jose. It was too small – and too small-time – for him. What he loved was the anonymity to be found down the coast in LA and in the rest of big-city America. There he meant nothing to Joe Briefcase or anybody else whose company he might stumble into. Great quote: 'I rate California very highly. The people are nuts, the birds had never heard of George Best but it didn't make any difference. It did my ego good to make it with girls who didn't know me from Alf Ramsey.'

That was one of the things he loved in the States: he could go into a bar with all these screaming Americans watching gridiron and he could dissolve, fade clean away. And if he got talking to somebody and they asked what he did for a living, he would make something up. He loved that anonymity because it also meant there was no one to shop him to the smudgers.

He liked to take off by himself; take the short hop on a plane to LA and check into a little motel down the beach. After his first stay in rehab, just after Calum was born, he stayed sober for nine months, bathing the baby, strolling the baby, posing for happy snaps which show him clean-shaven, dead-eyed, preparing to run. Which show him bewildered in this drift of normal life in which normal people are apparently happy to live. The happiness that reads white: a pure, polished, unembellished white, uncontaminated by the restless accidents of life. A tract house on a new subdivision with a wife, a baby, Dallas the dog. *And then . . . something: alcohol, a problem with alcohol, always alcohol.*

He hit bottom in early 1982. He was off the wagon and going pretty strong. He was on a roar. He was in a bar called Hennessy's on the beach in LA, sitting by himself at the bar as he liked to, and it was a small thing, not a crash of cymbals

moment or anything involving self-abasement or throwing up.

'Do you know who I am?' He had never said such a thing in his life. But he didn't mean it like that. He had been using Hennessy's a lot over the years. This same barman had served him many times. Now he didn't know who he was. 'I used to have Bestie's.' He was dishevelled, blurred, pasty, all bloated up. The stillness of the beachfront bar was strange and portentous. The look on the barman's face. Bestie the soccer-hero Brit. That was his moment of hitting bottom. A pretty sick man. Time to go home.

It was a time tunnel from that quiet moment to the echoing quiet of a holding cell, two years later, in London, in 1984. Same story. Drink, clubs, driving while drunk, champagne, women, a big roar. Except this time he headbutted a policeman. Already cuffed, he tried to deck one of the small army of Bill sent to arrest him.

It seems remarkable, given his career of writing off cars, philandering and domestic violence, and his multiple addictions to alcohol, gambling and sex, that he only went to prison once.

But it's an exchange that took place in the canteen at Southwark Crown Court before sentencing that has entered Best legend. Jeff Powell of the *Mail* and Hugh McIlvanney, then of the *Observer*, had been called as character witnesses. His friends and defence team were staring into the bottom of their coffee cups, with nothing to say. Then George glanced across at them with a smile. 'Well, I suppose that's the knighthood fucked,' he said.

Do you know who I am?

Did you get to be who you are?

He could put his hand up to that one. He could answer yes to that.

Ten

*The room was filled with objects on tasteful display. Flannel
jerseys draped along the walls, caps with souvenir buttons
pinned to the visors, there were newspaper pages framed and
hung. Brian did a reverent tour, examining autographed bats
ranked on custom wall fittings, game bats beautifully
grained, some with pine tar on the choke. There were stadium seats labelled like rare botanical specimens – Ebbets
Field, Shibe Park, Griffith Stadium. He nearly touched an
old catcher's mitt set on a pedestal . . . but he managed to
hold back. He looked at autographed baseballs in plexiglass
globes. He leaned over display cases that held cigarette
cards, ticket stubs, the signed contracts of famous players,
nineteenth-century baseball board games, bubblegum wrappers that carried the pinkish likenesses of men from Brian's
youth, their names a kind of poetry floating down the
decades.*

There was going to have to be a King of Collectors. And he
was going to have to be a bit of an oddball, along the lines of
old Marvin Lundy in Don DeLillo's vast novel *Underworld*. I
had decided that before I'd ever heard of Leslie Millman or
tried to track him down.

DeLillo is unparalleled as a media-age rune-reader and
surfer of the zeitgeist, and his instincts have been shown to be
dead-on, eerily right. The Twin Towers, for example, loom
large as symbols bristling with dark significance in DeLillo's
work dating back at least twenty years. He tackled the psy-
chopathology of collecting in his 1978 novel *Running Dog*.
But that was about a collector's panting eagerness to track
down footage of an orgy rumoured to have taken place in
Hitler's bunker under the Reich Chancellery in Berlin in 1945.

That would go under the heading of 'erotica' (dirty pictures for rich people).

Sporting memorabilia have surged in popularity in recent years. There has been a market boom in programmes, autographs, personalized boots. DeLillo's collector, Marvin Lundy, lives in a house 'steeped in aquarium dimness' whose basement contains his lifetime collection of baseball memorabilia. The jewel in the collection is the home-run ball with which the New York Giants beat the New York Dodgers in the dying seconds of a legendary game at the Polo Grounds in the Bronx in 1951. For the people in *Underworld*, the baseball with which Bobby Thomson wrote himself into history – 'The Shot Heard Round the World', the papers called it – has become a powerful symbol of the lost innocence of a pre-nuclear, pre-digitized world.

Over the years, collectors have competed to possess the ball because they want to possess a moment which remains pure, unreproduced except in memory, and is not available to be freeze-framed or focus-shifted or enhanced – *exhausting all the reality stored in its magnetic pores* – unlike the endlessly repeated news footage of violent tragedy and the sports instant replay.

'The scratchier an old film or audiotape, the clearer the action in a way,' DeLillo writes. 'Because it's not in competition for our attention with a thousand other pieces of action. Because it's something that's preserved and unique.'

As with the Bobby Thomson home-run ball, it occurred to me, so with George Best's boots. His boyhood boots with the teams and the goal tallies handwritten on the sides, which have never turned up. The boots are unaccounted for. You're looking at a £100K item, right there.

So it was a home-grown version of DeLillo's Marvin Lundy, as well as a lead on Best's palaeozoic-period leather boots, I was hoping to find on the day I got in a taxi to go and visit Leslie Millman at his house in the north Manchester suburb of Prestwich.

The further north we drove, past Strangeways and Lower Broughton, past Crumpsall and the Cliff and into Hilton Park with its big stand-alone houses and large population of Hasidic Jews, the more the driver was impressed. 'Nice. Oh, very nice.' He was Lithuanian, it turned out, a relatively recent arrival who spoke little English and depended heavily on his sat-nav device. He was particularly made-up that the small enclave where Millman lived squatted behind a pair of heavy, electronically controlled, intercom-activated gates. 'Very secured!'

It was a modern development of mini-townhouse properties, two-storeyed with balconied first-floor windows. The gates swung open and we proceeded to the end of the cul-de-sac, where Leslie Millman was waiting to meet us. 'Nice place! Very nice!' the driver called out. Millman stepped forward from his doorway looking suspicious and asked the taxi driver to set a time when he would come back and collect me. He wrote some digits down on a piece of paper, the entry code for the gate.

> Brian . . . wanted to talk about old ball-players, stadium dimensions, about nicknames and minor-league towns. That's why he was here, to surrender himself to longing, to listen to his host recite the anecdotal texts, all the passed-down stories of bonehead plays and swirling brawls, the pitching duels that carried into twilight, stories that Marvin had been collecting for half a century.

Leslie Millman was a man in his fifties, with a pale, wintering, convalescent look. He looked like a larger man who had recently lost weight, or a slight man who, late in life, was starting to carry extra weight around his middle. He seemed world-weary.

It was August 2005, the first Saturday of the new football season, although the papers were giving great play to the third Ashes Test at Old Trafford. United had just beaten Everton 2–0 at Goodison in a lunchtime kick-off. He had watched the game on a sofa pulled up close to the large television which seems to be the only modern piece of furniture he owns.

'I have a little bit of a museum you might be interested to see,' he had said on the phone. 'I have things belonging to both of them [Best and Edwards] that few people have ever seen.'

I got a sense of the museum in a room directly off the hall – dozens of neatly shelved books with red ManU spines, regimented ring folders, a cellophane-wrapped copy of Charles Buchan's *Football Monthly* with a fresh-faced Duncan Edwards on the cover, a glimpse of a table-top display case with a green baize bed. It was a room the developers had probably offered as a small utility room or shower room/toilet.

Millman led the way up a staircase hung with framed United memorabilia – black and white glossy photographs (Sir Matt signing Denis Law, Sir Matt with various trophies), programmes, prints of famous album covers depicting Best as either the fifth Beatle (on the crossing at Abbey Road) or as all the Beatles in a reworking of Klaus Voorman's iconic line drawing for *Revolver*.

A window was open, rippling the curtain behind the television, but the room felt airless. He collects art nouveau and Arts and Crafts-period furniture in addition to his footballing interests, and a number of heavy, dark wood cabinets and bureaux were crowded into the small space, like manual labourers standing shoulder-to-shoulder in the crush at the Stretford End or the Leazes or the Spion Kop. 'Don't put that there!' he cautioned sharply when I went to put my glass of water by my feet on the baby-pink carpet. 'You're sure to knock it over.'

'People collect, collect, always collecting. There's people they go after anything out of wartime Germany. Naziana. This is major collectors looking for big history. Does that mean the objects in this room are total trivia? What's the word I'm looking for that sounds like you're getting injected with a vaccine in a fleshy part of your arm?'

'Innocuous'.

'Innocuous. What am I, innocuous? This is history, back-page. From back to front. Happy, tragic, desperate.' Marvin shifted his gaze. 'In this trunk right here I have the one thing that my whole life for the past twenty-two years I was trying to collect . . . I tracked, I searched and finally I found it and bought it, eighteen months ago, and I don't even put it on display. I keep it in the trunk, out of sight . . . It's the Bobby Thomson home-run ball, which I traced it back starting with rumours in the business. It wasn't even a business back then, just a few interested parties with someone's telephone number or first name, the skimpiest kind of lead that I pursued with a fury.'

Millman went to his first match at Old Trafford in 1962 when he was twelve, the season of what he thinks of as one of the 'major cataclysms' in the club's history: the signing from Torino of Denis Law ('the original Cantona'). His first time. And yet it felt oddly familiar. He had this feeling – that he'd been there before. Perhaps it was genetic, something in the genes, passed down from the father to the son. His father had supported the club from the year dot, when they were a two-bit, Second Division side that hadn't won anything for years and City were the glamour team. From the age of no more than about six, his father would walk five miles across the city and duck in through a hole in the fence at the United training ground at Broughton Park.

But no, it wasn't about inheritance. Strange how you could forget, but he *had* been there before: 1958, in February, the first match after Munich, the FA Cup tie against Sheffield Wednesday when, as an eight-year-old, he had gone with his father to buy tickets – the same tickets, same flimsy pieces of pale green- or pink-tinted raffle-ticket-like paper that now change hands for hundreds of pounds. Anything to do with Munich. The tickets for the match against Red Star the night before the crash fetch thousands. *Stadion Jugoslovenske*

Narodne Armije – Kup Evropskih Sampiona. A red star on a blue field. A very rare item.

Copies of the programme for the game United should have played against Wolves on the Saturday, two days after their return from Belgrade, with the Babes all named in the team, fetch in the high thousands. Once the news reached them that the plane had crashed and it was looking serious, the printers, Nicholls, had ordered the whole print run of 30–40,000 to be destroyed. No more than fifteen to eighteen copies have ever surfaced, and a good number of them have, in one way or another, beaten a path to Leslie Millman's door. He was there. He is entitled.

> *When you see a thing like that, a thing that becomes a news-reel, you begin to feel you are a carrier of some solemn scrap of history.*

In the pubs, people said it was like those days in 1940 when a hush came over the whole place as soon as the BBC news bulletins came on the air. Glasses stopped clinking. Everybody stopped ordering drinks as the latest casualty lists came over. Men in dungarees flocked out of the factories on Trafford Park at five o'clock and stood in incredulous groups round the evening paper display bills. Girls stood sobbing under the giant stand. People rushed outside. People wanted to be together. The singular moment of city-wide post-war grief and anguish.

I asked Millman if it was correct to assume that a connection with Munich gave an item added value? 'Nothing has a value,' he said flatly. 'Nobody saw any value in these things. There was no market for this product. They were worth pennies. Literally pennies.' He murmured something under his breath about what sounded like 'people from Hampshire or the Cotswolds'.

'Programmes, tickets, photographs, magazines are available to anybody. *Anybody*,' he continued. 'The common man. They now all think – the auction houses and these – you're getting it every which way but loose.'

Every which way but loose. This put a different spin on him.

Maybe he had been in a beat combo in the sixties, maybe even in the Whirlwinds with Malcolm 'Waggy' Wagner, also from Prestwich, and the people who formed the rump of 10cc? The moroseness, the impatience, the art nouveau furniture, the melancholy junk from yesteryear decking the walls of his house like the content of his inner world had seemed to disqualify him from the casual pop reference. Far from it, however. In real life, as the business card he presented me with as I was leaving made clear, Millman is the MD of 'Streetwize Accessories', a division of the Ace Supply Company Ltd, a firm specializing in 'a wide and varied range of automotive products' designed 'to add quality and style to cars'. According to the Streetwize on-line catalogue, their products include 'exterior undercar neon lights, an extensive range of interior flexible lighting tubes, neon tubes and black lights, interior dash lights, neon dancing frames and LED phone holders that will make car interiors glow'. Also 'tie-downs, towropes, booster cables and adhesive tapes, exclusive designer car mats, steering wheel covers, horns and repair kits'. Everything, in short, for the boy footballer with aspirations to one day own his own Beckingham Palace. Tomorrow's collectibles today.

And there was a back room, because isn't there always a back room . . . and in the back room weren't the magazines cased in acetate folders; maybe these were rare issues or rare labels, or maybe the folders themselves were the fetish items here, dust-veneered, handled, nearly opaque some of them, a dullish sort of plastic with a faint odour and prophylactic feel, like condoms for reading matter, and maybe there's another room where you need to whisper a password and this is the room with folders only, empty folders, handled a thousand times . . . raincoated men with National Geographics, *furtively thumbing labels.*

'It's rocking-horse manure, this stuff,' Millman said. 'Some of it has been seen by nobody.' We had repaired to his little downstairs museum, where the many hundreds of items of his collection were all filed, indexed, cross-referenced, price-coded and precisely, protectively wrapped to professional museum standard. In fact, he said around a dozen pieces were currently on loan to the Manchester United museum at Old Trafford, volunteered out of the kindness of his heart. So it irked him (he was obviously still chafing) that, when Phillips auctioneers put the gems of the Leslie Millman Collection under the hammer in a special sale in a suite in Old Trafford's North Stand in 2000, the club charged him £10,000 for the privilege.

That sale had been forced on him by a divorce settlement. It wasn't the first. The collection we were standing in the middle of was the third he had pulled together. 'I had to sell the first time because I was broke, the second time because of the divorce,' he said, shuffling through the contents of a box file he had reached for from a shelf. 'But you realize it's only money. It'll come back. You're either a winner, or you're not. It's like: you've been on a team all your life, you've won World Cup, Champions League, Premiership medals and you move in the end to another team and you think, "What do I do?" So you do it all again. And you can. Because you're a winner.'

The task of reassembling his collection had been made easier by the fact that, rather than having to go back to scavenging among what others are busily engaged in throwing out or consigning to the incinerator, people now bring stuff to him. His reputation as the Reds' King of Collectors has spread far and wide, so people roll up at his door all the time – that is, at the estate's security gate – bearing intimate scraps of their own or other people's lives. He collects public documents: significant sporting luncheon and dinner menus, autographed by the guests of honour, team sheets, team photographs, signed contracts, players' passes from the pre- and immediate post-war years, rare bubblegum and cigarette cards, tickets; match programmes are the bread and butter.

But it's documents relating less to the public figure than the private person that he's constantly on the lookout for, and which fetch the highest prices. He dipped into one of his files and produced a coloured postcard, prophylactically wrapped. The front showed a picture of the modern, multi-storey hotel in the centre of Belgrade where the United team stayed the night before Munich. On the back were the signatures of most of the squad, including Duncan Edwards, Roger Byrne and the others who died in the crash. The autographs had been collected by an Irish pipe-fitter working in Yugoslavia at the time, a friend of Danny Blanchflower's, who was then playing for Aston Villa, and therefore a friend of Danny's brother Jackie, one of the founder Babes.

'He was made welcome,' Millman explained, 'walked into the hotel shop, bought two postcards, and got the team to sign them. He originally called me nine years ago and asked for two grand. I told him to call the club; he did and asked for five grand, and they sent him packing. The phone went again nine years later. No preamble. "Well, d'you want it?" He said he was in Salford and could be here in ten minutes. He ran in and left the taxi with its engine running. Turned out he'd lost one of the cards and said he was bound to lose the other. But I still wasn't going to pay what he was asking. As he dashed back to the cab, he stopped at the front door. "Five hundred? In cash?" I happened to have five hundred in the house.'

He plucked out a second postcard with the Babes' signatures on the back and the period picture of another hotel, this one in Madrid, on the front. It had been the property of a woman who had won a *Manchester Evening Chronicle* competition with a prize of a trip to the match in Spain. 'Went a bit mad at the end of her life,' Millman said. 'Thrust it on a man in the street. He was gay, and obviously had no interest in football. Gave him six hundred for it.'

'We're here in our basements with tremendous history on our walls. And I'll tell you something, you'll see I'm right. There's men in the coming years they'll pay fortunes for these objects. They'll pay unbelievable, because this is desperation speaking . . .

'Men come here to see my collection.'

'Yes.'

'They come and they don't want to leave. The phone rings, it's the family – where is he? This is the fraternity of missing men.'

The documents are here because the dead men whose traces they contain are not. A lot of what Millman owns is startlingly personal: he showed me photographs taken at Duncan Edwards's funeral, the order of service, family snapshots, personal letters (revealing signature only, not the content). Despite what he had said earlier about the Babes not adding value, materials bearing on their deaths and Munich seem to form a core of the collection. 'Edwards and four of the others who died', he said, 'were world-class. If they hadn't died, the little runt Charlton, a plodder like that, might never have emerged. There might never have been a George Best or a Denis Law because the others would have held their places for years. Bobby Moore wouldn't have got a sniff.'

'Who could be interested in a laundry list?' the eminent Edwardian historian Sir Paul Vinogradov allegedly exclaimed. The answer today is that many people could, and clearly are. Laundry lists, betting slips, holiday postcards, Christmas cards, cheques, certificates of birth, passports, certificates of death . . . Millman seems to see these forensic fragments of strangers' lives as if they were rooted in some meaningful way in his own.

It is a confusion which is one of the defining characteristics of a time when the line separating private from collective memory has grown blurred to the point where, thanks to media saturation, the collective memory of any recent generation has now become the individual memory of each of its members. Munich, the assassination of Kennedy, the death of Diana, 9/11: private memory has largely been subsumed in public spectacle.

I had one last question: the boots. Had he heard anything on the grapevine, rumours in collecting circles about the pair of football boots that George Best had customized in a personal way rather than have the people from Nike or Adidas do it for him? I imagined they would have enormous collector-appeal to a certain kind of yearning, backward-glancing collector.

'I'm interested in paper ephemera,' he said, 'as you could have noticed. Not medals. I can buy a [player's] shirt. [But] I'm not interested in buying it.'

Did he ever collect those kinds of things? 'I've got 'em rid. I have no player's personal items. They are a mark of their achievements. I did nothing to achieve them.'

A few days later I received an email from Millman:

. . . I have no problem with supplying material for any publication but please understand my stuff is expensive and in many cases are one offs, I would expect you to propose some deal if I am to advise and loan material . . . , I have worked in past with others and this is the correct procedure.

I am not looking for ridiculous numbers just a sensible and reasonable something. If you feel that you are unable to simply pay for anything that could be beneficial to you in a publication then simply leave the matter where it is.

I am not saying this for any personal gain, I will give whatever to Charity, I do not need to earn in this manner but I expect that my efforts/knowledge & collection have some value, and this is the only way I have worked with several others in the past, supplying images and some text for those persons, all of which made decent profits, but then you would with the two most powerful words in world football, "manchester united".

Regards
LESLIE

Brian was ashamed by other men's obsessions. They exposed his own middling drift, the voice he heard, soft, faint and faraway, that told him not to bother.

The legend of the holy drinker #46

The Phene

Sir Matt passed away in January 1994. When he died he was president of the club and had become, as his obituarist noted in *The Times*, 'part of the soul of Manchester'. Something that Busby had said in a speech he gave on the day he was made a Freeman of Manchester in 1967 was quoted by several of the papers: 'There are two . . . aspects of the game that have always impressed me. I love its drama, its smooth playing skill – and its great occasions, for example the Cup Final in the great arena at Wembley. I feel a sense of romance, wonder and mystery, a sense of poetry. On such occasions the game is larger than life.'

It was this sentiment which had been the bond between Busby, the stoic romantic who had established Manchester United's reputation as one of the greatest club sides in English football history, and the ruined romantic who, in the years since he ceased being one of the club's greatest-ever players, had been leading an aimless, itinerant and – at least viewed from the outside, seen from Matt Busby's perspective – a dissolute and pointless existence. What Best and Busby shared was a commitment to artistry and inspiration – a touch of show biz – combined with an innate distrust of the blackboard coaching, the numbers and systems that Busby's successors had brought to Manchester United ('All that bollocks about zonal defence and 4–4–2 and all that crap,' as Best once put it).

'Go out and enjoy it' had been the Old Man's only tactical intervention, and Best maintained to the end that he had decided to get out when the enjoyment disappeared. (Naturally, it was never this simple – the counter-claim that he was getting too out of it to enjoy it was also true, and is probably more relevant.)

He returned to Manchester for the funeral. It took place twenty years almost to the day after his last appearance in the

Old Trafford dressing room – the day which had ended with him sitting on his own in the darkened stadium knowing that he had ceased to be a part of Manchester United. The coincidence of dates pushed up the emotional temperature of an occasion which was already heavy with sentiment and sentimental associations.

He hadn't seen some of the 1968 team for years, and many in the crowds lining the route held black and white photographs of the Busby Babes up at the windows of their coach en route from the ground to St John's Roman Catholic church in Chorlton. Also scattered among the crowd were pictures, wilted by the rain, of their own, younger selves, the Boys of '68. It had been twenty-six years since the historic victory over Benfica; thirty-six years since Munich. Even before Munich, the precocious achievements of Busby's young, almost mythological heroes had been the talking point of millions. Even people who never normally thought about football had suddenly taken notice.

'The reason for their surge of popularity is quite simple,' the sports editor of the *Daily Telegraph* wrote in the wake of United's second consecutive League championship in 1957. 'Under the expert and fatherly guidance of Matt Busby, a happy band of young men have developed a team spirit and comradeship seldom equalled in any of our sports. They give all they have for the club, and in all circumstances they try to play football.' Bobby Charlton once gave a profound analysis of the reason for their excellence: he said playing well was the only means they had at their disposal of speaking to the manager; performance on the field was the way of bridging the gap between their own callowness and Busby's eminence. 'He was a legendary figure, part of the world we never stopped dreaming about. His presence seemed to electrify all of us. We would tear into the game like lions. It was the only way, in a sense, that we could communicate with him at that time. We would all have run ourselves into the ground for him.'

Lying in his bed in the Rechts der Isar hospital, Busby had

prayed to die, something which he afterwards said he felt ashamed to have done. He was given the last rites twice, but he survived. 'It is the object of life to build,' he said many years later. 'When I knew the worst at Munich I understood at last that to pray for death as I had done was wrong and cowardly. I knew somehow I must succeed again for the sake of those who died. Otherwise my life would have no meaning.'

It was clear Busby believed that, by murdering his talent, Best had sinned against something more fundamental than just a team or a sport; he had disappointed the best hopes of millions of ordinary people and, in the process, stripped his own life of dignity and meaning. There was that remark of his about Best and Edwards, made many years earlier: 'I suppose, in their own ways, they both died, didn't they?'

After the funeral breakfast at Old Trafford, a smaller group, with George Best included in it, followed Busby's coffin to its final resting place in a cemetery which Best had come to know well during his life in Manchester.

Mrs Fullaway's house in Aycliffe Avenue was just a street away from Southern Cemetery, and the bus stop where George would wait for the bus to take him to Old Trafford in those days when he was still too young to drive was on Moor Road, opposite the cemetery's main entrance. His home-from-home at Phyllis's was a short drive along Princess Road, past the cemetery's eastern perimeter wall.

As Best recalled: 'We passed so close to Mrs Fullaway's house that I could have reached out and touched the front door and we also went past the bus stop where I used to hide from Sir Matt. I thought of all the times I had seen him driving down that road and it made it all so much more emotional for me.

'I started thinking of all the fun times I had had during my time there and that first day at Mrs Fullaway's, when Eric McMordie and I had found Manchester so strange and decided to run away . . . Plus the times, later on, when I used to dodge police patrol cars on the way home from nights out.

My whole life flashed before me, even if it seemed like a life-time ago that I had lived in that house and first dreamed of being a star footballer . . . I had to dry my eyes before I got off the bus but the tears started again when they lowered Sir Matt into the ground . . . It was the hardest day I'd had to go through since my mother's death.'

A city as big as Manchester is a vast palimpsest in which one language is written – or scribbled – on top of another. Close to Aycliffe Avenue, and adjacent to the municipal allotments next to Southern Cemetery on Princess Road, was a piece of waste-land overgrown with weeds and shielded from the traffic by high hawthorn hedges which had long been a favourite haunt of the prostitutes from Moss Side and local courting couples. On a Saturday night in October 1977, a young Scottish woman called Jean Jordan had been picked up by a man and had driven with him to the allotments by Southern Cemetery. After he parked, she had led the way into the deeper darkness some yards from the car, and there had become the sixth vic-tim of the Yorkshire Ripper.

In the Nile and Reno clubs in Moss Side, in the days when Best and Mike Summerbee were regulars at the weekend-long shebeens, she had been known as 'Scotch Jean'. Speeding towards the M63 link with the trans-Pennine motorway direct to Leeds and Bradford, Jordan's killer had also passed so close to Mrs Fullaway's house that he could have reached out and touched the front door.

A week later he returned to the piece of wasteland on Princess Road in an attempt to retrieve the traceable five-pound note he had given Jean Jordan and, when he failed to find it, had mutilated her already badly decomposed body.

In the minds of many people, the cemetery area of Chorlton stopped being the place where Georgie Best once lived only a year after he had packed and moved away. He had given them great diversion, but he was history. The area had been over-written with a darker association. It had become the place where the Ripper once struck, instead.

At last, now, I was thoroughly conscious that I desired alcohol. But what of it? I wasn't afraid of John Barleycorn. I had associated with him too long. I was wise in the matter of drink. I was discreet. Never again would I drink to excess. I knew the dangers and the pitfalls of John Barleycorn, the various ways by which he had tried to kill me in the past. But all that was past, long past. Never again would I drink myself to stupefaction. Never again would I get drunk. All I wanted, and all I would take, was just enough to glow and warm me, to kick geniality alive in me and put laughter in my throat and stir the maggots of imagination slightly in my brain. Oh, I was thoroughly master of myself, and of John Barleycorn.

Jack London, *John Barleycorn*

It was no accident that Best got his first national write-ups for his performance in the away game against Chelsea in 1964, when both teams applauded him off at the end. It was one of the many great displays he would give over the years at Chelsea. 'Something about the ground used to lift him,' Matt Busby once remarked, 'make him play better. But I shall always remember that first time. Ever after that when we went to Stamford Bridge I thought I ought to have phoned the police and told them a murder was about to be committed.'

'I loved playing at Chelsea', Best said, 'because they were the glamour side of London.' Stamford Bridge was at the centre of what Christopher Booker in *The Neophiliacs* described scathingly as 'the shining, youthful, vigorous New England which had thrust its way irresistibly up through the decaying, class-ridden atrophy of the old . . . an England bathed in the dazzling release of unprecedented new talent and energy; the England of brilliant young playwrights, of irreverent film directors and television men, of a glittering new classless culture that was the cynosure of the world'. Booker's catalogue of the types of people who had equally helped to 'transform the flavour of English life' – the fashion designers, the hair stylists,

the cookery experts, the owners of antique shops, discothe-
ques, little restaurants, the interior designers, the television
conversationalists – could have been a roll-call of the new converts to football packing the private boxes at Stamford Bridge
on Saturdays. The pre-match lunches at Alvaro's on the King's
Road, where the likes of Terence Stamp, Michael Caine,
Michael Crawford and Cathy McGowan from *Ready, Steady,
Go* gathered to discuss Terry Venables's form and the new
paisleys at Granny Takes a Trip, were a central part of the
mythology of 'Swinging London'. Did Georgie want to take
his seat at the high table of the popocracy? Do bears shit in the
woods?

When he started to slip away to London to escape the mad
stranglehold his fame had put on him in Manchester, it seemed
natural that he would gravitate towards Chelsea and the
King's Road. In the late seventies he used to lay low in a pub in
Belgravia called the Duke of Wellington with Rodney Marsh
and Bobby Moore and other members of the Fulham team that
the press took to calling the 'Showbiz XI'. (Twenty-five years
later, the same pub would become the regular hang-out for
Paul Gascoigne when he was living with the millionaire entre-
preneur/disc jockey Chris Evans and his then wife Billie Piper.)
Belgravia, though, was way out of Best's league and so, when
he came back to England to live after his years in California, he
started looking a half a mile or so further west for a pub that
fitted him and a flat that was close enough to it that he would
be able to climb into the bottle with the least hindrance possible every morning.

For the best part of the next twenty years he was part of the
furniture of a small Victorian local tucked away well off the
tourist route in the maze of back streets between the King's
Road and the river. Anybody who wanted to get him – bailiffs,
football writers, the producers of television programmes from
which he was absconding – always knew they could get him at
the Phene. He would skip breakfast and be in the Phene drinking white wine at ten in the morning. He would stagger back

to his flat at four in the afternoon, collapse into bed for a nap and then return for the closing session. The Phene was the centre of his existence and he was content to spend entire days there, the days silting up into weeks and months, with the occasional foray to the betting shop, the off-licence on the corner, now and again (food was never high on the list of priorities) to Pucci's pizzeria on the King's Road. It was an everyday routine. The same, week in and week out, for years.

The nearby houses on Cheyne Walk, on the Embankment, were some of the most valuable real estate in Europe. Keith Richards and Mick Jagger had both owned houses there in the sixties; Guinnesses and Gettys had passed grand Cheyne Walk properties down through the generations. But Cadogan Estates, who owned most of this part of Chelsea, had made provision for a generous volume of public housing. The white stucco terraces and blocks of mansion flats were separated by several modern council estates and regular sets of red-brick Victorian 'dwellings'. It was this very metropolitan mix of high and low which gave the area its special character. In that sense, the Phene, the pub that Best sniffed out and managed (as he always managed) to bend to his ways, was a typical Chelsea local.

Essentially a single, smoky, small room with a circular bar, it stands on the corner of a little tree-lined street called Margaretta Terrace which was built in 1851 for prosperous tradesmen but whose elegance and proximity to Westminster made it popular with early Victorian MPs as a suitable place to set up their mistresses. George Melly rented a room in Margaretta Terrace for a number of years after the war, when he was singing with the Mick Mulligan band. Mulligan himself lodged round the corner with his girlfriend in a house owned by a couple called John and Buddy. The Bohemian demi-monde atmosphere as described by Melly in his autobiography is still clearly recognizable more than fifty years later:

'John was a very sweet shy man with glasses and a moustache who liked to play the trumpet. Buddy was a big positive woman whose charm and personal kindness just about made up for her extreme right-wing views. Even so we were always having terrible shout-ups, especially after several of the huge gin and tonics which were as much a part of the ambience as the click of the backgammon counters and the placing of bets over the telephone . . . Mick and Pam weren't at Buddy and John's very long. One night after a concert they had a terrible row, and Mick gave Pam a black eye and rushed out into the night. I was just about to eat a delicious plateful of cold roast beef in the kitchen . . . I put down my knife and fork and walked along the embankment. Mick was leaning on the wall staring at the oily water.'

Eamon Dunphy has described how, when he knew him, Best always liked bars that functioned as 'a home for those who didn't belong anywhere else . . . Bars where human vulnerability was not frowned upon, was, on the contrary, celebrated.' The playwright Ted Whitehead was a Phene regular, and Michael Angelis, who was in Whitehead's first play at the Royal Court in Sloane Square, had started to go in with his girlfriend Helen Worth, 'Gail Tilsley' in *Coronation Street*, who knew George from Manchester. The Phene attracted a constant through-flow of familiar faces from Granadaland, and they were never troubled by the hardcore of regulars, which was mainly made up of postmen, refuse collectors and local tradesmen who Best quickly established could be relied on for both their discretion and their practical help. Whatever he wanted doing – shelves built, a coat of paint thrown on the walls over unsightly blood spatters from the ruckus a few nights before, a lock changed after the latest girlfriend had walked or he had turfed her out – he could always find somebody in the Phene who could be depended on to do it.

It was a pub whose character changed with the seasons. In the winter months, with its burgundy flock wallpaper and gilded alcove moulding, it was dark, cave-like, clubby. But as soon as the days lengthened the large garden would fill up with City boys and Hoorays and 'Sloaney pony' girls loudly ordering kir royales and jugs of Pimm's. People wearing 'shades' indoors, air kisses at the bar.

The one constant was the grizzled figure at his corner table, half-hidden himself but with an unobstructed view of the door. He didn't invite conversation and, if the look he shot them over his glasses didn't deter unwanted visitors from invading his space, he didn't mind letting them have the rough edge of his tongue.

For somebody who, like his friend Rod Stewart, was rarely photographed without at least one generic blonde actress-slash-model in tow, Best was a man who seemed to luxuriate in his own company. Whenever I would see him in the Phene in the last years – old man's glasses low on his nose, *Daily Mirror* crossword propped up protectively in front of him – he'd remind me of the life-lagged narrator of Peter Handke's short novel *The Afternoon of a Writer*. After a day spent not getting any words down on the page, the writer of the title habitually hauls his carcass to the local 'gin mill' to lose himself among 'the faces that could be associated only with this particular room, with this smoke and artificial light': 'He recalled certain particulars concerning each one of them. Not a few had told him the whole story of their lives, most of which he had forgotten by the next day . . . For today he required no more, no sight or conversation, and above all nothing new. Just to rest, to close his eyes and ears; just to inhale and exhale would be effort enough.'

'Getting drunk: there was no doubt that that was always the quest,' Martin Amis once wrote of his father Kingsley. 'Being drunk had its points, but getting drunk was the good bit.'

First in and last out. Best liked to breathe in the opening-time cellar smells and observe the shapes the slanting light cut through the fixtures and fittings; he liked to stare into the distance and listen to London.

His friends lied on his behalf and said he wasn't there when wives, girlfriends and creditors were in hot pursuit on the phone; the bar staff laced his 'orange juice' with vodka and

tipped brandies into his coffee in the periods when he was supposed to be drying out. A charismatic, oddly shy, easily worried
creature, in an atmospherically controlled, security-patrolled,
guaranteed 70 per cent proof protected environment. The same
thing that makes you live can kill you in the end.

> *I spoiled this city for myself. I didn't realize it, but the days
> came along one after another, and then two years were gone,
> and everything was gone, and I was gone.*
>   F. Scott Fitzgerald, *Babylon Revisited*

He had announced his arrival in Chelsea by having a typically
crash-and-burn affair with a 'tempestuous' glamour model
called Angie Lynne, who had left the *Coronation Street* actor
Chris Quinten to move in with Best in Oakley Street. She was
his girlfriend when he went to prison for three months for
drink-driving and assault, and she flew with him to Mauritius
after he had trousered a cheque for telling the story of his life
inside, in early 1985. But it rained on their paradise island, he
drank after promising not to, they had fights, she gave as good
as she got, and he couldn't wait to get back to his place among
the regulars in his brown corner in the Phene. (Tony Adams
once said that he had found a definition of insanity that suited
him and his behaviour: making the same mistake over and
over again and expecting a different result.)

'"Hi, I've just earned fifteen grand for the story of our first
night together!" It was George on the phone,' Alex Best writes
in her book *Always Alex*, 'sounding incredibly pleased with
himself.'

In the last years most of his trips to exotic parts were as the
'guest' of one of the red-top papers, which became the vehicle
for the bathos-laden real-life soap that in the trade earned itself
the nickname 'BestEnders'. 'For our second wedding anniversary the *Daily Star* offered to take us to the beautiful island of
Mauritius . . . The *Daily Mail* asked to do a story about
George's rapid recovery and I'd always fancied Mustique . . .
In June we headed off to Corfu . . .' Between the accounts of

how she had been given black eyes and broken arms and had her hair hacked off in the night by her drunken husband, Alex Best's book is a litany of tabloid-funded trips to faraway places with George. A beating and a pay day. Another love-rat scandal, another 'BestEnders' episode sold to the pops. This was the very modern transactional mess that their nine-year-long marriage quickly turned into.

Without her knowledge, Best sold his account of the first 'night of passion' that he and Alex Pursey had together to the *News of the World*. She was shocked; she thought it made her sound 'cheap' and 'a bimbo'. But she learned. The heroic life consists of a very long afterwards, and even legends have to earn their corn. The eventless life that Best continually claimed to crave was one that he couldn't afford to live. His wife found out that he was planning to divorce her by picking up the paper. The last image of Best that we are likely to see – unless others besides his agent were busy with their camera phones in his ward in the Cromwell Hospital – is the terrible 'death bed' picture splashed across the front page of the *News of the World* on the last Sunday of his life.

Alex was an air hostess working for Virgin when they met. She was a Home Counties girl who had posed for photo love stories in comics such as *Jackie* and *My Guy* and had done some topless modelling. She had recently split up with the Wimbledon footballer John Scales and was twenty-six years Best's junior. He had set places he went looking for 'talent': Blushes on the King's Road, Blondes in Mayfair, Johnny Gold's celebrity hang-out Tramp in Jermyn Street and the Dover Street Wine Bar. He met Alex at Tramp and invited her over for a drink the next day.

As she later recalled: 'I remember thinking that we'd be meeting in some classy bar, full of beautiful people, as Chelsea is so up-market . . . But the reality couldn't have been more different. George had invited me to his local pub, the Phene, [and] as I walked in I don't know what shocked me most, the hideous flocked wallpaper and luridly patterned sticky carpet or the tables of very old men. There were even a few Chelsea Pensioners . . . George was sitting at what I would later discover was his table, with an enormous glass of white wine in front of him. I say glass, but it was actually more like a goldfish bowl . . . He didn't touch it for ages, then drank the lot in one go.'

He proposed to her in the Phene, they went into the Phene on the morning of their wedding and, when he came over to visit from California, Calum would have to sit in the Phene and watch his dad get drunk. Best would even take the shepherd's pies she had made into the Phene to share with the regulars, and only came home to sleep.

When he eventually took her to see his basement flat around the corner, it was also far from what Alex with her *OK!* ideas of fame and glamour had had in mind: 'The decor was shabby and looked as if it hadn't been touched since the Sixties; the grey carpets were threadbare and the furniture was falling apart. The boiler didn't work properly and in the summer you could only get hot water if the boiler was on, so if I wanted a bath the flat would end up sweltering and there wasn't even a garden to cool down in. The kitchen was so small it could barely fit two people. There wasn't even a washing machine so I would end up hand-washing [my underwear] in the sink.'

She was too well-brought-up to mention the vomit stains on the armchairs and sofa, but she would find out soon enough that's what they were. 'And this was all the property he had – there was no country mansion, no holiday home somewhere exotic . . . He certainly hadn't got the lifestyle that you might expect.'

On his return to the UK after his years in California he had been declared bankrupt for non-payment of tax. Throughout the eighties he had scraped together a living from a combination of exhibition matches and speaking engagements for not a lot of money at supporters' evenings and in working men's clubs. Mary Shatila, the woman he had been living with at the time Alex Pursey came on the scene (they had met in Blondes), had done her best to keep him afloat. But, by the mid-nineties, his right leg, which he had injured when he was still playing for United and which had later been further damaged by a severe thrombosis, was too far gone to allow him to play; his reputation for chronic unreliability and flakiness had seen the speaking engagements virtually dry up.

His father and some friends in Northern Ireland had organized a testimonial match and dinner for him in 1988, which had raised £110,000. But he had made his notorious *Wogan* appearance ('Terry, I like screwing, all right?' 'What do you do in your spare time?' 'Screw') eighteen months later and was back to blowing whatever money did come in in the casinos of the West End. He demanded to be paid in cash for any work that he did and loved showing off his 'wedge'. But Alex had opened the door on a number of occasions and found men threatening to take away their furniture for unpaid bills.

Together with his agent Phil Hughes, she decided that George 'was a class act and we didn't want him wasting his time in dives for no money'. He had done some radio work for the London commercial station LBC, and in 1995 he signed a lucrative contract to appear as a pundit on Saturday afternoons on Sky Sports. But as a precaution they always had either Clive Allen or Alan Mullery standing by in case the bottle (as it sometimes did) got to Bestie first. His tactics were simple: he'd go to the pub – sometimes the Phene, other times the Wellesley, another pub nearby – and refuse to come out. The car sent to fetch him would be outside with its engine gunning, but he would refuse to move.

'I prefer not to.' The famous mantra repeated by Bartleby the scrivener throughout Herman Melville's story of that name is the phrase nobody would have been surprised to have found engraved on George Best's heart. The thing Bartleby, like Best, preferred not to do was the task he had been hired to perform. Why Bartleby chose not to copy the legal documents his employer put on his desk is a puzzle that has occupied literary scholars for a full century and a half. Bartleby answers an advertisement, is hired and promptly sets to copying with boundless energy day and night, with no breaks for meals. One day, abruptly, for no discernible reason, he stops. He won't do his job. 'I would prefer not to.'

'One prime thing was this – he was always there – first in the morning, continually through the day, and the last at night', Melville writes. 'For long periods he would stand looking out, at his pale window behind the screen, upon the dead brick wall . . . in one of those dead-wall reveries of his.

'. . . At all events, he would do no copying. At last, in reply to my urgings, he informed me that he had permanently given up copying . . . "I have given up copying," he said, and slid aside.' All along the way, when asked for his reasons, Bartleby only says: 'I prefer not to.'

His giving up is unsettling; in a society geared to succeeding, to being 'cheerfully industrious', it is a dangerously transgressive act. Why does he do it? Maybe because he can. The 'arch refuser'. The serious artist who refuses to copy, who instead reaches out for originality. Frank Lentricchia has written that his employer senses, 'though he does not know that he does, some danger in Bartleby's sadness . . . In his heart he would cast Bartleby out to a place alone, "absolutely alone in the universe".'

The viewers of Sky Sports' *Soccer Saturday* watch a panel of ex-footballers watching football on television, giving them verbal updates on what's happening. By agreeing to take part, George was once again expected to perform as part of a team. A team of talking heads tied to their screens as effectively as supermarket assistants tied to their check-out tills; a panel of physically thickened, middle-aged men of mixed reputations all giving out this same message: Football is easy; life is tough.

Bartleby lurches deathward from the outset: the outcome of Melville's fable of existential refusal is that eventually Bartleby starves himself to death. Best's poison was drink.

He made attempts to stop – or, more accurately, gestures in the direction of being stopped. His friend Jimmy Greaves, a recovering alcoholic who has been dry for many years, was sceptical about the effectiveness of aversion drugs. 'It doesn't stop you thinking alcoholic and that's what you've got to get rid of before you can be cured,' he said. 'You can be off the drink for months and yet, subconsciously, be planning a collision with the stuff somewhere up ahead. The implant, which has a time span attached to its effect, encourages that thinking. I don't believe in it.'

From the eighties onwards, though, Best made regular trips to Denmark to have Antabuse aversion tablets sewn into pockets in the lining of his stomach. When the effects wore off and he was plunged into the cycle of bingeing and blacking out once more – or, more typically, *before* the effects wore off and he was gambling how sick it would make him to add just a little more wine to the white wine spritzer, to make that double brandy a treble – he would book himself a two- or three-week stay at a health farm and try to commit himself to the loneliness and monotony of the gym.

The objective of checking himself into the fat farms at Henlow Grange in Bedfordshire or Forest Mere in Hampshire was to rest his liver and give it a chance to heal. The reality, though, was inevitably very different: he would continue putting the drink away on or off the premises and leave feeling at least as beaten up as when he arrived.

Late in 1998, a court ruled that he had to give up the flat in Oakley Street that had been his refuge for fourteen years and really the only place he had ever thought of as his own. They moved in with Alex's parents in the Surrey suburbs, but he carried on with his routine, driving up to London to the Phene every day. Eventually she found them another flat which conformed to all the conditions of where he wanted to live: it was still in Chelsea, still close to his haunts, still within lurching distance of the pub.

They had a fight and she broke her arm soon after moving in. He threw her violently to the floor and stormed off to the pub, and she had to get herself to casualty. He was on spirits now as well as the wine; there was a bottle of Pinot Grigio by the bed to top up his insatiable thirst. He was preferring not to turn up at Sky most Saturdays, but when he did Make-up had to go to work: his skin was blotchy, his eyes jaundiced, his nose crusted with scabs. The programme-makers liked to joke that viewers tuned in just to see if George Best was still alive. One day Alex saw a pitiful old man in a whacked-out tracksuit collapse ahead of her in the street, stinking of drink. 'Ravaged' was the word. George.

His neighbours got used to seeing him on the street sometimes, just wandering, with a faraway look in his eyes. Like he didn't even see everybody watching him. Or they weren't there. After spending some time with Joe DiMaggio, the American writer Gay Talese thought that look was the consequence of fame. It was the same look Talese had seen in the eyes of Greta Garbo: 'Because when people got so famous that there was no one else on their level – no one else had a life at that pitch of hyperexistence – then, it was like the other people didn't quite have existence . . . they simply weren't there.'

The firefighters at Chelsea fire station, which was mid-way between the Phene and another pub that was part of his usual beat, would make him up a bed for the night if they came across him unconscious on a bench or saw him staggering home, looking excessively the worse for wear.

The stomach pains started early in 2000 – acute, stabbing pains which would make him vomit and cough up blood, and which he attempted to dose with brandy, which would simultaneously drown and inflame his spongiform, already largely necrotic, liver.

At his funeral, Professor Williams, Best's consultant at the Cromwell, an expensive private hospital in London, would recall the frisson of excitement that ran through his department when news got round that George Best was in for a consultation, although he himself wasn't entirely sure at the time, he said, who George Best was. A quarter of an hour after walking into 'the Prof's' office in March 2000 he was in bed in the liver unit, attached to a saline drip, and would remain there for two months. 'Professor Williams had made it clear that I couldn't drink again,' Best remembered, 'but I reasoned that doctors and their ilk always paint the blackest picture they can.' He sold the story of his cirrhosis to a Sunday paper on discharge and by July was hitting the bottle again.

After offering him a safe haven for much of what turned out to be the last year of his life, Stephen Purdew, the owner of Champney's 'spa retreat' at Forest Mere, would eventually evict Best, calling him 'a stumbling pathetic drunk'. A former hunting lodge on the edge of a lake, Forest Mere stands in 150 acres of woodland on the edge of the New Forest near Liphook. In an irony that certainly wasn't lost on Best, who was busy getting himself barred from every pub and wine bar in the area, the grounds at Forest Mere also accommodate Sporting Chance, the charity set up by the former Arsenal and England captain Tony Adams to help sportsmen with addictions.

When his teammate Paul Merson had come out publicly with his own addictions to alcohol, gambling and cocaine, Adams had seen it as the sign of a weak man. 'Personally I dreaded going into a treatment centre. That would have been total humiliation for a winner,' he wrote in his autobiography. 'Now I can see that a strong man is one who is open to his feelings, be they happy or sad, confident or vulnerable.'

Adams acknowledges that, for a time, he became a 'recovery bore' – 'so evangelical about this way of life that I was trying to give it to other people'. And there is no doubt that this would have been George Best's attitude towards him: his punch-ups on Sporting Chance's doorstep, at the Royal Anchor in Liphook, his marathon sessions at Folly's wine bar in Petersfield and sodden returns to Forest Mere were a calculated affront. Peter Kay, Sporting Chance's chief executive, said that Best had finally agreed to an assessment at the clinic shortly before the final relapse leading to his death. 'He was addicted to alcohol. But he had a secondary addiction and that was George Best. It's the pressure of being a genius. If you're a genius then you think you have to be a genius every day of your life.

'Alcoholism is a disease of denial. When George precluded himself from our treatment by going out on that bender [instead of coming in], we knew he wouldn't live much longer. We knew that was the end for him.'

By 2001, the setting was different – a cottage by the sea in a village called Portavogie in County Down, close to Carol, George's 'religious' sister – but the craving, and the routine, was grindingly, dismally familiar. At one point the local priest, foreseeing a site of pilgrimage, another Irish shrine (so Alex thought), came to the door to suggest that George might choose to be buried in the local churchyard. They went home to England to start another round of the Antabuse implants that were the only way he could stay sober enough for long enough to make himself a candidate for the liver from a cadaver donor which he and everybody else knew by then was the only thing that was going to keep him alive.

'First your talent goes, then your money goes, then your friends go,' goes the sporting adage. Best's friends had remained supportive and available, on the whole, in spite of his serial rejections and provocations. But his best friends for many years by then had been pubs rather than people. And, in the period he was out of circulation building himself up for his operation and then convalescing after it, the pubs that had so steadfastly stood by him, providing him with a psychic as well as a local bearing, began to either disappear or change so radically he barely recognized them.

The Beehive, for example, where he used to go to play pool in the afternoons, was demolished for a new townhouse development. The King's Head & Eight Bells on Cheyne Walk was given an eau-de-Nil exterior and relaunched as the Chelsea Brasserie. The Front Page became the (despite its name, much more upmarket) Pig's Ear, where the second-in-line to the

throne and his girlfriend were sometimes spotted. Most daunt-
ingly, and disorientatingly for him, though, was the way time
had moved on at the Phene during his absence. First, the pug-
nacious little guv'nor, for thirty years the central prop of the
place and George's co-conspirator, died. Then his widow
decided to sell. New people inevitably meant new ideas. The
flocking went, the comfortable but tatty bench seating went,
the gilded moulding went and everything was given a coat of
neutral, designer grey matt paint. Worse: the word 'gastro' was
introduced. The upstairs room became a restaurant specializing in Scandinavian cooking. Gravadlax and other health-pro-
moting fish dishes became available in the bar. The regulars
wandered further afield to other, unreconstructed locals. The
Phene, constant as the northern star, was now the Phene only
in name. It was like a death in the family.

There was a sense of shedding. Shedding and falling. Everything falling away. He was given the transplant in July 2002,
two months after his fifty-sixth birthday. He took the first step
on the road of drinking himself to death for a second time a
week or two after he turned fifty-seven. There was a lurid public bust-up with Alex, and a series of gruesome pictures in the
papers. The *Mail on Sunday* pulled the plug on his column and
his 'roadshow' with Jimmy Greaves had to be cancelled when
the public voted with their wallets and stayed away.

The shedding and falling, the subtraction, gathered pace.
His wife divorced him and disappeared on to prime-time television to conduct a public flirtation with an iffy earl called
Lord Brocket. He was arrested for drink-driving again while
Alex was on *I'm a Celebrity . . .*, which, if the papers were to
be believed, he was watching 'round the clock', and hit with a
twenty-month ban. His friend Stephen Purdew said he wanted
him out of Forest Mere.

So here he was. The lovable nogoodnik, lovable no longer.
He had no wife, no way of moving himself from A to B, no visible means of support, no house and no pub that he could
think of any more as home. He was a pariah; a compulsive

gambler, woman-beater and stumbling drunk, running out of reasons to remain alive.

'I'm a peasant,' the former heavyweight champion Mike Tyson said around this time, at the end of his last comeback fight. 'At one point, I thought life was about acquiring things. Life is totally about losing everything.'

Best ended up drinking in the company of a woman called Gina in a council house that was a dirty version – gerbils in a cage in the bath, the reek of cats – of the one he had grown up in on the Cregagh.

If life had taught him anything, it seemed to be the one thing he started off knowing: that he'd rather be nothing than a nobody.

Eleven

'The really gifted ones, the ones that make it out of here still on the upswing, if they get to the Show –'
'Meaning professional [tennis] you mean.'
'In the Show they'll get all they want of being made into statues to be looked at and poked at and discussed, and then some.'

David Foster Wallace, *Infinite Jest*

This space was clearly a model for how a body ought to be: enclosed, contained, sealed. The ideal body: without flesh of any kind, old or young, beautiful or battered, scented or smelly; without movement, external or internal; without appetites . . . Not a place of fluids, organs, muscles, tendons and bones all in a constant, precarious and living tension with each other, but a vacant, hollow, whited chamber, scraped clean, cleared of any evidence of the grotesque embarrassments of an actual life.

David Batchelor, *Chromophobia*

Because of the backwards-leaning angle the body makes in relation to the plinth – he is bearing all his weight on his left foot, his right foot pulled well back to hoof the ball the length of Market Street, skywards in the direction of Dudley Castle – it was necessary to insert a rod running right through his body from the left shoulder to his left ankle, with a metre or so left protruding for eventual insertion into the channel that had been prepared for it in the concrete core of the pedestal. Four further rods descend from the corners of the bronze base of the statue to reinforce its stability and unmovability.

Because it is hollow it is surprisingly light: it only weighs half a tonne. It was transported horizontally on a flat-bed truck from the foundry in Milton Keynes and lowered slowly into place by crane. It was then left wrapped in tarpaulin and rope overnight. In his closing remarks at the unveiling ceremony the following morning, His Worshipful the Mayor of Dudley Councillor Fred Hunt thanked Mrs Sarah Anne Edwards and Sir Bobby Charlton, the Revd Geoffrey Johnston of St Francis's, Dudley, his council colleagues who had helped make the emplacement of the statue of Duncan Edwards in the marketplace a reality, and then . . . and then he went on to thank the . . . the chap . . . the man who . . . 'the bloke what done it'.

It says a great deal about James Butler that he is able to relate this without rancour. Without, in fact, seeming to think it is particularly unusual. 'There were masses of people there,' he remembers. 'I've never seen so many people in the centre of Dudley. You couldn't move for people. I mean, a lot of them were great fans of Duncan Edwards. But they had also come to see Bobby Charlton, and wherever he went, the crowd sort of went with him. I was just a bystander. I made sure I was down in the crowd in case anything went wrong with the unveiling. I was ready to pull the cloth off, in case it got snagged or anything . . . "The bloke what done it"! It was great.'

Butler is a Royal Academician, which is only one of the things that makes him bang out of fashion. He's a figurative artist. He makes likenesses. In bronze. To public commission. Of the honoured dead, figures at the crossing point between the sacred and the secular; civic symbols of the virtues of public service and patriotic sacrifice. Generals. Prime ministers. Local worthies, like His Worshipful the Mayor of Dudley Councillor Fred Hunt. And also – although this is a recent development, coinciding with the increasing foreign influence in English football and the erection of towering, bone-white skeletal stadium structures, monuments to football's new status as a global sport owned by global telecommunications and media organizations – homegrown footballers of the old school and folkloric football-club managers and chairmen. In addition to Duncan Edwards, Butler's recent commissions have included statues of Billy Wright and Stan Cullis for the Wolves ground at Molineux, and Sir Jack Walker, the former chairman of Blackburn Rovers.

At seventy, Butler is the age Edwards would have been had he lived. He is of a time that pre-dates this time when, as an artist, 'you can send anything to Italy and the buggers'll carve it'. (He was speaking here of Marc Quinn's Trafalgar Square statue of the thalidomide victim Alison Lapper, which he describes as 'gruesome'.) 'Amazing. Amazing thing to want to put on a plinth,' he says, 'but then that's the way things are nowadays. Beauty is not something that is considered to be of any value. It's the reverse, isn't it? You never get beautiful objects any more. No one under the age of fifty does objects which are supposed to have beauty in them – everybody does things which are 'kin awful. We all know life is 'kin awful. [His swallowing the first part of the word is a period thing, a relic of a past where it was considered not done for a man to swear in front of a woman.] You don't need to tell me. You don't do a handsome-looking girl any more, you do one that's been disfigured in some way or other.'

The Beverley Sisters are the kind of girls Butler would have found handsome-looking in their time and, while appreciating the kitschness of it all, he was delighted when the three of them launched immediately into one of their fifties song-and-dance routines in the courtyard of the Warwickshire farm where he lives the time they came to see the Billy Wright statue he was working on in the studio. Wright, of course, got married to Joy, the non-twin Beverley sister, when he was still the England and Wolverhampton Wanderers captain, and the pair of them were a sort of Posh and Becks, if you can picture Posh and Becks re-imaged as a cardiganed Terry and a home-permed June, of that long-gone, infinitely more innocent time.

Wright was the player Duncan Edwards was expected to succeed as national-team captain. The FA apprenticed him to Wright. They trained together, they roomed together, they took the honours which were showered on them with the same modest grace. Wright was a pall-bearer at Edwards's funeral.

The Beverley Sisters cried when he showed them into the studio where the sculpted clay figure of Billy Wright stood, awaiting casting – 'wracked sobs'. Mrs Edwards cried when she came to view the figure of her son; she took his cold right hand, which was about on a level with her head, as she had when she said her goodbyes the last time she saw Duncan in the chapel of the Rechts der Isar hospital, and sobbed. 'She was looking at the hand, she didn't look at the head,' Butler says. 'A great old duck. A tiny little lady. And I said to her, "What d'you think, Mrs Edwards?" "It's amazing," she said. "It's wonderful. You've even got the veins in his hand." And I said, "What about the head, Mrs Edwards? Does it look like him?" And she looked up like that, and she said: "That's my boy.'"

How to present the dead as though they were still alive, while acknowledging that they are irrecoverably dead? It is the age-old problem of memorial art: we mourn the dead because they are gone but not (yet) forgotten, but also because we believe our mourning can bring them back to life. Butler's daughters have grown up with what their father does for a living; they aren't spooked by the studio with its dark, lifelike shapes and shadows. But they had friends, particularly when they were younger, who didn't like to go into the barn where likenesses, bagged in plastic when they weren't being worked, were being devotedly grown out of clay.

It is possible to take a photograph of Edwards's statue, head-on and from below with a tree in leaf behind it, which suggests it is in a *rus in urbe*, countryside-in-the-city, softly landscaped setting. It is, of course, only another piece of street furniture in a busy city street liberally littered with benches, bollards, waste bins and hectically competing commercial and council signage.

'There is nothing as invisible as monuments,' the Austrian writer Robert Musil once wrote. The day I went to visit James Butler in Warwickshire was farmers'-market day in Dudley, and a cable from the hog-roast stall had been threaded casually between the foot and the ball at the base of the Edwards plinth and plugged into a generator, which was pushed up hard against the other side of it. The inscription was hidden behind a metal sign giving the details and date of the next market.

A monument in its oldest and most original sense is a human creation, erected for the specific purpose of keeping single human deeds or events alive in the minds of future generations. Monuments owe their name to their function as agents of memory. 'I suppose a statue like that,' Butler says of his own statue of Edwards, 'I suppose it will live longer than the actual person, won't it? I mean, it will still be there when the memory of the person is fading. We all remember Duncan Edwards now. But in, say, fifty years, even thirty years, most people won't know about him. They won't have a clear idea of what he was. He'll just be a footballer. And then I suppose the new architect of Dudley will say, "We don't want that bloody thing stuck in the middle there, we'll shove it somewhere else."'

In the Lord Mayor's parlour at the reception which followed the unveiling, Butler got chatting to Sir Bobby Charlton, who had spoken so movingly about his relationship with Duncan. 'Mrs Edwards was sitting down having a cup of tea, and old Bobby Charlton, he said to me, "You see all the rings she's wearing?" And I looked, and she's got a hand full of really ornate heavy gold rings. He said, "That's her wealth. She carries all her wealth around in her rings." Wouldn't leave it at home under the bed or anything. He said that somebody had a go at her, trying to pull 'em off her, and she hit him with these bloody rings and ripped his face to pieces. He ran off screaming. She was an extremely tough old duck.'

Manchester United's first game after George Best died was away at West Ham on the Sunday. Sir Bobby put on his black tie and mourner's greatcoat to join Sir Trevor Brooking in a brief ceremony to honour Best's memory on the touchline at Upton Park.

Mrs Edwards had grown very close to Bobby over the years. He had first come to her house as a skinny schoolboy and had done as much as anybody to keep Duncan's memory alive; after herself, he had been the chief memory-keeper. But, ironically, he wasn't her favourite among the United players who had come after Duncan. She had a special favourite who never seemed quiet and shy to her, like Bobby, although he was. Who always seemed outward and fearless and full of everything. That was George.

The legend of the holy drinker #2

The Egerton Arms

It snowed in Manchester on the day of the funeral – big fat flakes drifting down in front of the big screen in Exchange Square which drew only a modest crowd of shoppers. Everything – shopping, eating, drinking, queuing for the tram – took place against a background of Christmas muzak, and most people were too busy getting ready for Christmas – too rushed and cold – to stop.

The street-sweepers started drifting into the Egerton Arms around eleven, just as the funeral was starting that Saturday morning. The televisions were on and tuned to MUTV, the club's cable channel, which was taking the BBC's feed of the service from Stormont. There were three sets, all mounted high on the wall among the Christmas lights and streamers – two in the main bar and one in a smaller room off it. This was a kind of shrine to United, with large framed team photographs and banners. It was occupied by mostly younger men – men young enough to still play in the pub's own team – who sat silently with their pints in front of them, eyes fixed on the television over the door. The street-sweepers in their yellow reflector visi-vests settled themselves in the other room and shook out their *Sun*s and *Mirror*s, concentrated on making their roll-ups and generally made it clear they had no interest in the ceremony which was blasting out in both bars.

The Egerton Arms is beneath the same railway bridge at Salford station that used to make the glasses tremble on the shelves at the Brown Bull when trains rolled across it. It is in a narrow cobbled street around the back of where the Brown Bull used to be, and where a B&B called The Copperheads now stands, packed into the same dark Victorian building, a traditional pub with thick etched windows and a suspicious, nicotined interior. Its closeness to the Granada studios is indi-cated by a mock-official, Rotary Club-style wooden plaque outside the men's toilets declaring that 'these new loos were opened in 1970 by Stan Ogden, Alan Howard and Billy Walker' – three *Coronation Street* stalwarts, noted drinkers on- and off-screen.

As more customers drifted in – they were all men, all old enough to be scowlingly out of sympathy with the new English fondness for shrines and breast-beating and public displays of emotion – everybody except the occupants of the small bar went on pretending to be too busy studying form or doing their numbers for the lottery to have any attention left over for the speechifying and the sentimental balladeering coming out of the television. Every so often, though – when Calum broke down in the middle of his tribute to his father, when Brian Kennedy changed the words of Don McLean's song about Vincent (one of Best's favourites) to include a direct reference to George ('When no hope was left inside, on that starry, starry night / You led your life as legends often do / Ah but I could have told you, Georgie, this world was never meant for one as beautiful as you') – then they watched over the rims of their glasses or shyly out of the corners of their eyes, resisting the direct engagement which could result in them welling up or, worse, be seen to be shedding tears.

The previous evening I had seen a man very like the men in the Egerton Arms loitering in an embarrassed way in the rain by the Best shrine at Old Trafford, which stretched the whole length of Sir Matt Busby Way. He waited until he thought nobody was looking and then quickly placed the bunch of red roses he had concealed inside his coat on the pavement next to a 1957 League Championship replica shirt. After a few minutes he went back and just as shyly tore the wrapping paper a bit so that the heads of the flowers could be seen. Attached to them was a note typical of the hundreds of poems and notes and messages inscribed on scarves and shirts and other treasured possessions that had been laid in the dirt and wet: 'Your with Sir Matt now George he will take care of you again,' it said. 'Thank you for living my dream.'

The bronze figure of Sir Matt looks out over the road that now bears his name, from a vantage point above the biggest football merchandise megastore in Europe. In the days following his death in 1994, the fans came in their tens of thousands, bringing back to the Old Man the souvenirs and mementoes they believed to be rightly his – the love of sport as an expression of the love of place.

In a poetic gesture which was also a literalization of 'Abide with Me', the traditional football hymn, the supporters' scarves and replica jerseys were washed in the club laundry after the funeral and then put into bales. The bales were embedded in the base of the statue of Busby outside the East Stand. And there, invisible yet tangible, like the memories invested in them, for the time being they remain.

Asked once while he was still a young man how he would like to die, Best replied: 'Sometimes when I think about my life I keep remembering a scene from that film *Charlie Bubbles*. It's right at the end when Charlie, who is proper pissed off with everything, finds a balloon at the bottom of the garden and just floats away in it.

'Occasionally, when I look into the future, I think that's how I would like it to end. Just floating away in a bloody great balloon with red and white stripes on it'.

> *Proudly, in spite of his tattered clothing, [Andreas] walked into a respectable bistro and sat down at a table – he, who for so long had only stood at bars, or rather propped his elbow on them. He sat. And since his chair was facing a mirror, he could hardly avoid looking at his reflection in it, and it was as though he were making his own acqaintance again after a long absence. He was shocked. Immediately he realised how for the last few years he had been so distrustful of mirrors. It was not good to see evidence of his own dissipation with his*

*own eyes. For as long as he had been able to avoid seeing it,
it was either as though he had no face at all, or still had the
old one from the time before he had become dissipated . . .*

'Wojtech got up out of his chair, ordered a couple of
Pernods, and was at the point of dragging Andreas up to the
bar to drink them with him. But just as Andreas gets up to
go to the bar, he collapses on the floor like a sack, and everyone in the bistro is alarmed, including Wojtech, and the little
girl most of all. And because there is no doctor close at hand,
and no chemist's shop, he is dragged across the square to the
church, to the vestry in fact, because even the unbelieving
waiters believe that priests know something about living and
dying; and the girl called Therese, she too accompanies
them.

'So they bring our poor Andreas into the vestry, and
unfortunately he's no longer capable of speech, all he can do
is reach for the left inside pocket of his jacket where he has
the money he owes his little creditress, and he says: "Miss
Therese!" – and he sighs once, and he dies.

'May God grant us all, all of us drinkers, such a good and
easy death!'

Joseph Roth, *The Legend of the Holy Drinker*

Sources and Acknowledgements

TEXT

I owe a real debt to:

A Strange Kind of Glory by Eamon Dunphy (Wm Heinemann, 1991).
The Football Man by Arthur Hopcraft (Penguin, 1968).
McIlvanney on Football by Hugh McIlvanney (Mainstream, 1996).
Football: The Golden Age, Ed. John Tennant (Cassell, 2001).

BESTIANA

Best: An Intimate Biography by Michael Parkinson (Hutchinson, 1975).
Anatomy of a Football Star by David Meek (Sportsmans Book Club, 1970).
Where Do I Go from Here? by George Best (with Graeme Wright)
    (Macdonald, 1982).
The Best of Times by George Best (with Les Scott) (Simon and Schuster,
    1994).
Blessed by George Best (with Roy Collins) (Ebury Press, 2001).
Bestie by Joe Lovejoy (Sidgwick, 1998).
George and Me by Angie Best (Virgin, 2001).
Always Alex by Alex Best (Blake, 2005).

MANCHESTER UNITED/FOOTBALL:

My Soccer Life by Bobby Charlton (Sportsmans Book Club, 1964).
The Team That Wouldn't Die by John Roberts (Arthur Barker, 1975).
The Day a Team Died by Frank Taylor (Souvenir Press, 1983).
The Lost Babes by Jeff Connor (Harper Sport, 2006).
Father of Football: The Story of Matt Busby by David Miller (Pavilion,
    1994).
Starmaker: The Untold Story of Jimmy Murphy by Brian Hughes
    (Empire, 2002).
Duncan Edwards by Iain McCartney (Britesport, 2001).
The Birth of the Babes: Manchester United Youth Policy 1950–1957 by
    Tony Whelan (Empire, 2005).
The Charlton Brothers by Norman Harris (Stanley Paul, 1971).
Jack and Bobby by Leo McKinstry (CollinsWillow, 2002).
Together Again by Willie Irvine (SportsBooks, 2005).
Always in the Running: The Manchester United Dream Team by Jim
    White (Mainstream, 1998)

The Boss: The Many Sides of Alex Ferguson by Michael Crick (Simon and Schuster, 2002).
Played in Manchester by Simon Inglis (English Heritage, 2004).
Engineering Archie: Archibald Leitch – Football Ground Designer by Simon Inglis (English Heritage 2005).
The Football Grounds of Great Britain by Simon Inglis (CollinsWillow, 1983).
Addicted by Tony Adams (with Ian Ridley) (CollinsWillow, 1998).
Rock Bottom by Paul Merson (with Harry Harris) (Bloomsbury, 1995).
Hero and Villain by Paul Merson (with Ian Ridley) (CollinsWillow, 1999).
Gazza by Paul Gascoigne (with Hunter Davies) (Headline, 2004).
Jackie Milburn in Black and White by Mike Kirkup (Stanley Paul, 1990).
The Glory Game by Hunter Davies (Weidenfeld, 1972).
People In Sport by Brian Glanville (Sportsman's Book Club, 1968).
Football Memories by Brian Glanville (Robson Books, 1999).
Soccer Focus by John Moynihan (Simon and Schuster, 1989).
The Perfect Ten by Richard Williams (Faber, 2006).

GENERAL
Air Disasters by Stanley Stewart (Ian Allen Ltd, 1985).
Triumph and Tragedy in Mudville by Stephen Jay Gould (Cape, 2004).
Football Against the Enemy by Simon Kuper (Phoenix, 1994).
How Soccer Explains the World by Franklin Foer (HarperCollins, 2004).
The Beautiful Game? By David Conn (Yellow Jersey, 2004).
Those Feet: A Sensual History of English Football by David Winner (Bloomsbury, 2005).
A Journey to the Heart of England by Caroline Hillier (Paladin, 1976).
English Journey by J. B. Priestley (Heinemann, 1934).
Granada Television: The First Generation, Ed. John Finch (Manchester University Press, 2003).
Manchester, England by Dave Haslam (Fourth Estate, 1999).
Halls of Fame by John D'Agata (Graywolf Press, 2001).
'Life Story' by David Shields (collected in *The Next American Essay*, Ed. John D'Agata, Graywolf Press, 2003).
The Four Seasons of Success by Bud Schulberg (Robson Books, 1974).
Namath by Mark Kriegel (Viking, 2004).
Joe DiMaggio by Richard Ben Cramer (Simon and Schuster, 2000).
Moneyball by Michael Lewis (Norton, 2003).
Underworld by Don DeLillo (Picador, 1998).
American Pastoral by Philip Roth (Cape, 1997).
Infinite Jest by David Foster Wallace (Little, Brown, 1996).
The Legend of the Holy Drinker by Joseph Roth (1939 / Chatto and Windus, trans. Michael Hofmann, 1989).
John Barleycorn by Jack London (OUP, 1998).

Bartleby by Herman Melville (Dover Editions, 1990).

The Emigrants, by W. G. Sebald (New Directions, 1996).

Arthur & George by Julian Barnes (Cape, 2005).

The Thirsty Muse by Tom Dardis (Abacus, 1990).

Celebrity by James Monaco (Delta, 1978).

Common Fame by Richard Schickel (Pavilion, 1985).

Owning Up by George Melly (Weidenfeld, 1965).

Air Guitar by Dave Hickey (Art Issues Press, 1996).

Crimes of Art and Terror by Frank Lentricchia and Jody McAuliffe (University of Chicago Press, 2003).

Imagined Cities by Robert Alter (Yale, 2005).

Theatres of Memory by Raphael Samuel (Verso, 1994).

Identity of England by Robert Colls (OUP, 2002).

In Churchill's Shadow by David Cannadine (Penguin, 2002).

Steps to an Ecology of Mind by Gregory Bateson (University of Chicago Press, 1972).

Chromophobia by David Batchelor (Reaktion, 2004).

Like a Fiery Elephant by Jonathan Coe (Picador, 2004).

Illustrations were taken from the following publications:

The Birth of the Babes by Tony Whelan (Empire Publications, 2005): 89

Duncan Edwards by Iain McCartney (Britespot, 2001): 31, 45, 60

Football: The Golden Age, Ed. John Tennant (Cassell, 2001): 18, 41, 130, 146

George and Me by Angie Best (Virgin, 2001): 209

Air Disasters by Stanley Stewart (Ian Allen Ltd, 1985): title page diagram.

Images: 41, 71, 81, 130, 146 © popperfoto.com

I would like to thank:

Mark Wylie and Gillian Moors at the Manchester United Archive and Museum, Old Trafford; Victoria Coxon and Sue Mills at Woodhorn Museum in Ashington; the staff of the Dudley Borough Archive and Local History Department.

The Revd Geoff Johnston of St Francis' Parish Church, Dudley; Malcolm Sier, Angie Butler, James Butler RA, Leslie Millman, Ged Murray, Bruce Mitchell, Clive Everton, Phil Yates, Dan Davies at Bonhams, Christopher Walker, Patricia Walker, Robert Colls, Bill Lancaster, Tom Pickard, Don Vent, Darren Heron, John Tennant, Jack Tennant, Jason Beard, Richard Clegg, Paul Green, David Robson.

My agent Gillon Aitken, and Ayesha Karim.

The following people at Faber and Faber made the book better at every turn: Jon Riley, who originally commissioned it; Lee Brackstone, Angus Cargill, Dave Watkins, Donna Payne, Anna Pallai, Kate Burton, Helen Francis. Also Chris Shamwama at Ghost, and Ian Bahrami for his copy-editing.

Alma Cogan

Winner of the Whitbread First Novel Award

In his debut novel, Gordon Burn takes Britain's biggest-selling vocalist of the 1950s and turns her story into an equation of celebrity and murder. Fictional characters jostle for space with real-life stars – from John Lennon to Doris Day and Sammy Davis Jnr – as Burn, in a breathtaking act of appropriation, reinvents the popular culture of the post-war years. As beautifully written as it is disturbing, Alma Cogan remains a stingingly relevant exploration of the sad, dark underside of fame.

'An extraordinary, unprecedented novel. Audacious, innovative and totally compelling.' William Boyd

'No other novel has displayed the originality and power of Gordon Burn's *Alma Cogan*. This is my book of the year, because it is the one I desperately wish I had written.' Hilary Mantel

'A novel to treasure. As a dark meditation on fame and its undertow, as a dangerous and loving vision of post-war England, as a ruthless antidote to nostalgia, it's unlike anything I've ever read.' Michael Herr

faber

Also by Gordon Burn

Somebody's Husband, Somebody's Son

It seemed the case of the notorious Yorkshire Ripper was finally closed when Peter Sutcliffe was sentenced to life imprisonment in 1981. But in the early 1980s, Gordon Burn spent three years living in Sutcliffe's home town of Bingley, researching his life. *Somebody's Husband, Somebody's Son* offers one of the most penetrating and provocative insights into the mind of a murderer ever written.

'A book which will with some justice be compared to *In Cold Blood* and *The Executioner's Song*. It's as if Thomas Hardy were also present at the writing of this account of the Yorkshire Ripper.' Norman Mailer

'Quite brilliant, written from a startlingly original viewpoint.' Antony Sher

'Gordon Burn's classic.' Blake Morrison

Also by Gordon Burn

The North of England Home Service

In a forensic dissection of Britain's souring landscape, Gordon Burn tells the tale of Ray Cruddas, a light entertainer effecting a semi-dignified retreat from his fading career, who returns to the unnamed northern town of his youth.

'Elegiac, grave and affectionate . . . The history he presents, at times wielding an Orwellian eloquence, is worth the price of the book itself.' Seán O'Brien, *Independent*

'It is a book that feels as if it were written on foot, every sentence exhibiting a lifetime of close observation and streetwise wit . . . Nothing, not a joke or a jogger, is let off lightly.' Tim Adams, *Observer*

'Burn carves a tale of mutual dependence between two also-rans – Ray, once a successful Geordie comedian, and Jackie, an almost made-it boxer . . . It is a book about ageing, about the long haul between what you hoped your life might be and acceptance of what it is – and about the loneliness of men.' Anna Raeburn

Also by Gordon Burn

Pocket Money

In 1985, following 'that' final between Dennis Taylor and Steve Davis, Britain suddenly found itself in the grip of a new sporting obsession. Snooker, or 'Coronation Street with balls', was big business, and with TV looking to cash in, 1986 was to be a crucial year. In one corner was Barry Hearn and his Romford mafia – Davis, Taylor, Griffiths – and in the other were the bad boys – Higgins, White, Knowles – threatening the game's good name and its earning potential.

For one year, Gordon Burn travelled with this snooker circus. With unprecedented access to the leading personalities, *Pocket Money* offers a unique snapshot of 1980s Britain.

'A classic.' Frank Keating, *Guardian*

'Unputdownable.' *The Face*

'Funny, incisive and hugely entertaining.' *Time Out*

faber

Also by Gordon Burn

Fullalove

Norman Miller used to be one of Fleet Street's finest. Now he's a middle-aged, burned-out hack with a gift for the sensational story, the shouting tabloid lead. But as he reports on a series of brutal murders and sex crimes, he's forced to wonder whether he is just a witness – or part of some deeper pattern of cause and effect . . .

'Remarkable . . . Devastating . . . Required reading for anyone interested in what British fiction should be doing today.' *Esquire*

'Prescient, compelling, enthrallingly written and profoundly disturbing . . . *Fullalove* is an extraordinary, gripping and chilling book which lingers disquietingly in the mind, like the echo of a nightmare, long after you have put it down.' *Financial Times*

'Extraordinary . . . One of the year's most richly imagined and provocative novels.' *New Statesman*

faber

Happy Like Murderers: The True Story of Fred and Rosemary West

In this controversial and seminal work of reportage, Gordon Burn reveals the strange inner dynamic of Fred and Rosemary West's relationship. Based on meticulous research, this dark history is told in a powerful, compelling narrative.

'With his forensic commitment to get behind the tabloid headlines . . . Burn brilliantly reinvents reportorial writing . . . Startlingly original.' Matt Seaton, *Esquire*

'Brilliant, bleak, unflinching.' Deborah Orr, *Guardian*

'One knew . . . that if a book of merit could be written about these crimes, Gordon Burn would be the man to do it. His achievement rests on two pillars – the novelist's acute glance at apparently inconsequential detail, and the researcher's bold determination to immerse himself in the fetid world it is his task to explain . . . It is brave, and by no means easy, to do this without prurience . . . A book of record.' Brian Masters, *Spectator*

Also by Gordon Burn

Born Yesterday: The News as a Novel

Born Yesterday does what the media do every day: blur the boundaries between what is real and what is invented.

Summer 2007 was an extraordinarily rich time for news. Floods. Foot and mouth. The disappearances of Tony Blair and Madeleine McCann. The arrival of Gordon Brown. Terror attacks in Glasgow. In this powerful and electrifying novel, Gordon Burn takes the news from that year and weaves the strands together into an essential story for our time. The characters in these long-running reality soaps are presented here in three dimensions, their stories told through revealing glimpses and startling insights.

'Gordon Burn is right. The news is now a novel.' Mark Lawson

'Wonderful . . . poignant, hilarious and, at times, uncomfortably true.' *Evening Standard*

'Original . . . [and] highly sophisticated . . . No one has written more shrewdly and knowingly about popular newspaper culture than Burn, but with this novel he taps into something more profound and sinister.' William Boyd, *Guardian*

faber